History and Historians
in Late Antiquity

History and Historians
in Late Antiquity

edited by

Brian Croke
and
Alanna M. Emmett

PERGAMON PRESS

SYDNEY · OXFORD · NEW YORK · TORONTO · PARIS · FRANKFURT

Pergamon Press (Australia) Pty. Ltd.
19a Boundary Street, Rushcutters Bay, N.S.W. 2011, Australia.

Pergamon Press Ltd,
Headington Hall, Oxford OX3 0BW, England.

Pergamon Press Inc.,
Maxwell House, Fairview Park, Elmsford, N.Y. 10523, U.S.A.

Pergamon Press Canada Ltd,
Suite 104, 150 Consumers Road, Willowdale, Ontario M2J 1P9, Canada.

Pergamon Press GmbH,
6242 Kronberg-Taunus, Hammerweg 6, Postfach 1305, Federal Republic of Germany.

Pergamon Press SARL,
24 rue des Ecoles, 75240 Paris, Cedex 05, France.

First published 1983

Copyright © 1983, Brian Croke and Alanna M. Emmett

Cover design by Robert Taylor
Typeset in Australia by Hexagon Press
Printed in Hong Kong by Warren Printing Co. Ltd

National Library of Australia Cataloguing in Publication Data:

History and historians in late antiquity.

ISBN 0 08 029840 0

1. History, Ancient — Historiography —
Addresses, essays, lectures. I. Croke, Brian.
II. Emmett, Alanna.

930'.07'2

Foreword

In recent years there has emerged among scholars a growing interest in late antique literature and history. A common field of interest and expertise within the period is that of historiography. Consequently, a conference on the theme of 'Old and New in Late Antique Historiography' was held at Macquarie University in Sydney on 17–19 July 1981. All the papers delivered at the conference are published here with the exception of those on Josephus and Eusebius by Neville Birdsall (Birmingham) and on Malalas by Elizabeth Jeffreys (Macquarie). They represent the results of research in various stages of completion. To expedite publication they appear here basically as originally delivered. We have added an introductory chapter to give the collection greater coherence and direction by setting it in the wider context of history writing in the late antique Graeco-Roman world.

The editors wish to thank Averil Cameron, Bruce Harris, Elizabeth Jeffreys, Edwin Judge and John Matthews for their support at various stages. Publication is made possible with the help of the Macquarie University Research Grant.

April 1983

Brian Croke
Alanna M. Emmett

Contents

Abbreviations

CCL		*Corpus Christianorum Series Latina* (Turnholt 1953–)
CIL		*Corpus Inscriptionum Latinarum* (Berlin 1863–)
DE		Eusebius, *Demonstratio Evangelica*
FGrH		F. Jacoby, *Die Fragmente der griechischen Historiker* (Berlin 1923–)
FHG		C. Müller, *Fragmenta Historicorum Graecorum* (Berlin 1841–70)
GCS		*Die Griechischen Christlichen Schriftsteller* (Leipzig/Berlin 1898–)
HE		*Historia Ecclesiastica*
HF		Gregory of Tours, *History of the Franks*
HL		Paul the Deacon, *History of the Lombards*
ILS		H. Dessau, *Inscriptiones Latinae Selectae* (Berlin 1892–1916)
MGH		*Monumenta Germaniae Historica*
	AA	*Auctores Antiquissimi*
	Ep.	*Epistulae*
	Poet.	*Poetae*
	Script.	*Scriptores*
MP		Eusebius, *Martyrs of Palestine*
PE		Eusebius, *Praeparatio Evangelica*
PL		J. P. Migne, *Patrologia Latina*
PG		J. P. Migne, *Patrologia Graeca*
RE		Pauly-Wissowa, *Realencyclopädie der klassichen Altertumswissenschaft* (Stuttgart 1893–)
VC		Eusebius, *Vita Constantini*

Historiography in Late Antiquity:
An Overview

Brian Croke & Alanna M. Emmett

One of the formative periods in the history of historiography was that from the third to the seventh centuries (*c.* A.D. 250–650), a span of time in which the classical Greek and Roman ways of analysing and writing about the past were transformed. In the absence of any detailed, systematic and comprehensive account of this whole process, this introductory chapter is designed simply to sketch in the general lines of historiographical development, to describe its broad trends and essential features — all with a view to providing the general context for the ensuing chapters.[1]

The Greeks and Romans for the most part regarded writing about and explaining the past as a literary activity which usually concentrated on near-contemporary wars and politics and was shaped by the models of Herodotus and Thucydides, to which the Romans might add Sallust. 'History' was not, strictly speaking, an independent and self-contained activity, but an integral part of rhetoric. Knowledge of the past helped to elucidate the standard authors that children studied, and later provided examples to be used in the traditional education in public speaking; historical works were written to be read to an interested and discriminating audience.[2] This tradition of classical historiography is summed up for us in the essay of Lucian of Samosata, *How to Write History*, written in the second century A.D.: a history must be truthful, and above all, useful; the historian must possess political understanding and an appropriate style; he should preferably be an eye-witness and possess the experience, especially military experience, necessary for his task; the historian must commence with a proper preface, arrange his events usually in proper chronological order, compose splendid speeches for his characters and weigh up his moral judgments.

In the course of the fourth century, however, in both the Greek East and the Latin West, a profound transformation had begun to take place in the Roman world, a transformation which influenced significant areas of public and private life including the writing of history. The adoption of Christianity by the Emperor Constantine in 312 hastened the conversion of all levels of society, bringing with it a view of man and the world different from that of most Romans. At the same time the urban civilisation of Rome began to be threatened and disrupted by a succession of barbarian raids which resulted in the permanent settlement of whole barbarian nations on imperial territory. Most of the changes which occurred in the period from the fourth to the seventh centuries in the way history was written and explained can be ascribed to the influence of these two factors.

———————————

The fourth-century senatorial aristocracy of the Roman West, whether Christian or pagan, still learned its history from the Livian tradition and from Herodotus, among others.[3]

Consequently it could easily appreciate the traditional reading of a history of recent times by Ammianus Marcellinus in the 390s.[4] Although the surviving books cover just twenty-five years from 353 to 378, Ammianus' history apparently began in A.D. 96 where Tacitus left off. Though he is in some respects influenced by Suetonian-style biography, Ammianus' close attention to the traditional canons of historical composition is evident throughout his work: he sets himself (formally at least) against biographers and epitomators, thereby prescribing the genre of his own history; he constructs his speeches with great attention and employs the rhetorical handbooks when praise of his hero Julian is called for; and he displays his erudition in a variety of digressions and is ready to mete out praise and blame.[5] So far as we can tell, Ammianus was almost alone as a historian in his age. Very few others wrote on the scale and in the classical mould of Ammianus. At any rate no other works have survived and only a handful are known to have been written.[6]

By Ammianus' day, however, many of the Roman aristocrats were more interested in racy biographies than history and they preferred their history in a biographical form as provided for example by Aurelius Victor or the author of the *de viris illustribus*. At the same time, the intrusion of so many who lacked the customary Roman education into senior positions in the army or imperial administration meant that there was now an unprecedented demand for shorter works which summarised the basic facts of Roman history. A work like that of Eutropius or, more particularly, the *Breviarium* of Festus could provide vital background data for new or inexperienced imperial officials.[7] When the same demand eventually arose among Greek speakers it was simplest just to translate handbooks like that of Eutropius whose work is known in no less than three different Greek translations.

Although the western aristrocracies still knew and studied history of the traditional Roman kind, Christianity now confronted them with a whole new concept and range of history. The past was now important because it had a theological meaning and to understand it fully one had to appreciate the totality of human history from Adam to the present-day. Romans could now discover this in Jerome's translation of the *Chronicle* of Eusebius of Caesarea, an annalistic record of all known nations from Abraham to Eusebius' time which Jerome continued down to his own day (A.D. 378). So it was that late fourth-century aristocrats could be found busying themselves with studying the *Chronicle* and using it as an ancillary research tool in order to illuminate the Christian scriptures.[8]

Certainly the formative period in Christian historiography had been in the late third/early fourth century and in the East where Eusebius was responsible not only for the *Chronicle* but for another new kind of history as well — the history of the Christian Church or, rather one might say, of the Christian nation. Jerome later contemplated writing such a history himself for the Latin-speaking world (*vita Malchi* 1) but apparently abandoned the project. Instead, the work was made available in the West through the updated translation of Eusebius by Jerome's one-time rival, Rufinus of Aquileia. Finally, the aristocracy's apparent penchant for biography could now be channelled into another new Christian form of recording and interpreting the past, namely through the lives of famous holy men modelled on the life of the monk Antony by Athanasius.[9]

When we look at the West about half a century after the time of Ammianus and Jerome we find it vastly changed, socially and politically. Not only was the majority of the population now Christian but the grip of the imperial administration had been considerably loosened. Increasingly, local bishops became the effective leaders of their communities, the Roman army was dominated by barbarian officers and whole nations like the Visigoths now occupied large tracts of Roman provinces, while other tribes raided deep into Roman territory, threatening both town and countryside. In other words the settled prosperous pattern of villa and urban life that still largely prevailed in the late fourth century had now begun to disintegrate. Disruption to the traditional pattern and rhetorical emphasis of Roman education was inevitable. This, combined with the receding reality of an 'Eternal Rome', severely reduced the study let alone the composition of traditional Roman histories.[10] Yet the great crises of the day still called for a full-scale historical treatment in the classical tradition. However, the few who were capable of it like Sidonius Apollinaris, declined to take up the challenge: Sidonius turned down an offer to write the history of King Attila's adventures in Gaul and politely refused another similar request from a minister of the Visigothic king Euric, pointing out that historiography was not an appropriate activity for clerics.[11]

History was, nonetheless, a live issue in the Christian societies of the West. The sack of Rome by the Visigoths in 410 had a profound impact on contemporaries, Christian and pagan alike, weaned on the idea of 'Eternal Rome'. With a direct knowledge that stretched back only two or three generations to guide them, many Romans, including perhaps some wavering Christians, could not help but trace this unprecedented disaster to Rome's attachment to Christianity. Believing that an elementary knowledge of Roman history would lay this view to rest, Augustine of Hippo shaped his vast *City of God* in answer to the accusation that Christianity was to blame for Rome's humiliation, and developed the idea that God's community transcended that of man and certainly that of Rome.[12] Although Augustine was arguing that it was pointless to believe that Rome should last forever, he still commissioned a Spanish priest, Orosius, to assemble a world history in which it would be made clear to everyone what the best educated Christians already knew, that is, that equally terrible, if not worse, experiences had been endured in Rome's past; so recent misfortunes could hardly be blamed on the Christians. Orosius' straightforward *Historia contra paganos* (History against the Pagans) was to prove one of the most important historical textbooks of the Western Middle Ages. Augustine and Orosius regarded this kind of compilation as a factual coverage with which all Christians should be familiar and able to consult. History was no longer the preserve of the literary élite.

The emerging Christian culture of the Latin West was characterised by a quest for simplicity. A distaste for rhetoric and rhetorical education gave rise to a less elaborate kind of literary language (*sermo humilis*) which aimed to interpret, among other things, Christian history and scripture for a wider audience.[13] Relative simplicity was also a hallmark of the annalistic chronicles which became the most popular form of history-writing in the West. These were basically local continuations of the *Chronicle* of Jerome, although that of Prosper of Aquitaine was a new world chronicle in its own right. Each of these chronicles represented an attempt to relate local Italian, Gallic or Spanish events to universal history and to demonstrate the continuity in history as a whole. As a result they were kept up to date. Hydatius, for example, updated his to 469, Prosper twice continued his: from 433 to 443 and then to 455. Likewise successive chronicles were preserved and copied in a single manuscript, and thus a sort of continuous history by different authors was built up. Just as Prosper continued Jerome, he was himself continued in the sixth century by the African bishop Victor then exiled in Constantinople; while Victor was himself continued in turn by a

Spanish bishop John of Biclaro in the late sixth century.[14] There was now a type of history not designed to be read aloud at all.

Of all the late Roman chroniclers, especially in the West, very few are known by name. Chronicles like those of Jerome, Prosper, Marcellinus (actually an Easterner writing in Constantinople), Victor, not to mention the later ones of Cassiodorus, Isidore and Bede, survive in numerous manuscripts because they became recommended reading in medieval monasteries. Yet one must recognise that they represent merely the tip of an iceberg of chronographic production. There must have been a host of other local chroniclers who sought to update the better known chronicles or else combine them with each other or even add to them entries culled from some other source. Enough of these anonymous chroniclers have survived to suggest that the possibilities for combining and interpolating chronicle manuscripts were unlimited. This practice was widespread so that what now remains is a bewildering variety of chronicle continuations, interpolations and extracts. The functional nature of the chronicle meant that in practice almost every single manuscript came to represent a unique chronicle in itself.

In studying the chroniclers of late Antiquity, therefore, one must always begin with the manuscripts and versions. So, although for the sake of simplicity some chronicles go under a generic name such as *Chronica Gallica* or *Chronica Italica*, the reality is that such labels conceal a variety of unrelated anonymous versions and extracts preserved largely in the manuscripts of the major chroniclers. For example, *Cod. Univ. Matritensis* no. 134 (s.XIII) covers the period from Adam to 511: it comprises Jerome to 378, then a version of Hydatius followed by an anonymous Gallic chronicle to 511,[15] which is combined in turn with that of *BM 16974* under the rubric *Chronica Gallica*.[16]

From the mid-fourth century onwards conditions in the East were considerably different — politically, socially and economically. There political stability had been maintained despite occasional invasions of the Balkan provinces and campaigns against the Persians on the eastern frontier. Urban life had not become as disjointed as it had in the West, nor had large numbers of barbarians become permanently settled in the Roman provinces. The East was still Roman with the imperial Court firmly in control and government effectively maintained by a considerable bureaucracy. Further, the Court at Constantinople had gradually adapted itself to the imperial theory articulated by Eusebius whereby the emperor was the vice-gerent of God on earth and took the instrumental role in preserving doctrinal harmony.[17]

The Court, Senate and bureaucracy of the East placed continuous demands on the traditional curriculum. A consummate grounding in rhetoric and the law, based on classical literature, was still the prerequisite for high office. In the East too the fusion of Christianity and Hellenic culture had been fairly satisfactorily accomplished without serious prejudice to the continuity of the classical tradition. In this atmosphere the grooves of classical Greek historiography still ran deep. Thucydides and Herodotus remained the basic models into the seventh century and way beyond.[18] As long as Rome was likely to be at war with Persia there would always be an aspiring Herodotus or two. John the Lydian, John of Epiphaneia, Evagrius and Theophanes of Byzantium were all attracted to this challenge in the sixth century.[19]

Unlike history written in the West, history in the East continued to be written largely by men involved in some way in the events they describe and it remained concentrated on recounting the recent past in order to throw light on the present.[20] Olympiodorus of Egyptian Thebes and Priscus of Panion in the fifth century, as well as Nonnosus and Peter the Patrician in the sixth century, wrote histories that were based on or included their role as emissaries to foreign potentates. Procopius of Caesarea as secretary to Justinian's general Belisarius figures largely in the first-hand accounts of imperial campaigns in Africa, Italy and the East, and even sedentary historians like Agathias find some space for themselves in their narrative.

The writing of history demanded a mastery of the classical models and the most intense rhetorical and stylistic training. So it is that we find history being written by sophists like Priscus, Malchus of Philadelphia in Lydia and Eunapius of Sardis, or by practising advocates like Agathias and gentleman advocates like Menander in Constantinople. Histories still began with a highly-wrought preface setting out the scope and aims of the author and were executed on the pattern of their classical models with elaborate speeches and set pieces. A siege, for example, was written up as if it were Plataea all over again; an emperor needed a wise adviser just as Xerxes did; learned digressions were carefully composed, and so on.[21]

The adaptation of this tradition to Christian culture and history presented some difficulties. Although historians themselves were now Christians their attention to the necessity for a thoroughgoing classical style was scarcely compromised. In this tradition Christian terms had to be qualified and Christian subject-matter rigorously excluded.[22] In time, however, tensions appeared in matters of both style and content. This was evident in Malchus and increasingly so in Procopius, Agathias and Menander until finally it was resolved by the time of Theophylact in the seventh century when Christian themes and terms were fully and naturally incorporated into a stylised history of the classical kind.[23] A Christian historian with his heightened awareness of the past and of the role of Divine Providence, not to speak of the intervention of the Almighty in human affairs, could not, however, subscribe to classical notions of 'Fate' or 'Fortune' as causal factors in history. The *tyche* still evident in Procopius, for instance, is quite clearly embedded in a Christian system of explanation, albeit inconsistently.[24] By the time of his successor Agathias, however, it was perfectly possible to jettison the concept altogether and replace it with a simple Christian sin/punishment explanation.[25]

The profound currents of intellectual and social change running through late antique life still affected those who regarded themselves as defenders of the old ways. In this sense it becomes difficult to maintain that historians like Ammianus were purely 'classical'. As has been observed, the general increase in religion and magic at large in the fourth century is reflected in the greater emphasis on these matters in Ammianus and the author of the *Historia Augusta*, among others.[26] Likewise, we find a greater devotion to miracles and the role of Providence in history among some of the fifth-century historians so that a fiercely pagan historian like Zosimus can appear to have closer formal affinities to the church historians than to his classical predecessors.[27]

Although the continuing fortunes of the Christian nation could not be accommodated within conventional histories, the story of the growth of the church and its relationship with the imperial government came to be contained in the new genre of ecclesiastical history established by Eusebius. His purpose had been to reinforce the church's identity, delineate its relationship to external factors and establish a lineage of orthodoxy in order to mark off the boundaries of deviant doctrine; and he employed the method (largely novel to history) of quoting original documents in full. During the fourth century and beyond, the size, spread and influence of the Christian community changed dramatically. From a nation of believers quite distinct from the secular state the church came to transform the state itself to such an extent that it became increasingly artificial to speak of a dichotomy between Church and State. Both were interwoven in the fabric of the new Christian Empire.[28]

When others came to continue to their own day the *Ecclesiastical History* of Eusebius they were faced with describing a vastly different community. By now it was necessary to include a history of the Church, the piety and religious policies of Emperor and Court, and to trace the increasingly complex doctrinal controversies which, at least in the East, seem to have absorbed so much of a Christian scholar's time and energy. The relationship of the great bishoprics (Rome, Constantinople, Antioch, Alexandria, Jerusalem) with the Court and with each other was now a paramount concern too, and it was important to demonstrate above all how the guiding hand of Divine Providence continued to manifest itself in the affairs of both Church and State. The whole of public and private life was slowly being fused into a Christian amalgam that was to emerge fully later in the intensely theocratic style and propaganda of the age of Justinian.

Eusebius did find imitators in the latter part of the fourth century such as Gelasius of Caesarea who continued Eusebius' work through the reign of Constantine and beyond, but it was in the reign of Theodosius II (402–50) that the Eusebian continuators flourished. Firstly, Socrates wrote early in the 440s his *Ecclesiastical History* covering the period 306 to 439 and this was followed soon after by Sozomen who insisted on securing the imprimatur of the emperor in 443, a new development in historiography. Sozomen made extensive use of Socrates. Then there is Theodoret bishop of Cyrrhus whose history was also written in the 440s. All three demonstrate a certain uniformity of style and format which they inherited from their common model Eusebius. Their works were divided up according to the reigns of emperors and made extensive use of documentary evidence frequently quoted in full. Above all they ranged back beyond the present and immediate past.

The use of an imperial framework in the ecclesiastical histories provided a natural focus for the increasingly elaborate and influential role of the emperor in the church. Pious orthodox emperors enjoyed significant political successes and their reigns saw wonderful miracles; heterodox emperors suffered vengeance from the Almighty and endured all kinds of adversity. In this new Christian history Divine Justice was the essential force. The 'Fate' and 'Fortune' of the classical historians had no place in ecclesiastical history but their influence could not be entirely dispelled. Accordingly, Socrates, for example, relied on the no less conventional notion of *kairos*, a key time when the fortunes of civil and ecclesiastical life coincided.[29]

Although Eusebius was essentially a Christian scholar at the time he originally planned and wrote the *Ecclesiastical History*, while Theodoret and Gelasius of Caesarea were bishops and Theodore Lector a cleric, church history was not the exclusive preserve of clerics. Socrates and Sozomen, like Evagrius at the turn of the seventh century, were lawyers, that is to say they enjoyed the advantage of the best education available in their day — four years of rhetoric and three of law. So they were able to make extensive use of the law codes when relevant to Christian affairs. Their knowledge of the Christian scriptures and history was acquired separately.

Despite the fact that by the mid-fifth century ecclesiastical history had come to embrace a large part of what we might call 'secular' history, it remained a clearly distinct genre. Socrates and Sozomen were roughly contemporary with Olympiodorus but there was no scope for confusion between their works. Even a century later the boundaries were still reasonably firm. Procopius, for instance, who gave scarcely any space to Christian events in his lengthy histories, apparently regarded writing on ecclesiastical matters as something quite separate (*Wars* 8.25.13). Yet, as with style, there was increasing uneasiness about the parameters of content. Just as in real life the boundaries between secular and religious affairs, at least in the Christian Roman Empire of the East, were becoming less obvious, so in historical accounts the differences between secular and ecclesiastical history were becoming more blurred. To maintain them now required considerable restraint.

Socrates was criticised for including too much secular material in his history (*HE* 5. 1). His audience perhaps failed to appreciate the difficulties involved. Sozomen then tried studiously to preserve a strict concentration on ecclesiastical affairs only but his final books show that he was unable to sustain it. By the time of Evagrius and the Syriac church historians John of Ephesus and Zachariah of Mitylene, however, the tension had more or less resolved itself. Secular and church matters were now so closely interconnected that their strict separation was meaningless. In this sense, therefore, Evagrius is the most 'secular' of the early church historians and could quote Zosimus, Priscus and Eustathius of Epiphaneia as a matter of course.

Indeed the artificiality of maintaining distinct historiographical genres eventually proved altogether too inconvenient so that by the early seventh century both traditions had come to an end. A fundamental societal change now prevailed in the East as the communities of church and state had become fully and smoothly integrated into a single Christian imperial realm.[30] Theophylact is the last of the classical historians of the late antique tradition and Evagrius was to have no successor for another eight hundred years.

What had emerged in the East to replace both secular and church histories was the Christian world chronicle. Such chronicles had come to fulfil best the historical demands of this integrated Christian society for it was in them that a coherent picture of the past could be found. Rather than just tell the story of one's own generation or bring some previous work up to date which was the habit of chroniclers in the increasingly fragmented societies of the West, the Eastern chronicler's purpose was to set the present in the context of the whole of human history in a different way. Although Eusebius believed that human history really only began after the Fall and thus had commenced his chronicle with Abraham, subsequent computational advances had enabled the delineation of a Year of Creation to be established so those who followed Eusebius, such as the Alexandrians Panodorus and Annianus in the late fourth century, were able to fill out the picture from what was conceived of as the earliest epoch of recorded time.[31] Unlike the chroniclers of the West who set out to continue Jerome or their own immediate predecessor, the eastern chroniclers continued to go over the same ground, that is from Adam, and only really offered new material as they approached their own day. This apparent waste of effort remained a firm and important part of the whole of the Byzantine chronographic tradition. The Byzantines clearly felt it important to try to modify or improve on the productions of their predecessors.

Unfortunately, most of the earlier Byzantine chronicles do not survive in any form so we have only the names of authors to go on: Panodorus and Annianus of course, together with the fifth-century sophist Helikonios whose ten-book chronicle went from Adam to Theodosius II,[32] and the chroniclers cited in the sixth-century chronicle of John Malalas — Domninus and Nestorian. In fact it appears that the chronicle of Malalas marked a new departure for the emerging genre of the Byzantine world chronicle. Certainly his work profoundly influenced subsequent writers in the various languages of the Byzantine world and encapsulated well the Eastern view of world history, in which classical Greek and 'western' Roman history hardly figured. However, just as the western chroniclers differed from one another in their local bias, so too in the East the chronicles invariably reflected a local perspective. Except for the latter books, particularly the final Book 18, Malalas is decidedly Antiochene and most of his successors such as the Paschal Chronicler (seventh century) were Constantinopolitan in their slant. Whereas, in terms of authorship and content, the western chronicles may well reflect a clerical composition for an audience of limited education, the Eastern chronicles were not predominantly monastic nor do they suggest a lowbrow audience.[33]

————————

By the end of the fifth century there was no longer a Roman Empire in the West, the previous Roman provinces now being under the hegemony of various barbarian kings. The old Roman schools of Gaul and Italy which still flourished a century before and which had sustained the learning and composition of Roman history for generations were few and far between. Gregory of Tours' famous claim that classical learning had all but disappeared in Gaul only underscores the fact that classical historiography faded out when 'the ancient [literary] public died of shrinkage'.[34] Christian culture found all the history it needed in the Scriptures and the available chronicles, just as Gregory himself based the first part of his history on the Bible and the *Chronicles* of Jerome and Sulpicius Severus. Although with Christianity the educational aspirations of the majority had widened there was still no formal Christian curriculum. Students were now largely taught at home or in a monastery. Typical of the *literati* of his age Gregory of Tours was educated primarily in a monastery and he had to rely on his own resourcefulness to acquire his knowledge of classical authors like Sallust. Although the traditional pattern of education had all but died out in Italy too, Pope Gregory the Great and Venantius Fortunatus managed to receive a sound classical training.

The disappearance of the emperor removed the essential rationale for Roman history, but the composition and government of the Roman provinces had been slowly changing throughout the fifth century so the disappearance of the Empire in the West was hardly noticed. Orosius was writing for Romans in a time of crisis and faced a problem in trying to fit barbarians into Roman history, but by the end of the century it was no longer possible to describe events in that frame of reference. Salvian, a little earlier, had found room for the barbarians by proposing that they served God's purpose by helping re-invigorate a decadent Rome. By now Romans had fused with Goths, Franks, Burgundians and others to form new societies ruled by barbarian kings and operating in the channels of late Roman administration.

Long before these various nations had penetrated the Roman Empire they had established an heroic oral tradition which they passed on from one generation to the next. With their conversion to Christianity they too acquired a new history as part of God's people. When they came under the spell of Rome they also felt the need to acquire a more respectable past and relate it to that of the Romans, and their recollection of their pre-Roman past soon grew hazy.[35] Cassiodorus, for instance, as the instrument of the Ostrogothic Court in Italy, wrote a twelve-book history in which he aimed 'to make Gothic history Roman' (*Variae* 9.25). The Goths wanted to know about their own exclusive past and Romans were interested to see how it fitted into theirs. This curiosity is reflected in the circumstances of Jordanes being commissioned to write a summary history of the Goths in 551[36] and of Isidore of Seville being requested by the Visigothic king to explain how the various barbarian kings before him had ruled Spain.[37]

In the East, where the barbarian nations (even the most powerful like the Avars and Huns) failed to gain a permanent foothold until the seventh century, it was still possible to write history in the classical manner with the barbarians being treated as outsiders, although there is gradual increase in the scope given to non-Roman history in the period up to Agathias and then on to Theophylact. By contrast, Isidore's *Histories* of the Goths, Vandals and Suevi, prefaced by an encomium on Spain, is a clear indication that its author saw himself as living in the post-Roman era. Just as Spain had long existed and once been taken over by Rome, so now Roman rule was superseded by that of the Goths. The only genuine continuity was in the geographical entity of Spain. What is striking about Isidore's work is the smooth and effortless way that secular and ecclesiastical history are combined.

Just as in the East, the new political and social consensus of post-Roman society in the West could be reflected in its historiography. The level of explanation is quite simple. Pious Catholic kings are the most successful in battle; heretical or immoral monarchs are not so rewarded. For Isidore and his contemporaries this was the only way a detailed historical account could be written — a Christian society in a region ruled by a barbarian king under God's providence. This new kind of history in which all previous national and religious elements are combined is equally visible in the *History* of Gregory of Tours. Despite its popular title, it is not a history of the Franks but of Gaul in the fifth and sixth centuries in the context of world history.[38] In this account of the new Christian society at all social levels, in countryside as well as in town, Gregory was followed by Bede whose work is as much a history of English society in its period as of the English church in particular. It is certainly not an ecclesiastical history in the Eusebian tradition.[39] In fact the strong eastern tradition of church history was never replicated in the West. No one else apparently felt the need to continue Rufinus, let alone Eusebius. Indeed, the gap was only filled in the later sixth century when Cassiodorus arranged for a translation of a conflated version of the histories of Socrates, Sozomen and Theodoret — the *Historia Tripartita*. What had happened of course is that the West had experienced the effective integration of ecclesiastical and secular life, which eliminated the rationale of the church historian, a century or more before that process was fully accomplished in the East.[40]

By the early seventh century the styles and patterns that were to dominate historiography throughout the middle ages in both East and West had settled into position. The turbulent period from the beginning of the fourth century had witnessed the eclipse of classical history-writing throughout the Roman world. In its place stood an unprecedented variety of historiographical genres which ultimately converged in a common goal, to tell the story of salvation and to demonstrate the ways of God to men both now and since time immemorial.

Notes

1. This paper is inevitably shaped by, and should only be read in conjunction with, three important studies by A. Momigliano: 'Pagan and Christian Historiography in the Fourth Century' in A. Momigliano (ed.), *The Conflict Between Paganism and Christianity in the Fourth Century* (Oxford 1963), 79–99 (rp. in *Essays on Ancient and Modern Historiography* (Oxford 1977), 107–26); L'età del trapasso fra storiografia antica e storiografia medievale (320–550 d.C.)', *Rivista Storica Italiana* 81 (1969), 286–303; 'Popular Religious Beliefs and the Late Roman Historians', *Studies in Church History* 8 (1971), 1–18 (rp. in *Essays*, 141–59). See also A. Demandt, 'Geschichte in der spätantiken Gesellschaft', *Gymnasium* 89 (1982), 255–72.

2. G. Press, 'History and the Development of the Idea of History in Antiquity', *History and Theory* 18 (1979), 289–91; A. Momigliano, 'Tradition and the Classical Historian', *History and Theory* 11 (1972), 279–93 (rp. in *Essays* (n.1 above), 161–77), and 'The Historians of the Classical World and Their Audiences: Some Suggestions', *Annali della Scuola Normale Superiore di Pisa* ser. 3, 8 (1978), 59–75.

3. Teachers like Staphylius at Bordeaux knew the whole of Livy and Herodotus (Ausonius, *Prof.* 20.8), while Ausonius himself confesses to owning complete copies of Herodotus and Thucydides (*Ep.* 10.32).

4. Libanius, *Ep.* 1063 (Förster) records the reading of instalments of Ammianus' history at Rome.

5. For detailed bibliography on Ammianus see the articles below by Matthews (pp.30–41), Emmett (pp.42–53) and Austin (pp.54–65). A major study of Ammianus by John Matthews is forthcoming.

6. E.g. Nicomachus Flavianus' *Annales* (*ILS* 2948). Protadius contemplated writing a history of Gaul (Symmachus, *Ep.* 4.18 cf. 4.36) but we do not know if he finished it. Naucellius translated some Greek history (Symmachus, *Ep.* 3.11) and himself wrote a Roman history of some kind (Symmachus, *Ep.* 9.110 cf. Alan Cameron, 'The Roman Friends of Ammianus', *Journal of Roman Studies* 54 (1964), 18).

7. Alan Cameron, 'Paganism and Literature in Late Fourth-Century Rome', *Entretiens sur l'antiquité classique* 23 (Geneva 1977), 8–9; W. den Boer, *Some Minor Roman Historians* (Leiden 1972); B. Baldwin, 'Festus the Historian', *Historia* 27 (1978), 197–217; P. G. Michelotto, 'Note sulla storiografia del IV sec. d.C.', *Centro ricerche e documentazione sull'antichità classica. Atti* 9 (1977/8), 91–155; G. Bonamente, 'La dedica del Breuiarium e la carriera di Eutropio', *Giornale Italiano di Filologia* 29 (1977), 274–97; R. Browning, 'History' in E. J. Kenney (ed.), *Cambridge History of Classical Literature* II (Cambridge 1982), 735–42.

8. For details see the paper by Croke, below, pp.116–31.

9. On the *Church History* of Eusebius: R. M. Grant, *Eusebius as Church Historian* (Oxford 1980) and T. D. Barnes, *Constantine and Eusebius* (Cambridge, Mass. 1981), 126–47; and for saints' lives: R. Browning, 'Biography' in Kenney, *op. cit.*, 723–31.

10. T. Haarhoff, *Schools of Gaul* (Oxford 1920), 43ff., 174ff.; P. Riché, *Education and Culture in the Barbarian West* (Columbia 1976), 139ff., 208ff.

11. Sidonius, *Epp.* 4.22, 8.15. Known historians from the time are Sulpicius Alexander and Renatus Frigeridus whom Gregory of Tours (*HF* 2.8–9) used for events in the late fourth/early fifth centuries.

12. R. A. Markus, *Saeculum. History and Society in the Theology of St Augustine* (Cambridge 1970).

13. See the paper by Rousseau, below, pp.107–15.

14. The chronicles are best edited by Mommsen (*MGH. AA.* IX, XI, XIII), except for Hydatius: A. Tranoy, *Hydace. Chronique*, 2 vols (Paris 1974).

15. Mommsen, *MGH. AA.* IX, 626.

16. *ibid.*, 620.

17. For the historiographical elements of this east/west cleavage: W. H. C. Frend, 'The Roman Empire in Eastern and Western Historiography', *Proceedings of the Cambridge Philological Society* n.s. 14 (1968), 19–32 (rp. in *Religion Popular and Unpopular in the Early Christian Centuries* [London 1976]).

18. R. Scott, 'The Classical Tradition in Byzantine Historiography' in M. Mullett and R. Scott (eds), *Byzantium and the Classical Tradition* (Birmingham 1981), 61–74.

19. John Lyd., *de mag.* 3.28.5; John Epiph., *Hist.* I (*FHG* IV, 272–6); Evag., *HE* 5.20; Theoph. Byz. (*FHG* IV, 270–71).

20. R. C. Blockley, *The Fragmentary Classicising Historians of the Later Roman Empire* (Liverpool 1981); for individual authors: H. Hunger, *Die hochsprachliche profane Literatur der Byzantiner* I (Munich 1978), 279–319 to which add the studies by B. Baldwin: 'Olympiodorus of Thebes', *Antiquité Classique* 49 (1980), 212–31; 'Priscus of Panium', *Byzantion* 50 (1980), 18–61; 'Malchus of Philadelphia', *Dumbarton Oaks Papers* 32 (1978), 101–25. For more general analysis see Z. V. Udal'cova, 'Le monde vu par les historiens byzantins du IVe au VIIe siècle', *Byzantinoslavica* 33 (1972), 193–213 and J. A. S. Evans, 'The Attitudes of the Secular Historians of the Age of Justinian towards the Classical Past', *Traditio* 32 (1976), 353–8.

21. For these tricky literary problems see R. C. Blockley, 'Dexippus and Priscus and the Thucydidean Account of the Siege of Plataea', *Phoenix* 26 (1972), 18–27; L. R. Cresci, 'Aspetti dell'arcaismo negli storici tardo-antichi. Malco', *Atene e Roma* 24 (1976), 44–50; plus the paper by Adshead, below pp.82–7.

22. Averil and Alan Cameron, 'Christianity and Tradition in the Historiography of the Late Empire', *Classical Quarterly* n.s. 14 (1964), 316–28 rp. in Averil Cameron, *Continuity and Change in Sixth-Century Byzantium* (London 1981).

23. Averil Cameron, *Agathias* (Oxford 1970), 136.

24. Again the fundamental work has been that of Averil Cameron, 'The "Scepticism" of Procopius', *Historia* 15 (1966), 466–82 (rp. in *Continuity and Change* n.22 above). See also J. A. S. Evans, 'Christianity and Paganism in Procopius of Caesarea', *Greek, Roman and Byzantine Studies* 12 (1971), 81–100.

25. Averil Cameron, *op. cit.* (n.23 above), 92ff.

26. Momigliano, 'Popular Religious Beliefs . . .' (n.1 above), 145.

27. L. Cracco Ruggini, 'The Ecclesiastical Histories and the Pagan Historiography: Providence and Miracles', *Athenaeum* n.s.55 (1977), 107–26 and 'Zosimo, ossia il rovesciamento delle "Storie Ecclesiastiche",' *Augustinianum* 16 (1976), 23–6.

28. The best introduction to the ecclesiastical historians is R. A. Markus, 'Church History and the Early Church Historians', *Studies in Church History* 11 (1975), 1–17. See also G. Downey, 'The Perspective of the Early Church Historians', *Greek, Roman and Byzantine Studies* 6 (1965), 57–70. For a more comprehensive account see F. Winkelmann, 'Die Kirchengeschichtswerke im öströmischen Reich', *Byzantinoslavica* 37 (1976), 1–10, 173–190 and G. F. Chesnut, *The First Christian Histories* (Paris 1977). Among the too few studies of individual historians note P. Allen, *Evagrius*

Scholasticus. The Church Historian (Louvain 1981) and 'Zachariah Scholasticus and the *Historia Ecclesiastica* of Evagrius Scholasticus', *Journal of Theological Studies* n.s.31 (1980), 471–88, plus F. Winkelmann, 'Charakter und Bedeutung der Kirchengeschichte des Gelasios von Kaisareia', *Byzantinische Forschungen* 1 (1967), 346–85. Unfortunately we have not yet seen S. Calderone (ed.), *La storiografia ecclesiastica nella tarda antichità* (Messina 1980).

29. G. F. Chesnut, 'Kairos and Cosmic Sympathy in the Church Historian Socrates Scholasticus', *Church History* 44 (1975), 161–6; cf. Chesnut, *op. cit.* (n.28 above), 179–89.

30. Averil Cameron, 'Images of Authority: Elites and Icons in Late Sixth-Century Byzantium', *Past and Present* 84 (1979), 3–35 (rp. in *Continuity and Change* [n.2 above]).

31. A. A. Mosshammer, *The Chronicle of Eusebius and Greek Chronographic Tradition* (Lewisburg/London 1979), 77–8, 147–8.

32. Suda, E 851 (ed. Adler, II, 247).

33. E. M. Jeffreys, 'The Attitude of Byzantine Chroniclers towards Ancient History', *Byzantion* 49 (1979), 29–83; C. Mango, *Byzantium. The Empire of New Rome* (London 1980), 189–200 and H. G. Beck, 'Zur byzantinischen Mönchschronik' in C. Bauer (ed.), *Speculum Historiale* (Munich 1965), 188–97. A team of Australian scholars under the direction of Elizabeth Jeffreys and Roger Scott is preparing a translation of Malalas, together with a substantial introduction and commentary.

34. E. Auerbach, *Literary Language and its Public in Late Antiquity and in the Middle Ages* (London 1965), 334.

35. W. Goffart, *Barbarians and Romans A.D. 418–584. The Techniques of Accommodation* (Princeton 1980), 5–24.

36. A. Momigliano, 'Cassiodorus and Italian Culture of his Time' in A. Momigliano, *Studies in Historiography* (London 1966), 181–210.

37. J. N. Hillgarth, 'Historiography in Visigothic Spain' in *La Storiografia Altomedievale* (Settimane di Studio del centro italiano di studi sull'alto medioevo) (Spoleto 1970), 261–311.

38. J. M. Wallace-Hadrill, 'Gregory of Tours and Bede: their views on the personal qualities of kings', *Frühmittelalterliche Studien* 2 (1968), 31–44 (rp. in J. M. Wallace-Hadrill, *Early Medieval History* (Oxford 1975), 96–113); F. L. Ganshof, 'L'Historiographie dans la monarchie franque sous les Mérovingiens et les Carolingiens' in *La Storiografia Altomedievale* (n.37 above), 631–85.

39. R. A. Markus, *Bede and the Tradition of Ecclesiastical History*; Jarrow Lecture 1975 (Jarrow 1975); J. M. Wallace-Hadrill, 'Bede and Plummer' in *Early Medieval History* (n.38 above), 76–95.

40. In addition to the useful remarks of R. W. Hanning, *History and Theory* 12 (1973), 419–34 see the papers below by Gardiner, pp.147–54 and Moorhead, pp.155–68.

Christian Innovation
and its Contemporary Observers

E.A. Judge

I: What the historians could not see

Can the question of old and new in fourth-century historiography be related to that of the changes in the fourth-century world as a whole? In particular, what is the basic effect, in cultural terms, of the establishment of Christianity, and what does that have to do with the observations of Eusebius and Ammianus?

At the most obvious level, the struggle over Christianity centred on the relations between divine worship and the public life of the community. Both sides agreed that the welfare of the nation depended upon worshipping the right deity. Custom had traditionally supplied a simple answer to this problem. One's public duty was to respect the gods of one's ancestors. Insofar as Christianity restricted the choice to one God, it was introducing only a qualified novelty, for unitarian ideas were common, and the Christians accepted the traditionalist terms of the argument: 'Our worship can be shown (historically) to be the oldest anyway.' If this had been all there was to it, the fourth-century revolution would have been essentially a fortifying of the old order, as indeed many observers from both the classical and the Christian sides, both then and now, have held it to have been.

But insofar as Christian beliefs rested, not on custom, but on arguments about theology and about man's place in the world, it also came into conflict with the philosophical tradition of antiquity. At this level reconciliation was far less easy to secure. More important still for socio–cultural history is the fact that Christianity made a vastly more determined effort than other philosophical systems to remodel the ethical life (or at least the ideals) of the general community.

The almost total success of this effort points to a development probably without adequate parallel till then in human affairs. A conceptual system which claimed to explain and predict everything about human life was actually being put into some kind of general effect, contrary to the prevailing outlook. The ideas of an intellectual élite were being passed on to the whole community, and even imposed by the government as the new ordering principle of its life. We may thus locate the beginning of modern western history in the fourth century. From this point governments and traditions compete with organised systems of thought for control of the community. The dualistic pattern which has imprinted itself on the character of western social and cultural life has been established.[1]

The confusion of this development with a change in religion, shared as it was in the fourth century by writers from either side, prevented it being seen this way. Not that the religious change was a superficial element in the process historically. It was the familiarity of religious practice which provided the means by which the ideological reordering of the whole community was effected. Religion, however alien to Christianity, conferred social power upon it.

13

Contemporary observers show their consciousness of the fact that a fundamental social change was at stake by speaking of the Christians as a separate nation. This was of couse in itself a traditionalist device: nations are the entities which are entitled to have different customs. But since Christians had no national past or homeland, the conception of them as a nation represents also a provocative assessment of what was happening. The Christians had successfully created within the Roman world a range of social institutions on a national scale which were essentially at variance with the traditional pattern of life. The disruptive flourishing of monasticism and synods, for example, precisely in the face of the new establishment, suggests that in the last resort Constantine and Theodosius were the followers and not the makers of the basic split that was taking place in the structure of the civilised community.

Eusebius and Ammianus, being not simply honest men but historians, both suffer from the compulsion to limit their view of developments in their own day to what can be anticipated from the past. This book is concerned with changes in historical method. But since one might have hoped that, if historians were capable of adapting their techniques at all, they might have done so in a way that would do more justice to what was actually happening, one may begin by posing that question.

Ammianus

The historians would surely not have objected to the question, accepting as they did the principle of τὸ ἀξιόλογον, or concern for the things that were 'narratu . . . digna', as Ammianus puts it (28.1.15).[2] Behind his frequently invoked principle of fidelity, there seems to lie a basic appeal to *veritas*, which he perhaps formulated in the lost Preface.[3] The concern for the ultimate truth of history may of course have led Ammianus, as it probably did Eunapius, deliberately to refrain from giving special attention to Christianity. (Or was there a digression devoted to that subject in the lost books?) But the basic desire to assimilate what is feared as novel comes through alike in the pained reproaches of Ammianus and in the outbursts of Eunapius.[4]

Like some of the Christian apologists of his day, Ammianus is happy enough to accept the identification of Christianity with religion in the Roman sense. If the function of the gods is to protect the civil order, why should anyone object to Rome's enjoying the patronage of a new and manifestly successful power in the heavens? Ammianus can even tolerate (or is it irony?) the murderous competition for succession to the see of Rome. Given the political and social rewards, including the generosity of rich matrons, it was explicable, within the traditional understanding of the place of religion in politics, that men should compete for such a prize (27.3.14). Certainly they would have been truly happy if they had preferred the more morally consistent restraint of provincial bishops (27.3.15). But Ammianus had less understanding of the argumentative confrontations over orthodoxy, which engulfed the court of Constantius and exhausted the public transport system with repeated synods. He could not see the importance of trying to persuade everyone else to one's own opinion. It was a mere battle of words, an old woman's superstition, compared with the simplicity of pure Christianity (21.16.18). Yet when you got them together, as Julian well knew, they were worse than wild beasts to each other, says Ammianus (22.5.4). The author of the *Historia Augusta* agreed. He makes Aurelian complain that the way the senators were going on one might have thought they were debating in a church (20.5).

Our historians are both touching the point and missing it at the same time. The kind of open contention that had once been possible in the Senate was in fact now occurring in the churches. And because serious ideological struggles about the place of man in the world do tend to impose themselves upon public life, the churches were becoming a political arena.

Ammianus has fundamentally mistaken what is happening because of his very readiness to accept Christianity as a religion in the Roman sense. The same mistake of understanding had led to the failure of the persecutions. It was not just a matter of adapting the pantheon to a new manifestation of 'the highest divinity'.

What we are witnessing is the challenging of civilisation for the first time by something which *we* now call a religion, that is, by a comprehensive set of beliefs on man and the world which is capable of determining the pattern of one's life even in contradiction of the estab-lished social order. The western cultural tradition derives much of its vitality and argumen-tativeness from this phenomenon. W. Cantwell Smith has proposed that Manichaeism is historically the first example of a religion in this western sense.[5] It would have been easier for us and for Ammianus if the peculiarly Roman term 'religion' had never been taken over by Christianity in the fourth century. Manichaeans and Christians alike, and their critics, had already formulated an agreed terminology which more adequately described the situation: they were a new race or nation, complete with gods and customs of their own, but paradox-ically residing within no national boundaries. They cut across the existing pattern of political communities. Hence the bewildering climax of the persecutions. But the solution to them did not work either. The attempt to make Christianity into the religion of the Roman Empire broke down on the incompatibility of the phenonenon with religion in the existing sense. The truth was that Christianity was also incompatible with the State, so long as it retained within itself the seeds of all this trouble: the doctrine of a predetermined revelation of the truth about man and the demand that his life be conformed to it. Hence, in spite of the best efforts alike of Constantine and of Julian, such mind-bending fourth-century phenomena as synods and monasticism.

Eusebius
In his *Ecclesiastical History* Eusebius is fully aware of being a pathfinder from a literary point of view, in that no other writer had previously collected the kind of material he pro-poses to bring forward (*HE*.1.1.3.4). But there is a double reason why his mind has not moved on to the possibility of using this opportunity to analyse the essential novelty of the great change he witnessed in his own day.

In the first place, although he could not deny that the race of Christians was new (νέον ὁμολογουμένως ἔθνος, *HE* 1.4.2), their way of life (ὁ βίος ... καὶ τῆς ἀγωγῆς ὁ τρόπος, 1.4.4) went back to creation, just as Jesus should not be thought of as novel merely because of the date of his incarnate *politeia* (*HE* 1.4.1). Raoul Mortley has recently argued that this by now familiar position was already worked out by Clement of Alexandria, who presented the Christians 'as a lawful people under the quasi-kingly regime of Moses'. Since Plato, of course, was only 'Moses atticising', one could thus use history to represent the apparently novel race as the true heirs of the founder of the common culture of the hellenising world.[6]

Secondly, a major purpose of Eusebius in composing the *HE* was to insist that it was the same word of God which had guided the churches to his own day, in defiance of gnostic innovators (*HE* 1.1.1). It is no doubt his concern for orthodoxy that has led him to what has been hailed as a fundamental innovation in historiography, the extensive citation of primary documents.[7] Citation of texts had always been part of the business of proof, for example in law. The conversion of history into a technique of testing the truth in disputed cases is itself a mark of the invasion of classical culture as a whole by arguments about ultimate truth. Eusebius is probably at both levels practically unaware of the historical significance of what he was caught up in. But it was not lost on everyone at the time. Both the philosophical and the political critics of Christianity displayed some sense of the profound changes that threatened the social order of their day.

II: How the philosophers saw it

The collapse of the persecutions did not mean the end of the campaign against the churches. The basic objections had not been met by the political compromise, and there were other ways by which they could be pursued. Constantine hints several times at the sceptical observers whose criticisms he feared (Eus. *HE* 10.5.21, *VC* 2.60.2; Letter to Aelafius, *CSEL* 26.205). At some stage, perhaps prior to Nicaea in 325, he had condemned the work of Porphyry, *Against the Christians,* to be burnt (Soc. *HE* 1.9). Constantine proposes now to call the Arians 'Porphyrians'. Their books are also to be surrendered for burning, subject to the penalty of death. Eusebius was aware that the 15 books of Porphyry had been written long before (about 270, in fact). But he seems not to have had to come to grips with them personally until the persecutions were over, which was after Porphyry had died (in 308). In his work *Against Hierocles* Eusebius thinks he is dealing with propaganda based on Celsus, but it is clear that the philosopher of the persecution had based his *Logos Philalethes* on Porphyry. It was not long before Eusebius discovered the significance of the latter.[8] Jerome records (*de vir. ill.* 81) that he then produced 25 books against Porphyry. Apollinarius (*de vir. ill.* 104) was later to produce 30.

In the second decade of the fourth century, the influx of new members into the churches led Eusebius to compose an elaborate introduction for them, the *Preparation for and Demonstration of the Gospel.* It was to deal in an orderly way with the whole range of intellectual difficulties which might face the new believers. In it Eusebius constantly refers to Porphyry, and at the very beginning of the *Preparation* it is from Porphyry that he draws the vivid summary of the objections of the Greeks (1.2.1–5).[9] 'They say that we neither think like the Greeks nor act like foreigners. What then is it that is alien about us, and what is the novelty of our lifestyle?' The answer to this question is not that the Christians thought like Jews and lived like Greeks. Eusebius goes on to a series of questions which stress the unpardonable atrocity: the Christians have abandoned their national gods, to whom they are indebted for protection, and 'by a mindless and unexamined act of faith' (1.2.4) adopted the universally condemned mythology of the Jews, who are the impious enemies of all peoples. But (and this is the heart of the objection) the Christians do not even apply themselves to the God of the Jews in the way their customs require, but follow a novel and solitary path of their own, respecting neither Greek nor Jewish ways (1.2.5).

Porphyry

Did Porphyry go on to define or analyse this novelty? Probably not, for, with the characteristic conservatism of classical antiquity, he simply could not take seriously the possibility of an alternative way of life. Eusebius turns back on him his own catalogue of the methods of euthanasia amongst barbarian peoples (1.4.7). He claims that they have given up these atrocities solely on the strength of the teachings of Jesus as they have spread around the world. Eusebius thus admits the charges against 'Christianism', and offers it as an alternative to Hellenism and Judaism, 'its very name advertising its novelty' (1.5.12). But the rest of his *Preparation for the Gospel* is nevertheless not devoted to questions of social life, but to basic points in the doctrine of God. He endeavours to show up the weaknesses of polytheism together with its oracles and underlying fatalism (Books 1–6), and the superiority of Hebrew wisdom, which is in agreement with the best Platonic philosophy (Books 7–15). Of the 20 books of the *Demonstration of the Gospel*, the first 10, which alone are extant, deal with the reasons why Christians reject Moses and with the proofs of the divinity of Jesus from Hebrew prophecy. The lost books 11–20 probably continued this theme before finishing with the origins of the church. It is not impossible that Eusebius here attempted an assessment of the peculiar character of 'Christianism', or he may have done it in the *Praeparatio* and *Demonstratio Ecclesiastica*, to which Photius refers, if indeed these works are not simply the product of confusion on Photius' part.

On the other hand, the fragments of Porphyry's work (mainly from the *Apocriticus* of Macarius Magnes, who was answering an early fourth-century critique of Christianity, assumed to have been a digest of Porphyry) confirm that the intellectual issues were paramount. The scale and seriousness of his attacks confirm the impression given by Eusebius. Porphyry was basically concerned with the 'mindless and unexamined act of faith' upon which the peculiar life of the churches rested. He clearly recognised the power exercised over the minds of believers by the teaching of the Scriptures in church. He does not seem to have anticipated that religious sociology might want to find other explanations of the success of Christianity. Nevertheless, his criticisms frequently involve him in comments on contemporary church life, which show that he was an acute observer of what was going on there.[10]

Knowing the doctrines of Scripture as well as he did, Porphyry could see the inconsistency of Christians imitating the temples with large buildings of their own, even though they had no idols or sacrifices, and nothing prevented their praying at home, since the Lord would hear them anywhere (fr. 76). But he was also aware of the teaching activities that went on in the churches, for he understands the distinction between the catechumens and the 'faithful' (fr. 26), who were fully initiated. He does not consider even bishops and presbyters fit to count among the 'faithful' (fr. 95), since they did not live up to the gospel test of the grain of mustard seed (Matt. 17:20). He also considers that Mark 16:17–18 would be a good test of fitness for the 'priesthood' (he does not here use the Christian term), and especially of those competing for bishoprics (fr. 96). He knows that the churches uphold a 'canon of truth' (fr. 38) handed down from Jesus, and is not impressed by the 'tens of thousands' (fr. 36) who perished for it, which was pleasing neither to God nor to a reasonable man (fr. 64). Porphyry also recognises the universal spread of the gospel (fr. 13), which only goes to show the falsity of the prediction in Matt. 24:14, since the end has still not come.

But the most illuminating comments from the social point of view are perhaps those relating to the place of women and their property in the churches. In an earlier work, the *Philosophy from Oracles*, Porphyry had recognised the tenacity of Christian women (Augustine, *de civ. Dei* 19.23).[11] A husband asked the oracle which god he should propitiate to retrieve his wife from Christianity. Apollo replied that it was easier to fly or write on water than recall to reason an impious and defiled woman – therefore leave her to her folly, for she mourns a dead god, condemned as he was by good judges and dishonourably executed in his prime. In *Against the Christians* (fr. 97), Porphyry alleged that women constituted their 'senate' (so Jerome, who warns against the danger), dominating in the churches, and that the preference of the women 'passed judgement on the priestly rank'. The voting power of women was not seen as a sign of social progress, however. There was nothing surprising in Paul's having conquered the world (fr. 4). It was all done for profit. Men who were by origin peasants and paupers had used the familiar magic arts to induce 'rich little women' to hand over their wealth. Porphyry took the saying about the camel and the eye of the needle (Matt. 19:24) as a claim that the poor had privileged access to heaven (fr. 58). It was too immoral for him to credit it to Jesus. It must have been invented by certain paupers who coveted the property of the rich. Similarly, the challenge to the rich young ruler (Matt. 19:21), which was to become the charter of monasticism, must have been invented by a distressed gentlewoman, like the ones Porphyry knew of, who had been persuaded to distribute all their property to the poor. The women had then started raising funds, abandoning their freedom for indecent begging, and adopting a pitiable appearance instead of happiness, and had moved into the houses of those who still had them. It was the ultimate outrage. Having given up their own property on the pretext of piety, they had been driven by want to covet that of others. Porphyry also knew of women committed to virginity who made a boast of it, claiming that they were filled with the Holy Spirit like 'the one who had given birth to Jesus' (fr. 33). Porphyry's contempt for such women is clear. Did he fear the challenge their new way of life made to the accepted social order? Yet a generation later he was to write to his own wife against marriage and in favour of reducing one's material needs to the minimum. The ideals of the Christian women were probably closer to his own than he would have liked to admit.

The prevailing sarcasm of Porphyry's approach to Christianity probably prevented his making any rational appraisal of the contemporary social phenomenon. It also registers his concern at what he sensed as a form of religious mania. He had criticised the classical conception of the gods as well, and had given offence in that quarter. He was not concerned, as Celsus had been, with the national interest.

Celsus

About the time of the great persecution there were published at least three philosophical critiques of Christianity. One was the digest of Porphyry to which Macarius Magnes later replied, of unknown authorship. The second author, likewise unidentified, wrote the three books 'against the Christian name' which are referred to by Lactantius (*div. inst.* 5.2). The latter regards him as a power-seeker and profiteer masquerading as philosopher, and holds that his work was written in ignorance of what it was he was attacking. The only hints as to its contents do not rise above the usual stereotype — Christianity was a superstition suited to old women; the world would be better off when everyone attended again to the cult of the gods.

The third author, also described by Lactantius (*div. inst.* 5.2.12), can be safely identified with Hierocles, an experienced provincial governor who advised Diocletian on the opening of the persecution (*mort. pers.* 16.4). He went on to govern Egypt, and was a particularly provocative persecutor there. The two books of his *Logos Philalethes*, addressed not 'against', but 'to' the Christians, are said by Lactantius to have concentrated on the inconsistencies of Scripture with such penetration that one might have thought he had once belonged to 'our sect'. He was especially hard on Peter and Paul, and the other apostles, who were common and uneducated men, and who were mostly fishermen (Lactantius adds that this lack of culture is a good assurance against their having been liars!). As for Jesus, he was the leader of a brigand army of 900 (a novelty in the tradition of polemics), and not to be compared for miracles with Apollonius of Tyana. Lactantius also tells us that the work contained the praises of 'the highest God' — the same style Licinius was to use in the prayer he was given for his troops before their battle with Maximinus. Eusebius (*contra Hieroclen* 1) claims that the work was a blatant plagiarism, taken from Celsus. He was at this stage no more able than Lactantius to recognise the hand of Porphyry behind the work.

It may be, however, that the shadow of Celsus lay more heavily over these debates than has been thought. As late as 335, when Eusebius delivered his speech 'In Praise of Constantine' at the dedication of the Church of the Holy Sepulchre in Jerusalem, he still thought it important to come to grips with a number of the criticisms that had been first raised by Celsus.[12] It would perhaps be going too far to say that he was working from Celsus. But the similarity of the arguments that Eusebius faced is clear. The philosophical critique as he deals with it is inspired by two major sentiments. The first is a frustration with the fact that so many people should have been persuaded to accept a view of God that was intellectually untenable. It was quite arbitrary of the Christians to have singled out Jesus for divine honours when the world was rich in heroes, and polytheism corresponded well with the diversity of things. The incarnation was an impossible and unnecessary contamination of God's perfection, while the humiliation of Jesus on the cross proved that he could not have been divine anyway.

The second kind of argument to which Eusebius replies is inspired by concern over the social promiscuity of the Christian movement. In contrast with the universal judgement that one should associate with God what is best in life, the Christians deliberately cultivated the worst people. Jesus himself was of mean origin, and the disciples paltry. Yet this vulgar company, appearing only the day before yesterday, and in a backward corner of the Empire, had had the impertinence to call in question hallowed national customs, and to address themselves without discrimination to people of any national tradition. This was a profanation of the State, stripping it of its divine sanctions. But in any case, the perverse judgement of the Christians had not been vindicated by their God in the passage of time. Andresen has argued that Celsus, in response to the novel development of a theology of history by Justin, had reacted uniquely amongst the critics of Christianity against the Greek tradition of understanding the cosmos in metaphysical categories.[13] But arguments from social and historical reality lack the security of the timeless. The remarkable shift of fortune which Eusebius had witnessed enabled him to convert the social deficiencies to which Celsus had appealed into trump cards. Celsus had mocked the Jews as frogs holding sanhedrin round a pond, while the Christian worms held their ecclesia in the dung-heap, arguing about which of them was the worst sinner. God had larger things to think of. Plotinus, the teacher of Porphyry, though by no means hostile to Christians, would have agreed. It was absurd to call the least of men brothers and deny this name to the sun and the heavenly bodies. It was all a gross anthropomorphism, hopelessly overestimating the importance of man in the cosmos. But if the universe is stable, remarkable things still happen in the world of men. History might yet reveal the hand of God. In Eusebius' day the worms had suddenly turned, to rule the world.

Julian

With Julian we meet at last a spokesman whose voice has not been stifled. We could hardly wish for a better qualified informant. Standing where he does, at the centre of power, and at a time when the significance of the recent changes must have been apparent to anyone with an eye to see, and above all with his close personal involvement, he must have known the answers to our questions. Yet Julian is equally clearly an untypical if not unique participant. His acute sensitivities sharpen all the issues, but no doubt overstate them too.

Taking up the old complaint, he reproaches the Christians with 'the spirit of apostasy' from the national religion (3.388).[14] The same idea had already been turned against him by his half-brother, Gallus (if the letter is genuine), in response to the rumour that he was thinking of abandoning the religion of his family (3.288). As the heirs of Constantine, their personal and national obligation now lay where Constantine's choice had fallen. In making his way back to Hellenism, however, Julian conceived of himself as called by Zeus and the other gods for the restoration of the true and truly ancient religion. He sets this out in a lengthy parable (2.130–148; cf. 3.12, 26, 148). At a critical point in his career he had prayed to the gods for a sign (2.282), and at other times received one apparently unsolicited (2.486: 3.4, 8). Julian's mind was highly alert to the need for guidance. Homer and Plato are bound to him personally, like amulets (3.98). He was no doubt familiar with the practice, documented by the many extracts from the Bible preserved on folded pieces of papyrus, whereby believers literally bound themselves to the words of God. The Bible had made a deep impression on Julian too. He alludes to passages of Scripture, expecting his non-Christian readers to understand the point (2.6, 36, 298, 304, 308). It was said that in his youth he had learnt it all by heart (Eunapius, *vit. Soph.* 473).

The ancient religion, however, which he was determined to restore, or, as he called it, 'Hellenism', could no longer be taken for granted. For all his intense conviction of its truth, Julian did not attempt to conceal from himself or anyone else the widespread disbelief and even disloyalty he faced. He defended himself with insults. 'Dogs relieve themselves on the pillars in front of the schools and courts' (2.8). He admits the fact that the prefect of Egypt is openly ignoring his demand for the banishment of Athanasius (3.142). In the *Misopogon*, the satire on himself by which he reflects his frustration, he no doubt even exaggerates the degree to which the citizens of Antioch found his image and policies ridiculously outdated (2.470). But the omission of the city council to provide sacrifices for his visit to the temple of Zeus at Daphne, where it was left to the priest to find a goose from his private means (2.486), represents a tacit opposition to his wishes. He must have seen that it put a large question mark over the future. The temple of Apollo at Daphne had already been stripped for building materials (3.98).

But Julian was actively encouraging the development of a national community ('koinon', 3.28) of the Hellenes, which could also claim its dedicated patronesses (3.136). As the sole ruler of the Roman Empire, with the prospect of a long life ahead of him, he must have seemed to many a figure to be seriously reckoned with. He speaks of the unusual sight of crowded temple precincts, as people and magistrates hastened to applaud him and listen to his reproachful speeches (2.438). There were even bishops who kept their options open. Pegasius of Ilium had all along been a secret admirer of the old gods, and was now free to take up a priesthood publicly (2.48–54). George, the Arian bishop of Alexandria, assassinated by the Christian mob, had possessed a good classical library which Julian had used in the past, and which he now hoped to rescue (2.74, 122). Even Basil, the future bishop of Caesarea and formerly a fellow-student of Julian's at Athens, received an invitation to Court, with a public travel voucher into the bargain. Julian hoped for friendly academic debate (3.82).

Like his intellectual predecessors, and fortified in this no doubt by his Christian upbringing, Julian was fully conscious that the 'madness of the Galileans' (2.36), by which they had introduced a novel 'kerygma' and teaching (3.142) and inflicted a disease on the community (3.144), sprang from the study of Scripture. He recognised the passion for learning and argument that gripped the church at Alexandria, and the strong supply of teachers in it (3.150). But he also challenged the Galileans to put the matter to a proper educational test. Train a sample group of children in Scripture only, he proposed, and see whether they turn out any better than slaves (3.386). True to the philosophical ideal, Julian believes that knowledge is only possible for an élite. The Galileans were creating a false expectation amongst the people. For the same reason Julian objected to the Cynics taking seriously the opinions of common people (2.46). The churches, he rightly detected, had been tacitly relying upon the classical tradition to help them come to terms with educated society. But Jesus had only been known for 300 years, and his followers were really leeches, who sucked only the worst blood from the Jewish tradition to which they had attached themselves (3.376). He and the 'fishermen-theologians' (3.188) had only been interested in the sinners, to whom Jesus immorally offered forgiveness (2.412), and in mean activities like curing cripples and blind paupers. You confined yourselves to backward peoples and places like this, Julian reminds them, because you never expected that 'you would one day arrive at the position of power you now have' (3.376).

Yet in spite of his contempt for their vulgarity, Julian recognised that the attraction of the churches lay partly in their charitable work (2.302, 336; 3.68–70). He recognised the power of Jesus' command to 'sell what you have and give to the poor', even though he could see that it made economic nonsense (3.430). He complained that the councillors of Antioch who neglected the sacrifices nevertheless allowed their wives to empty the cupboards to feed the poor — and to enjoy the reputation they won from it (2.490). The same women were allowed to 'govern themselves' and have control over the bringing up of the children (2.472). Julian was enraged that Athanasius should have baptised 'eminent Greek women' during his reign (2.142). Although he regarded the life of women as pitiable and emotionally unstable (2.64, 440), he knew their importance in the spread of the gospel (3.376). He also recognised the solidarity of the social classes created by Christian belief (2.474), in spite of the economic conflicts and exploitation in which the groups concerned were involved (2.502–512).

Features of church life new to his era also took Julian's eye. He was by no means confined to the conventional objections to Christianity. The insubordination he faced in Alexandria and Antioch made clear to him the fact that the governing classes in such cities were now closely connected with the bishops. If his policies were frustrated, he could assume that the bishops and presbyters had been sitting in secret session with the local administration (3.46). When the people of Alexandria had tried to stop the dismantling of the temples, the prefect had turned his troops on them, 'perhaps because he feared George more than Constantius' (3.62). The troubles at Alexandria and elsewhere made clear another novelty of the age, the state of civil war between rival Christian orthodoxies. Julian knows the technical terminology, and his sharp tongue does not spare the atrocities either of 'heretics' (3.128) or of 'clerics' (3.130). Neither Jesus nor Paul had authorised them to slaughter each other 'because they did not mourn the dead body [of Jesus] in the same way' (3.376). Julian loved to depict Christianity as a cult of death. He was familiar with the fetishism of the cross (3.372), but above all his barbs were directed at the cult of the martyrs. He hinted that the Christians had turned out to be polytheists after all (3.374). Because the bones of the martyrs were kept there, he called the churches 'tombs' (2.134, 484; 3.134). By seeking the inspiration of the dead in this way the churches were breaking the scriptural ban on sleeping among the tombs

(3.416). 'You have filled everything with tombs and monuments, but it is nowhere prescribed for you that you should abase yourselves before them and revere them' (3.414).

Apart from the petition of Isidore of Karanis (P. Col. 171), Julian is our earliest independent authority for monasticism. He admired asceticism as a philosopher. Marcus Aurelius 'displayed a beauty beyond invention by the very fact that he kept himself uncared for and unadorned'; 'His body shone with transparent light, most pure and clear, from lack of food' (2.371). Julian's chosen company of seven at Antioch pursued a kind of collective asceticism (2.466). The people of Antioch found his matted and lice-infested hair and beard revolting, together with his long nails and ink-stained hands (2.422–424). They objected to his sleeping alone (2.442). But he did not admire the monks. He knows of the Antonian type of hermit, 'surrendered to the possession of evil spirits and driven by them to hatred of mankind' (2.296). He has also long known of the 'apotactites' (2.122, taking the revised reading of Bidez). They are frauds. By giving up a few things, they attract support from all sides, and have everyone dancing attendance upon them. Julian likes to insult the Cynics by calling them 'apotactites'. Their traditional calling had been to 're-coin the currency' (2.82), or to create an alternative lifestyle, as we should now put it. The comparison suggests that Julian was sensitive to the challenge presented by monasticism to the established social order. But he draws two vital distinctions. The Cynics did not go in for giving oracular advice, nor did they raise funds for the needy out of 'mercy', as the Galileans called it. Here once more we find the two distinctive hallmarks of Christianity, this time explicitly identified for us by a peculiarly well-qualified disbeliever: the doctrine of revelation, and care for those in need.

Although Julian was heir to the military burden of the Roman Empire, and lost his life campaigning against the Persians, he was not seriously concerned with Christianity as a threat to national security, as had been the persecuting emperors. Religion was not for him in the first place a matter of the public interest. Julian was concerned for the intrinsic truth of 'Hellenism', the recognition of which he believed to be central to the integrity of the classical tradition. His onslaught on Christianity set a style that was to find echoes amongst Greek writers of the old persuasion for a century or more. They immortalised their hero, and retreated into their academic preserves, prepared to sit out the siege indefinitely.[15] Julian's older contemporary, Libanius, the great rhetorician of Antioch, taught the generation of classicising bishops that followed them. Yet he did not hesitate to take up Julian's criticisms of Christianity, as his speeches gave him opportunity. He was no campaigner, but the hypocrisy of the rabble-rousing monks, 'the men clothed in black', especially incensed him. Eunapius, though, like Julian, a pupil of the Christian sophist, Prohaeresius, at Athens, spoke out in very similar terms. In his *Lives of the Sophists* he gave expression to his sense of the importance for Greek education of the élite succession of scholars. The rhetorician Themistius, however, who worked for both Constantius and Theodosius, attempted no direct criticism of Christianity. Reversing the attitude of Julian, he advocated a philosophical education that would make ethics popular, in the hope of creating a cultural bond between ruler and subject. He was content to praise Constantius, Julian and Theodosius alike as philosophers. Such a spirit of compromise, which earned him the contempt of the intransigent sophists, secured the future of Hellenism more effectively than confrontation could ever have done. He showed the way to the Greek-Christian symbiosis of Byzantium.

III: How the policy-makers tried to stop it
The philosophical critique of Christianity tells us how the movement was viewed within a

limited circle of intellectuals. But their ongoing preoccupation with its illogicality and vulgarity, I believe, correctly identifies the mainspring: the beliefs of the Christians contradicted both the accepted ways of understanding the world and its hierarchy of social values. Beliefs and social action, moreoever, were coupled together in a unique manner, with effects unknown before in classical antiquity. An alternative form of community life was being created, and had begun seriously to disorient those who valued the old city-based culture. The persecutions demonstrate the fact that this threat not only arose in the conceit of philosophers, but was taken to heart by government and public as well. The reasons are also clear. The concern was for national security, a fully traditional reaction.

But in the immediate aftermath of the persecutions we find a quite distinct kind of response at the public level, and one which is new to the classical tradition. If the Christians will not associate themselves in the proper way with the general community, they had better be excluded from it. The choice is now between full assimilation and apartheid. Coupled with this demand are attempts to generate a renewal of community support for the national cults. Their prestige had been injured by the capitulation of the government to the Christians. Now they are to be regenerated, but in a novel way. They will be reorganised so as to capture some of the sources of community strength and solidarity that had been effectively demonstrated in the organisation of the churches.

Maximinus

It is not clear who first thought of this method of treating the problem. As soon as the death of Galerius became known in May 311, Maximinus Daia moved to occupy Asia Minor. He had given effect to the edict of toleration by a rather more guarded circular issued to the governors of the East by his Praetorian Prefect, Sabinus (Eus. *HE* 9.1.3–6). Eusebius himself alludes (9.2) to a period of six months' respite for the churches. We may then imagine that the return of the exiles, and plans for the rebuilding of churches, would soon have created tension with those who had profited from their suppression.[16]

According to Lactantius (*mort. pers.* 36.3), Maximinus then arranged for deputations from the cities to seek from him a ban on the construction of meeting-places ('conventicula') by the Christians. This was followed by the creation of high priests for each city. They were to be selected from the leading citizens, and were to sacrifice daily to all the gods. The existing priests of the various cults were to be subordinate to the high priest, and together they were to be responsible for preventing any meeting places being built by Christians, and indeed for preventing their meeting at all.

The high priests of the various cities were grouped into provincial hierarchies, under a metropolitan. Eusebius stresses the novelty of these procedures (*HE* 9.7.1). The assimilation of the priesthoods to the pattern of civil authority parallels the development of such a pattern that had occurred amongst the churches. It represents a bid to upstage the Christians.

At Antioch the campaign was originated by Theotecnus, the city treasurer. He is presumably the imperial *curator civitatis*, which might support the assumption that the ultimate initiative came from above, though by this stage the post was usually filled from the local nobility. Like Epitynchanus,[17] he was able to produce oracles to give himself credence (9.3). They were presumably issued in the name of Zeus Philios, whose cult he managed. The cult-name is perhaps significant: the Christians are to be driven out in the name of the god of hospitality.

Eusebius says (*HE* 9.4.1) that the fashion of appealing to Maximinus for the exclusion of

Christians spread from Antioch, and he stresses the selection of civil leaders as the new city and provincial high-priests (9.4.2). They had guards, and a military escort (8.14.9).

The campaign of Maximinus had also embraced public education. Fictitious Acts of Pilate and Jesus were devised (Eus. *HE* 9.5.1). They were to be officially displayed by means of inscriptions, and used as teaching material in schools, to be learnt by heart by the children. Maximinus also published in every city and place the revelations (extorted, according to Eusebius, by the military governor of Damascus) of public prostitutes on the indecencies which were performed in 'the Lord's houses' (*HE* 9.5.2). Roman tradition was familiar with the public display of eulogistic treatments of history, but the convention had been to condemn the memories of the losers to oblivion. Now, however, the sense of ideological competition is apparent. The paradox of the deified criminal, which we know from the philosophers was a major source of offence in Christian doctrine, is to be dealt with openly, using even the elementary means of persuasion available through the schools. Does this reflect an awareness of the influence of Christian doctrine on children? Their enemies were ahead of the churches in recognising the uses of education for indoctrination. This must mark the beginning of what has become a major feature of western civilisation: the commitment of the state to a deliberate inculcation of its version of the truth, and the conversion of education to this purpose. The ideologising of society is then, by reaction, one of the most far-reaching consequences of the dogmatic drive of the churches.

Licinius

Although Licinius is seen by Eusebius as the vindicator of the Christian cause over Maximinus, one may reasonably assume that the concerns of the cities upon which his campaign had rested remained the same, and that the new ruler would for political reasons at least be obliged to take them seriously.[18] As the tension built up towards his final conflict with Constantine (in 324), moreover, he must have found it prudent to cultivate anti-Christian opinion, given the strong personal commitment of Constantine to the churches. Eusebius says that he came to admire the anti-Christian policies of his predecessors in the East (*HE* 10.8.2). He began to 'besiege' the Christians gradually, and without drawing too much attention to it (10.8.8). First, he removed all Christians from his household (10.8.9). He then excluded from service (although Eusebius uses the term 'soldiers', this should probably be taken as a reference to the civil service) and downgraded those who would not sacrifice (10.8.10). Worse was to follow, but 'must I recall all his deeds in detail?', asks Eusebius, 'and the unlawful laws of that most lawless man?' (These remarks are important, in view of the claim that the *HE* does not justify our accepting the measures registered in the *VC* as authentic.) There was a ban on taking food to prisoners or those in chains. No one was to be allowed to do good to his neighbour. Those who attempted this ministry were to be made subject to the same suffering they sought to relieve (10.8.11). The emotional reaction of Eusebius (more extensive than indicated here) shows that Licinius had put his finger on a sensitive spot. Presumably he recognised the social influence established by the charitable practices of the Christians, and quietly cut the nerve of their ministry.

Eusebius then refers (without detail) to the elimination of the most reputable bishops by having the governors lay traps for them. Unheard of means of death were employed (*HE* 10.8.14). The details given suggest only local atrocities on the part of the governors (10.8.17). Eusebius implies that the basis for the action was that the Christians were believed to be praying for the victory of Constantine (10.8.16). In Amasia, and other cities of Pontus, some churches were demolished, others locked up (10.8.15). There would have been a general persecution had not Constantine's victory intervened (10.8.18–19).

Although Eusebius was clearly not very well informed at the time of his final revision of the history (soon after 324?), the *Life of Constantine* (even if genuine, published apparently only after Eusebius' death in 339?) provides striking additional details. The Eusebian authorship of this work has been seriously challenged on grounds of style and composition, which are rejected, with argument, by the latest editor.[19] He also dismisses, though without giving reasons, the objections brought against the details of the persecution in particular, which have been held to be a fabrication, based upon the attested policies of Theodosius against the heretics.[20] It is not possible here to debate this argument, but instead I propose to ask the question whether the details can be given a plausible explanation in relation to what Eusebius tells us in the *HE* of the policies of Licinius.

But first, what of the documents in the *Vita Constantini*? The letter which is said to have been sent by Constantine to Eusebius himself and to all the other bishops on the repair and extension of neglected church buildings (*VC* 2.46.1–3), although it refers to the restoration of freedom from 'that dragon' (Licinius), nowhere suggests that any buildings had been destroyed, nor that there had been any confiscations. What has to be made good is the result of neglect, based partly on the fear of possible action against the churches.

Destruction of buildings is likewise not mentioned (though confiscation is) in the 'complete provision' (*VC* 2.41) for restoration of rights which Constantine made in an edict addressed 'to the provincials of Palestine' (*VC* 2.24–42), and which is said in one group of manuscripts to have been 'the first letter sent after his victory over the tyrants by Constantine, Emperor of the Romans, to those in the eastern land'. This is the edict of which 'Eusebius' claims to have a personal signed copy. Its authenticity has been established by the identification of a fragment of it in P. Lond. 878. It directs that the following 'cruel outrages and punishments' are to be reversed (26.2). On the personal front, the penalties specified are: exile beyond the frontiers (30.1); banishment to islands (31.1); condemnation to labour in mines or public works (32.1); loss of civil rank (32.2); loss of status in the government service (33); loss of social rank (34.1), with consequential condemnation to work in women's apartments or linen factories (34.1) or reduction to the status of servant of the treasury (34.1); reduction to slavery (34.2). On the property front the penalties are: compulsory enrolment as councillor (which carried financial obligations) (30.1); confiscation of all property (30.2); confiscation of the deceased estates of martyrs (35.1) (next-of-kin are now to inherit or, in their absence, the churches); confiscation of church buildings, lands and orchards (39); confiscation of martyrs' graves (40). In all these cases, restoration is required whether from individuals (37.1), who may have obtained the properties at auction (38), by purchase (41) or as gifts (41), or from the treasury (39).

It will be apparent that this list implies a far more extensive range of action than Eusebius had indicated in the *HE*. It is hard to think that it was the result only of individual initiatives by the governors. That no particular prominence is given to the death penalty confirms the suspicion that in the *HE* Eusebius was making the most of it. On the other hand, the extensive range of status degradations and confiscations suggests a planned drive to reduce the wealth and social dignity of the church community. Two points not mentioned in the *HE* are particularly tell-tale. The compulsory enrolment of Christians as councillors presumably reverses the immunity granted to Catholic clergymen by Constantine in 313 (Eus. *HE* 10.7), and reinforced in 319 (*Cod. Theod.* 16.2.1, 2), though by 320 Constantine himself had had to stop the flight of propertied persons from their civil obligations by confining access to the clergy-posts to those too poor for council service (*Cod. Theod.* 16.2.3). Secondly, the confiscation of martyrs' graves presumably represents the same line of attack which had opened the campaign of Maximinus in 311. Thus although this catalogue does not, and being a list of individual penalties at law, could not substantiate the other measures attributed to Licinius in the *VC*, its diversity, and the emphasis on the social effects of the policy, certainly justifies serious consideration of the others.

The first 'law' attributed to Licinius (*VC* 1.51.1) is a ban on the bishops' meeting in synod, or even visiting each other for consultation. The author notes (51.2) that this is the only legitimate method by which ecclesiastical decisions are made. If this act is authentic, it is a well-calculated move to break down the extraordinary international nexus which had been created amongst the bishops, and to which Constantine had quickly learnt to subject himself for guidance in matters ecclesiastical. Even the reorganisation of religion along provincial lines by Maximinus had not ventured to go so far. One can easily imagine how the tumultuous series of synods at Alexandria over Arianism may have given Licinius the excuse for a ban. Given the vast power which was shortly to be demonstrated by the councils, it could even be rated far-sighted. But quite apart from the threat of a state within the State, the socially disruptive factionalism in church life justified a curb on the politicking of bishops. It has been held that the purpose of the measure would have been to provoke the bishops into self-incriminating acts of retaliation.[21] In that case it would be amongst the 'traps' alluded to in *HE* 10.8.4

The second 'law' (*VC* 1.53.1) prevented women meeting for prayer with men, and excluded them from attendance at 'instruction in virtue'. The bishops were not to catechise women, but other women were to be selected to teach the women. Cataudella assumes that this represents a desire to prevent the kind of sexual scandals of which Maximinus had publicly accused the churches (*HE* 9.5.2), and that it must be unhistorical because the churches would not have found such a measure unwelcome in the circumstances assumed. But it is notable that in spite of gossip the Fathers of the church were generally inclined to justify the close associations they maintained with the patronesses who supplied them with funds and social prestige, while the orders of widows and virgins provided the backbone of the caring ministry of the churches. It might be sounder to suppose that the object of such a measure by Licinius would have been to break down this very effective system of social relations. One may also perhaps suspect in it an outworking of the contempt for the intellectual capacity of women which is a feature of the philosophical tradition, if not of the ecclesiastical one (Eus. *PE* 1.4.14, 5.3). By making the women undertake the teaching of women, may not the hope have been that some of the impetus would be lost to the life of the churches through the intellectual degeneration which would follow on the notoriously productive female side?

One of the historically troublesome aspects of these extra measures attributed to Licinius in the *VC* is their complete lack of attestation from other sources. It may be noted here, on the other hand, that a recently published papyrus documents a circle of women who ranked as 'teachers' in the church (P. Strasb. Gr. 1900). The editor dates this text to later in the fourth century, and attributes it to heretical circles, who are known to have been willing to use women as teachers.[22] But the date should perhaps be reconsidered in the light of a possible *Sitz im Leben* during the campaign of Licinius.

A third measure requires church meetings to take place outside the city-gates in the open air (*VC* 1.53.2). This is explicable in terms of the petitions to Maximinus requesting the exclusion of the Christians from the cities, while the denial of building rights may have been intended to cripple the charitable (or even indecent) activities which were associated with church buildings.

These three items are the major additions of the *VC* to the account of the policies of Licinius given by Eusebius in the *HE*. None of them is inconsistent with the picture presented there of a ruler gradually limiting the risks of a programme he knew from experience could easily back-fire. We know that Eusebius of Nicomedia retained the confidence of Licinius throughout, and that a relative of this bishop, the Praetorian Prefect Julius Julianus, was honoured by Constantine with the consulship immediately after his defeat, and married into his family to become the grandfather of the Emperor Julian. It is clear therefore that Licinius had been following a policy of compromise rather than full confrontation. There is no reason to suppose that he was deliberately seeking a collision with Constantine: the pace was being set by the other side. But given the coming struggle he was bound to make the most of those who would not welcome the victory of the great patron of the churches. We should also not exclude the possibility that the main grievance of Licinius in ecclesiastical matters was with those who opposed Eusebius of Nicomedia as an Arian. Eusebius of Caesarea, however, has cast him as a total renegade, thus fully endorsing the propaganda of Constantine. Neither Eusebius nor any other author, composing the *VC* from that point of view, would have been likely to invent such peculiar and unspectacular offences on Licinius' part as the three measures peculiar to the *VC*. The very difficulty of explaining them obliges the modern historian to consider more carefully the possibility that they are actual relics of the policy of Licinius. Any rhetorically capable writer in antiquity would have had far more sensational allegations ready to hand had he needed to invent them.

The difficulty of correlating the measures with other evidence for the history of the church in these times is a danger sign, of course. The innocent testimony of Isidore of Karanis (P. Col. 171) makes it quite certain that there was no serious constraint on church life in his corner of Egypt, and the same seems to have been the case with Alexandria. But we should remember that we do not know the chronology of the acts of Licinius. It is perfectly possible that a more detailed knowledge of the timing would enable us to fit in both the evidence for ecclesiastical freedom and the acts of repression. The same applies of course to the possibility that the policy was applied in different ways in different places. The *VC* says that some of the measures were greeted with ridicule. We may imagine that they were only successful where there was public support, and administrators willing to gamble on a victory for Licinius. The situation everywhere must have been confused. From the city of Hermopolis Magna, in Egypt, we possess from about the year 320 the correspondence of a lawyer, Theophanes.[23] He was a cultivated man, with religious interests that are difficult to pin down, and had made a journey to Antioch to intervene in some questions of injustices arising from religious causes. Some editors have put him on the Christian side, others amongst their opponents. His sons say that they owe to their father an ability 'to think little of those who think differently'. Two correspondents address him as their 'beloved brother', and another speaks of 'the highest God' and yet another of 'the grace of the Almighty God'. But another correspondent again is certainly a 'chief prophet' in the cult of Hermes Trismegistus. There may have been more realism in the attempt of Maximinus to affiliate all beliefs into one social structure of religion than church critics could allow. Licinius appears to have made a distinctive and more limited attempt to curb the social independence of the churches.

Although not a Christian, and necessarily dependent upon the support of the classical gods in his conflict with Constantine (*VC* 2.4; 2.5.2), he does not seem to have attempted to revive the city and provincial high-priesthoods of Maximinus. That, along with other more radical measures, was reserved for Julian.

IV: Who saw best what was going on?

The conclusion then is this. Neither Eusebius nor Ammianus seems to have been in a position to see directly the basic nature of the changes going on. Eusebius was too preoccupied with the need to demonstrate the maintenance of the orthodox succession against innovators to appreciate the ways in which the struggle over orthodoxy was itself shifting the centre of power in the community out of the hands of the civil rulers. The official status accorded the churches, and their mass following, subsequently made it easier for Ammianus to see them as occupying an acceptable place within the old Roman pattern of religion. He failed to recognise the historical importance of things which repelled him, notably their argumentativeness, and assumed that it was an aberration rather than of the essence of Christianity. But the philosophers, and especially those who apparently had inside knowledge of the movement, Porphyry, Hierocles and Julian, saw the need to cripple the intellectual drive of the churches by discrediting Scripture. They saw the new pattern of social alignments which it generated, and clearly sensed the threat to the very integrity of classical civilisation. At the practical level, Maximinus and Licinius attempted to save the day by imposing a uniform religious structure on the community, and breaking down the institutions through which an alternative pattern of society was being built up within the Roman world.

History was not repeating itself. Insofar as fundamentally new arrangements for life were being introduced, especially in the West, classical historiography ceased to provide useful conventions for viewing it. The new ecclesiastical history failed to expand its horizons far enough to take in the full range of public life. Chronography provided a step in the right direction, towards a teleological explanation of man's progress through time, but its skeletal form left it too far short of the full analysis of the significance of the changes.

Notes

1.   A. Dihle, 'Antikes und Unantikes in der frühchristlichen Staatstheorie', in D. M. Pippidi (ed.), *Assimilation et résistance à la culture gréco-romaine dans le monde ancien* (Bucharest 1976), 323–32; E. A. Judge, *The Conversion of Rome: Ancient Sources of Modern Social Tensions* (North Ryde 1980).

2.   H. Drexler, *Ammianstudien* (Hildesheim 1974), 3.

3.   G. Sabbah, *La méthode d'Ammien Marcellin* (Paris 1978), 19.

4.   *ibid.*, 55.

5.   In a lecture at the XIVth International Congress of the International Association for the History of Religions, in Winnipeg on 21 August 1980.

6.   R. J. Mortley, 'The past in Clement of Alexandria: a study of an attempt to define Christianity in socio-cultural terms', in E. P. Sanders (ed.), *Jewish and Christian Self-Definition* (London 1980), 186–200.

7.   A. Momigliano, 'Pagan and Christian historiography in the fourth century A.D.', in *The Conflict between Paganism and Christianity in the Fourth Century* (Oxford 1963), 79–99, drawing attention (91) to Josephus as representing a similarly apologetic use of documents in history.

8.   For the chronology I follow J. Sirinelli's introduction to the *Sources Chrétiennes* edn (1974) of Eusebius' 'Preparation for the Gospel'. But it is now claimed that Eusebius had made extensive use of Porphyry 'Against the Christians' in the first edition of his Chronicle (*c.* 300 or even as early as 280) : so B. Croke, 'The Era of Porphyry's Anti-Christian Polemic', *Journal of Religious History* 14 (1984).

9.   U. von Wilamowitz-Moellendorf, 'Ein Bruchstück aus der Schrift des Porphyrius gegen die Christen', *Zeitschrift für die neutestamentliche Wissenschaft* 1 (1900), 101–5.

10.   Yet Harnack's classification of a few fragments under this heading is arbitrary; the allusions may well have been only incidental to his main attack on Scripture : A. von Harnack, *Porphyrius gegen die Christen* (Berlin 1916); T. D. Barnes, 'Porphyry *Against the Christians* : Date and the Attribution of Fragments', *Journal of Theological Studies* 24 (1973), 424–42; A. Benoit, 'Le *Contra Christianos* de Porphyre : où en est la collecte des fragments?' in *Mélanges Simon* (Paris 1978), 261–75.

11.   J. M. Demarolle, 'Les femmes chrétiennes vues par Porphyre', *Jahrbuch für Antike und Christentum* 13 (1970), 42–7.

12.   C. T. H. R. Ehrhardt, 'Eusebius and Celsus', *Jahrbuch für Antike und Christentum* 22 (1979), 40–9.

13.   C. Andresen, *Logos und Nomos : die Polemik des Kelsos wider das Christentum* (Berlin 1955).

14.   All references to Julian are to volume and page in the Loeb edition of W. C. Wright.

15.   For Libanius, see P. de Labriolle, *La réaction paienne*[9] (Paris 1950), 429–33. For Eunapius, see I. Opelt, s.v., *Reallexikon für Antike und Christentum* 6 (1965), 18–36, and R. T. Ridley, 'Eunapius and Zosimus', *Helikon* 9/10 (1969/70), 574–92. For Themistius, see G. Downey, 'Themistius and the Defense of Hellenism in the Fourth Century', *Harvard Theological Review* 50 (1957), 259–74.

16.   Moreover, H. Castritius has shown, in *Studien zu Maximinus Daia* (Kallmünz 1969), how the general economic interests of the cities were closely tied to the festivals and other commercial aspects of the public cults.

17.   For his inscription as 'first high-priest, saviour of his country, and legislator', found near Acmoneia in Phrygia, see H. Grégoire, 'Notes épigraphiques I : La religion de Maximin Daia', *Byzantion* 8 (1933), 49–56.

18.   That he did so is implied by Libanius, *Or.* 3.6 (ed. Foerster, p.190).

19.   F. Winkelmann, *Über das Leben des Kaisers Konstantin* (*GCS* 1.1) (Berlin 1975).

20.   M. R. Cataudella, 'La persecuzione di Licinio e l'autenticità della Vita Constantini', *Athenaeum* 48 (1970), 48–83, 229–59.

21.   H. Feld, *Der Kaiser Licinius* (Diss. Saarland 1960).

22.   M. Nagel, 'Lettre chrétien sur papyrus (provenant des milieux sectaires du IVe siècle?)', *Zeitschrift für Papyrologie und Epigraphik* 18 (1975), 317–23.

23.   E. A. Judge and S. R. Pickering, 'Papyrus documentation of church and community in Egypt to the mid-fourth century', *Jahrbuch für Antike und Christentum* 20 (1977), 47–71.

Ammianus' Historical Evolution

John Matthews

Ammianus Marcellinus ended his history with the battle of Hadrianople and the death of Valens in August 378, and with the immediate sequel to these momentous events. In a brief postscript he challenged historians of the rising generation, men in the full vigour of youth and learning, to continue his work (31.16.9). But he has a warning: if they do attempt the task, they should ensure that they master the higher style appropriate, as Gibbon put it (conveying an irony not present in Ammianus himself), for the 'more glorious history of the ensuing reign'.[1] As Gibbon remarked, the 'rising generation' did not seem disposed to accept the challenge; so that Ammianus, the first major Latin historian of the Roman Empire since Tacitus, is also the last of the line.

Even had Ammianus not been unique, his achievement would still have been an extra-ordinary one from the point of view of his linguistic and cultural background. He had written, as he explains in his postscript, as a former soldier and a Greek: 'ut miles quondam et Graecus'. It has been suggested that Ammianus is here stating his double qualification as a historian — practical experience as a soldier, allied to the literary and rhetorical training essential for the proper performance of the historian's task.[2] There is something to be said for this view. What, after all, was the purpose of history except as a moral lesson (drawn for contemporaries from the past or from contemporary events for the future) and what is more central to this essentially persuasive task than the deployment of traditional rhetorical skills? It was not for nothing that oratory and history were considered related and adjacent arts, or that Ammianus himself could once refer to his narrative as 'oratio' (14.6.2) and also in another passage compare his history, though true and based on the best evidence, with panegyric (16.1.3 see below, p.34). As for the first part of Ammianus' self-identification, it was of course assumed that the historian of contemporary affairs should possess the practical experience which qualified him to pass judgment on them.

Others (most recently Robert Browning) have taken Ammianus' expression 'ut miles et Graecus' rather in a concessive or apologetic sense, as if he were excusing himself as a *mere* soldier and Greek, for his effrontery in writing Roman history — an occupation (as Browning suggests) more characteristic of civilian, even aristocratic, pursuits than of the military profession.[3] That Ammianus himself may have meant the phrase in this sense seems to me to be suggested by his openly apologetic remark, which follows immediately, that he had written 'as well as my abilities permitted'('per virium explicavi mensura').There is indeed something paradoxical about Ammianus' claim, at more than one level. To take only the most pragmatic of these, it is hard to see the 'soldiers' portrayed in Ammianus' own narrative as sensitive, erudite men of literary gifts, likely to have produced histories. More typical of the class is the 'subagreste ingenium' of the Emperor Valens and others (31.14.8) — an expression more precisely defined in one case, that of a career bureaucrat who supported Valens, as involving the absence of the 'polish' imparted by the reading of Classical authors: 'subagreste ingenium, nullis vetustatis lectionibus expolitum' (30.4.2).

The paradox in Ammianus' statement that he had written as a 'Greek' is still more conspicuous in his decision, for whatever reason, to write in Latin. Ammianus' example, though neglected by historians, was as it happens matched by a poetic successor of the 'rising generation', Claudian of Alexandria — who (we may recall) in Gibbon's estimation 'soared above his feeble contemporaries and placed himself, after an interval of three hundred years, among the poets of ancient Rome'.[4] Yet Claudian too was unique, and he hardly goes far to explain Ammianus, of whom there is no evidence that he was at all aware. More typical of Ammianus' Greek contemporaries was his Antiochene fellow-citizen, Libanius, who resisted Latin and feared it as a language of bureaucrats and lawyers connected with the imperial administration. Libanius' influence as a teacher of rhetoric, though extensive, was confined to the Greek establishment of the eastern Roman Empire, just as his travels — in striking contrast to those of Ammianus — were confined to the great cities of the East.[5]

Yet, considered more deeply, the paradox in Ammianus' self-identification is less blatant than I have implied so far. Ammianus' military rank, as *protector domesticus*, means that he belonged to an officer élite. Promotion to the rank of *protector* involved for its recipients the ceremony of *adoratio* as conceded, in the words of a law of A.D. 387, to those favoured officials 'thought worthy to touch Our Purple' (*Cod. Theod.* 6.24.4). Ammianus' attachment to Ursicinus, mentioned at his first personal appearance in Ammianus' history as it survives (14.9.1), is an instance of the procedure, also mentioned in the Theodosian Code (6.24.5), by which a *protector* might be assigned, or 'deputed', by an emperor to serve under a general in the field. Ammianus' attachment to Ursicinus as a member of his personal staff goes far towards explaining his obvious partisanship for him against real or imagined criticism and intrigue, and means also that he was well placed in relation to some of the more important military events of the day in which Ursicinus was involved. It explains, too, the adventurous and often dashing nature of Ammianus' own exploits under Ursicinus' command. Ammianus appears in some of these as something very unlike a regular soldier of the ranks, if that is what the average reader would understand by 'miles'.

Ammianus' age when he first appears in the history as already *protector domesticus* in 354, also marks him as being out of the ordinary. To hold this rank, as Ammianus did, at twenty-five or under, implies certain initial advantages, for it was more usually achieved only after years of loyal, painstaking service.[6] One exception was Herculanus, described still as a 'young man' in 363 and already *protector domesticus* in 354 (Amm. Marc. 14.10.2). He was the son of the *magister equitum* Hermogenes who was killed in riots at Constantinople in 342. The young Jovian, made emperor after Julian's death in 363, had by then become head (*primicerius*) of the *domestici*. Born in 331, he was the son of Varronianus, a well-known general (25.5.4). So too the most likely explanation of Ammianus' early promotion is surely parental influence.

To look now at the second part of Ammianus' self-identification, there is no need to doubt the natural assumption that he underwent a normal Greek literary education at Antioch. I suspect, as others have, that he had there met as a fellow-student the future satrap of Corduene, Jovinianus, whom he later visited on a fascinating reconnoitring mission on behalf of Ursicinus (18.6.20ff.). Jovinianus had been a hostage in Syria, and was there bewitched by love of the liberal arts, so much so that even as satrap of his native principality he wished 'with a burning desire' to return to the Roman Empire (18.6.20). It is a curious perspective on a Kurdish chieftain who is otherwise recorded, in an eastern source, as settling Bedouin Arabs on land under his authority.[7]

At the same time, Antioch was in Ammianus' day not simply a great Hellenistic city enjoying a late flowering of its own Greek culture. It was a Roman administrative centre of the first importance. The Praetorian Prefect, his deputy the *comes Orientis*, and the *magister militum* of the East had their head offices there. The city was a frequent imperial residence, as the focal point of the emperors' preparations for campaigns against the Persians; this was true of much of the first half (337–350) of the reign of Constantius — that is, during Ammianus' own childhood and youth there; and of course it was also true of the great Persian campaign mounted in 363 by Julian. And the presence of the imperial administration and army means, in the fourth century, something of immense importance for the under-standing of Ammianus Marcellinus: the widespread use, in government circles and in the city of Antioch, of the Latin language. 'Look at this man', wrote the cleric John Chrysostom, giving a selection of the possible careers which a man might choose, 'he has learned the language of the Italians, and shines in the imperial palace!' (*adv. oppug. vit. mon.* 2.10; [*PG* 47.357]). If Ammianus, as I have suggested, owed to paternal influence his early advance-ment to the rank of *protector domesticus*, then his links with the imperial administration reached back to the previous generation; and so too, his links with Latin-speaking court circles at Antioch. This is important, for if true it follows that Ammianus' command of Latin, far from being acquired in adult years or during his two-year stay in Gaul between 355 and 357, derives already from his childhood upbringing.

Ammianus' history, like Ammianus himself, must be understood in terms of a fusion of the two elements, Greek and Latin, in his cultural formation. Both come out on a variety of levels, literary and linguistic, but I shall limit myself in this paper to a group of passages which seem to me to be especially revealing of the wider issue. Introducing his account of the exploits of Julian as Caesar in Gaul with a long digression on the origins, organisation and character of the Gallic provinces and their inhabitants (15.9–12), Ammianus remarks that this was a subject left incomplete by other writers: 'notitiam reliquere negotii semi-plenam' (15.9.2). This situation was rectified by Timagenes, who is described as 'in diligence and in language, a Greek': 'et diligentia Graecus et lingua' (Timagenes, who came from Alexandria, was a writer of the late Republican and Augustan age, known for his contentious character and disagreeable end as well as his depth of learning; he choked to death while trying to vomit at a dinner-party).[8] Ammianus justifies his use of a digression at this point. He wishes to avoid the situation of a seafarer who has to make running repairs in a storm, when he could with forethought have prepared himself safely in advance of the danger. The digression itself has, in a recent discussion of Ammianus as a military historian, been adjudged relevant and helpful to Ammianus' narrative of the campaigns which follows, and of course it is indeed this.[9] Yet, at the same time it goes far beyond what could ever be considered as strictly necessary for an understanding of the military and geographical setting of the cam-paigns. It resembles in this the still longer excursus on Persia, with which Ammianus prefaces his account of the Persian campaign of Julian (23.6.1–88), and in which he exceeds still more lavishly what is actually needed in order to understand the campaign. Ammianus remarks in his introduction to this digression that while his text may seem on the long side ('prolixior'), this will be to the advantage of 'complete knowledge': 'ad scientiam proficiet plenam' (23.6.1). Writers on Gaul before the Greek Timagenes, Ammianus said, had left behind them knowledge that was 'incomplete': 'notitiam reliquere . . . semiplenam' (15.9.2).

    The expression, 'scientia plena', so contrasted with 'notitia *semi*plena' has rightly been taken to exemplify Ammianus' ideals as a historian, but not always with due appreciation of the fact that he uses it to justify the inclusion, not of detailed political or military narrative, but of a *digression*.[10] This sense of the need to explain a military narrative by placing it in nothing less than its entire geographical and cultural context would itself have been enough to establish Ammianus' claim to be considered within the tradition of Greek historiography. There were of course digressions in Latin historians of the Classical period, but not of the number, variety or scale of treatment offered by Ammianus, nor displaying his range of erudition. The contrast in this respect between Ammianus and the Latin historiographical tradition of his own day hardly needs stating (see below, p.37).

    Ammianus' commitment to Roman attitudes and ideals is equally persistent and obvious to the reader, particularly in his admiration of Rome itself, the Eternal City, which 'will live as long as there are men': 'victura dum erunt homines Roma' (14.6.3). Ammianus' famous onslaughts on the immoralities of members of the upper and lower classes of Rome spring directly from his outrage that the historic distinction of the ancient assemblies of the Eternal City is so betrayed by men 'who do not consider where they were born' (14.6.7). His description, which immediately precedes this passage, of the process by which Rome, growing from infancy and youth to adult maturity and now in serene old age, has secured her eternity by conveying her inheritance to the Caesars 'as to her children', is from the point of view of Ammianus' political attitudes one of the most interesting passages of the history. It is also profoundly Roman in conception and expression (14.6.5). The same is true of what must be the best-known single passage of the history, Ammianus' account of the triumphal arrival and reception at Rome of the Emperor Constantius in 357 (16.10.1ff.). This is a passage which, I suspect, has many levels of resonance in Ammianus' mind. If, as in my view the evidence suggests, Ammianus was offering recitations from his history at Rome in or very close to 390, then the visit to Rome of the Emperor Theodosius in summer 389 was a near-contemporary event.[11] To its reader (or hearer) Ammianus' description of the visit of Constantius must surely have evoked the more recent event; not surprisingly, Ammianus' account has some affinities with the panegyric delivered to Theodosius in 389 by the Gallic orator Pacatus (*Pan. Lat.*, ed. Galletier, XII). Further, it seems at least possible that in evoking so vividly the impact upon Constantius of the ancient monuments of Rome (see especially 16.10.13ff.), Ammianus was also recalling the feelings of admiration which he had himself experienced in arriving at the city for the first time a few years before. It is hard to believe he can have written this passage before he had himself ever set eyes on Rome.

    The 'Greek' and the 'Roman', then, exist together at various levels in Ammianus' writing — which, it is hardly worth saying, must be understood, not in terms of one or the other, but of the combination of the two aspects. The question I wish to pose in this paper is a more specific one. Were the two elements present at the beginning of Ammianus' historical conception? Or is it more likely that his understanding of what a historian should aspire to developed over a period of time? And, in the case of the second of these possibilities, can we distinguish the earlier from the later stages of his development? To put these questions more concretely: why did Ammianus decide to write history at all? And, this decided, why did he write the type of history that he chose to write — a major history, in Latin, of nearly three centuries of the Roman Empire?

Now, it seems clear to me that there are two fundamental elements in Ammianus' historical conception. The first of these was his personal experiences, which take Ammianus and Ursicinus from the East and Antioch to Milan, then for two years (355-7) to the Gallic provinces, and then back to the East. The climax of this phase was the siege and capture in 359 of the city of Amida, from which Ammianus cleverly escaped as the city fell while the other *protectores* captured there, as Ammianus explains with possibly unconscious irony, were led into captivity in Persia, hands bound behind their backs (19.9.1). In the second phase, the Persian campaign of Julian in 363 (Books 23-25), Ammianus' personal presence is much less obtrusive. Though his standing as an eyewitness of the campaign is clear, and fundamental to the nature of his account, his own experiences do not occupy the prominent position which they had during his earlier service under Ursicinus, and he does not seem nearly so close to the centres of power and decision.[12]

Now, the events in which Ammianus was involved were certainly in their different ways important; the trials conducted at Antioch by Gallus Caesar, the suppression of Silvanus and early campaigns of Julian in Gaul, and above all the great Persian invasion of 359 – all of these events would properly form part of any history of the Roman Empire, written by a contemporary. The siege of Amida, indeed, seemed to Ammianus to have drawn upon this single region the misfortunes of the entire Roman world (19.1.4). Yet the prominence of the personal memoir indulged in by Ammianus is disconcerting. His exploits, often resembling tales of excitement and adventure reminiscent of a Hollywood screenplay rather than solemn Roman history, are something of an idiosyncrasy even among those ancient historians who, like Polybius, allow themselves to make personal appearances in their works. What we have to explain is the evolution of a Roman history reaching back to A.D. 96 (the principate of Nerva), and for this we need something more than personal memoir, however significant the events surrounding it. This wider perspective is provided, I believe, by Julian the Apostate, whose Persian campaign of 363 is the second phase in which Ammianus' personal experiences and the main course of Roman history converge.

The importance of Julian in Ammianus' historical conception is obvious, and can be demonstrated, not only from the actual attitudes expressed towards Julian by Ammianus (as we shall see, these are surprisingly ambiguous), but from the formal aspects of his presentation. Introducing the excursus on Gaul with which he follows Julian's elevation as Caesar, Ammianus invokes Vergil to set the scale of the higher theme now in store: 'ut Mantuanus vates praedixit excelsus, maius opus moveo, maiorque mihi nascitur ordo' (15.9.1). The allusion is to the words with which Vergil brought in the wars fought by the followers of Aeneas after their landing in Italy (*Aeneid* 7.44f.) – an appropriate introduction to the narrative of heroic military exploits on which Ammianus is now set to embark.

After the digression, Ammianus resumes his narrative, remarking that he will require the full resources of his modest talent: 'instrumenta omnia mediocris ingenii, si suffecerint, commoturus' (16.1.2). He adds that what follows will read like panegyric, though based on the best documentary evidence (16.1.3).

This rhetorically framed introduction to the regime of Julian is balanced by a similarly contrived treatment at its close. Ammianus' formal obituaries of emperors generally proceed in a straightforward manner, setting out the virtues of the emperor in question followed by his shortcomings – the latter often supported by literary *exempla* which make them appear more substantial than is really justified by the content of what is said. This device is particularly obvious in the obituary of Julian's predecessor, Constantius (21.16.1–19). The obituary of Julian has a more elaborately refined scheme, which from the start prevents it from being other than a panegyric. Ammianus begins by listing the four cardinal virtues defined by the 'philosophers': 'temperantia, prudentia, iustitia, fortitudo'. To these are added four subsidiary virtues — or rather, external manifestations of virtue: 'scientia rei militaris, auctoritas, felicitas, liberalitas' (25.4.1). Julian's actions are then set out to illustrate his possession of these virtues (in 14 sections), and this is followed by a brief statement of the emperor's few shortcomings (in 5 sections). Ammianus then adds a defence, against its critics, of Julian's disastrous Persian campaign, arguing that it was not Julian but Constantine who had provoked war with Persia, and that Julian would have been successful had the fates been in his favour (25.4.23–6). The laudatory framework of this obituary is as obvious as the special pleading with which it closes.

Ammianus' account of Julian's shortcomings, brief as it is, raises curiously intractable difficulties in considering his attitude to an emperor whom he, almost literally, heroised ('heroicis connumerandus ingeniis', 25.4.1); for his criticisms in effect undermine the fundamental principles of Julian's attempt at the restoration of traditional practices and beliefs, based as this was on the total renewal of the civic life and culture, secular as well as religious, of the Roman Empire. Ammianus criticises Julian for his excessive reliance on omens and portents, characterising his religious observances as 'superstitious' rather than 'legitimate' in their lavish intensity (25.4.16). He denounces Julian's famous prohibition of Christians from teaching grammar and rhetoric, a law which Ammianus says was 'intolerant' ('inclemens'), and in a still stronger passage that it should be 'buried in perpetual silence': 'obruendum perenni silentio' (25.4.20; 22.10.7). He questions Julian's strict insistence on the performance of civic duties by candidates who were properly exempt (25.4.21). Under Julian, writes Ammianus elsewhere, no candidate for curial service, once sought by his town council, was able to escape, whether on grounds of origin, imperial service, or exemption granted by favour (22.9.12; cf. 21.12.23). Valid exemptions ought no doubt to be recognised; yet Ammianus should have acknowledged that Julian's entire policy depended on the restoration of the civic as well as the religious integrity of the Roman Empire, and that the evasion of curial service by candidates well able to serve was one of the chief obstacles to its achievement.

Further, Ammianus remarks on Julian's excessive fondness for popularity, in pursuit of which he affected intimacy with the unworthiest of men. Julian was here declaring himself against the pomp and ceremony of the imperial office of the fourth century, sustained by Julian's predecessors and specifically approved by Ammianus in the case of Constantius (21.16.1). Julian, in Ammianus' view, was reducing the imperial position to below its proper dignity, but again, his policy was deliberate, part of his attempt to restore the imperial office to something more like the 'civil magistracy' which it had been (in theory at least) in the days of Marcus Aurelius. It was this contrast between civil magistracy and regal despotism, exemplified by the elaborate dress and ceremonial manner affected by the emperors since Diocletian that Ammianus (15.5.18) and other writers saw as symbolising most clearly the transition between what a modern historian would call the 'early' and 'late' Roman Empire.[13]

Ammianus' admiration for Julian is therefore qualified by fundamental criticisms of all major aspects of his policies (religious, civic, and cultural) and of his conception of the imperial office itself. Whether Ammianus himself fully realised this, or, if he did, how he reconciled himself to it, I do not know. Yet whatever the explanation of the ambiguities in

Ammianus' attitudes, Julian was an exciting and challenging figure, and remained so despite his increasingly obvious failures of judgement and the ultimate collapse of his policies. He exacted comparison with the past — with the dynasty of Constantine the Great, whose religious and military policies he had tried to reverse, with the Tetrarchy of Diocletian and his colleagues, and looking further back, with Marcus Aurelius — for whom, in his work the *Caesars* (written at Antioch in the winter of 362/3), he expressed such intense admiration. In his preface to Book 16, Ammianus too referred to Marcus, as the emperor whom above all others Julian tried to emulate in every way: 'ad cuius aemulationem actus suos effingebat et mores' (16.1.4). If this was so for Julian, so, too, for Ammianus himself. I would suggest that the figure and personality of Julian provided the link between his own experiences as described in the earlier of the surviving books and the broader course of Roman history. This was the emperor who, to quote the prophecy of an old woman of Vienne when Julian first entered the city, would 'restore the temples of the gods' (15.8.22), put the barbarians to flight and restore the old standards of integrity to the imperial office and provincial government. The earlier stages of this project, witnessed by Ammianus himself during his tour of duty in Gaul in 356 and 357, seemed to him to demonstrate all that was best and most admirable in the reign of Julian. — the more remarkable because, as he put it, his success was so totally unexpected (16.1.5).

If I am right in this, then both Ammianus' original conception of history and its enlargement to include the earlier centuries of the Roman Empire as well as Ammianus' own time are developments which were integral to himself and his own experience, and do not of themselves require the intervention of other historiographical models. Yet, irrespective of its original conception, the writing of history is a highly elaborate and self-conscious enterprise, not to be carried on in isolation from existing literary models; and it still remains to ask where such models might fit into Ammianus' evolution as a historian.

Towards the end of 392 Libanius wrote from Antioch to his compatriot in Rome a letter in which he responded to news which he had been brought of Ammianus' recitations there (*Ep.* 1063, Foerster). From the other circumstances mentioned in the letter — men returning from Rome to Antioch with their reports of Ammianus' success — the recitations themselves appear to have taken place in 389 or 390, at a time when the imperial court of Theodosius was located at Milan and Rome received many visitors from the emperor's entourage.[14] The men returning to Antioch in 392 could well be seen as supporters of Theodosius making their way further east after the emperor's return to Constantinople in the summer of 391. Now, Ammianus himself had come to Rome in or shortly before 384, when he was, say, 55 years of age. Since his retirement from the army in 363, he had travelled widely — certainly to Egypt (22.15.1) and southern Greece (26.10.9), to the Black Sea (22.8.1), possibly to one of the battlefields of the Gothic Wars of 376–8 (31.7.16), and surely to Constantinople.[15] Unless these travels were entirely pointless and random, by the time of his arrival at Rome his plans as a historian were, I suppose, already quite far advanced. How much was already written up in its final form is a rather different matter, though it would obviously be prudent for an aspiring historian to have some samples of his work ready for inspection by men whose goodwill he might require, as eyewitnesses of events for which he did not yet possess full information. On any account, there remained much material still to gather. Ammianus' accounts of the administrations of successive prefects of Rome, beginning already with Memmius Vitrasius Orfitus in Book 14 (6.1) clearly presuppose his presence at Rome, as in a different way do his criticisms of the moral delinquencies of the senators and people of the capital (14.6.2ff. and 28.4). Apart from the sense of personal animus in these passages, in the first of them Ammianus refers to an expulsion of foreign visitors from Rome during a corn shortage which had occurred 'not so long ago': 'haud ita dudum' (14.6.19). The most convincing date suggested for this expulsion is 384.[16]

It is obvious that substantial portions of Ammianus' later books – to take some examples from many, the prosecutions for magic and adultery conducted at Rome by the agents of Valentinian (28.1.1–57), the description of that emperor's frontier works in the north (28.2. 1–10), the complaints of the citizens of Tripolitania to the imperial Court (28.6.1–30), the campaigns of count Theodosius in Mauretania (29.5.1–56) – cannot have been written before Ammianus had come to the West and secured access to western sources of information. But this observation can be pressed a little harder, for it is worth noting that such passages, incorporating information which Ammianus is likely to have acquired relatively late in his historical development, occur not only in the later but also in the earliest of the surviving books (cf. 14.6.1–26), and also, by reasonable inference, in the now lost Books 1–13. Ammianus found living at Rome the eunuch Eutherius, a former adviser of Caesar Julian in Gaul (16.7.2f.). This at least seems a fair inference from the biographical sketch which Ammianus provides of Eutherius. Born of free parents in Armenia, Eutherius had been brought as a boy slave to the court of Constantine, and there advanced through his culture, intelligence and prodigious memory ('immensum quantum memoria vigens', 17.6.5). He had also served the Emperor Constans and, now living in old age at Rome, was admired by men of all social ranks: 'colatur a cunctis ordinibus et ametur' (16.7.7). Surely Ammianus was himself among these admirers, and if so, it would be natural to suppose him to have exploited Eutherius' powers of memory for information about Roman emperors whom he had known, as far back as the reign of Constantine.[17] Similar possibilities are suggested for the surviving books by the figure of Praetextatus, the great pagan senator who died as consul designate towards the end of 384. Ammianus records a number of episodes from the reign of Julian at Constantinople in 362, of which only one – the arrival at Constantinople of the philosopher Maximus – is recorded by any other ancient source.[18] Ammianus adds that Praetextatus, then at Constantinople on private business but soon to be made proconsul of Achaia, had witnessed these episodes: 'his omnibus aderat Praetextatus . . .' (22.6.6). So as late as 384, Ammianus was able to acquire additional material relating to the policies and character of Julian.

If Ammianus could after his arrival in Rome add information of quite a substantial nature, not only relating to recent events but going back to the reign of Constantine, then it is reasonable to ask whether his historical conception was itself still open to modification. What literary and historiographical influences might still have exerted themselves on Ammianus as his writing developed and moved into its final phases towards the year 390?

I have already suggested that the closest affinities to Ammianus' historical manner are in the Greek tradition. The truth of this is strikingly emphasised when one looks at the actual Latin historical productions of Ammianus' own day – epitomisers like Aurelius Victor (mentioned by Ammianus at 21.10.6), Eutropius and Festus, historical romancers like the author of the *Historia Augusta*, antiquarians like (in my view) the senator Nicomachus Flavianus, who wrote *Annales* dedicated to the Emperor Theodosius in or very close to 390.[19] Now the Greek historiographical tradition had produced a sequence of major works which in effect, by Ammianus' day, made up a continuous history. So, to take only the

Roman imperial period, Cassius Dio was succeeded by Dexippus, Dexippus by Eunapius, and he in the fifth century by Olympiodorus of Thebes, the forerunner of a great and still continuous tradition of Byzantine military and diplomatic history. If this Greek tradition of continuous historical writing is taken and applied to Ammianus, we will be bound to consider what most of his students assume by sheer instinct, linking him with his great Latin predecessor, Tacitus.

There is in one sense a very good reason for this. In the epilogue to his history, Ammianus, as we saw, invited others to resume the story where he left it in 378. With the loss of the first thirteen books, we are without the preface to the entire work, in which Ammianus would presumably have declared how he saw his own work in relation to his predecessors; but the epilogue, in directing us back to the reign of Nerva, evokes the model of Tacitus, whose *Histories* had ended at precisely this point.

It would be doing an injustice to Ernst Stein's magnificent judgment of Ammianus as the greatest literary genius between Tacitus and Dante,[20] and indeed an injustice to common sense, if we were to deny altogether that Ammianus knew or was conscious of the example of his Latin predecessor. But I think that it is worth considering very carefully how profound the influence of Tacitus might be.

First, on the assumption which I, though not all students of Ammianus, accept, that the period from A.D. 96 to 353 was described in the lost thirteen books and did not form an entirely separate work,[21] it is unlikely that the earliest part of Ammianus' history, in which the comparison with Tacitus would have been most clearly invited, was in scope or manner much like his predecessor's writing. If, on a rough calculation, the period from 96 to the death of Constantine in 337 was narrated in the first ten books of the history, the proportion of nearly twenty-five years per book in that section (as opposed to one and a half years per book in the surviving part) would contrast sharply with Tacitus. Ammianus could certainly improve on the pitiful tradition of late Latin historiography, above all by his use of the Greek sources on the second and third centuries, and so would have been rather more than the 'superficial epitome' of Gibbon's conjecture;[22] yet even so, his account of these centuries would have been much less expansive than Tacitus' account of the first century. To pass from the end of one author to the beginning of the other, one would not have guessed from the style or manner that one was reading Tacitus' continuator.

Second, as we saw, Ammianus came to Rome in about 384, having travelled very widely in the Empire, with much material still to collect but with much already assembled and — one would assume — the main outlines of the history already clear in his mind. Now I have suggested that the origins of Ammianus' conception lie in his own experience, and in the figure of Julian the Apostate, who challenged comparison with earlier emperors and so linked Ammianus' experience with the broader course of Roman history; and also that the most obvious historiographical models were provided not by the Latin but the Greek tradition. How necessary is it, if these suggestions are true, to think of Tacitus as an influence on Ammianus except in detail and at a relatively late stage? It may well be that the year 96 was suggested as a starting point by the example of Tacitus — supported by that of Suetonius, whose unworthy successor, Marius Maximus, Ammianus denounces in a well-known passage (28.4.14) on the trivial reading habits of members of the Roman aristocracy. But in a brief account of two centuries and more, written in, say, ten books, it would not much matter exactly where one began. Given the admiration of Julian for Marcus Aurelius it would be essential to include the reign of that emperor, and Hadrian would be irresistible for an author interested in the culture and religion of Roman emperors (at 25.4.17 Julian's superstition is compared with that of Hadrian, as his excessive sacrifices are to those of Marcus), and in restless travel through the regions of the Empire. The reign of Hadrian was equipped by Ammianus with a generous digression on Egypt (22.15.1). I suspect that the choice of A.D. 96 precisely, suggested by the double influence of Tacitus and Suetonius, was otherwise relatively unimportant, perhaps occurring to Ammianus quite late in his planning and without substantial influence on the manner and style in which he wrote.

So, to summarise: I have argued that the 'Greek' in Ammianus' self-identification is the dominant literary influence on his manner of writing, in its scale and generosity of treatment, particularly evident in the digressions; but at the same time that the Latin language was far deeper in his experience than is usually appreciated. As a product of a great Roman administrative capital in an age when the language of administration in the East was Latin, Ammianus acquired in boyhood and youth an affinity with Roman ideals together with his familiarity with the language. And thirdly, I have argued that the transition which is required between Ammianus' personal experiences, as he told them in Books 14–19 of his history, and the writing of Roman history on the grand scale, is provided, not by any purely 'historiographical' influences but by the figure of Julian the Apostate, in the challenge which he posed to the Christian establishment of the fourth century, and the comparison which he invited with the emperors of an earlier age. It was the career of Julian, not the writings of Tacitus, which turned Ammianus' mind to the history of the earlier Roman Empire.

I have to say that I am still puzzled by Ammianus' apparent lack of awareness of the fundamental nature of his reservations on the policies of an emperor whom he continued to admire as much as he evidently admired Julian. I am fascinated too by the ultimately inaccessible question of the evolution of his personal feelings over the years, as he advanced from early manhood towards old age, and as the figure of his dead hero receded into the past and his ideals of the restoration of the old ways yielded to the weight of a further generation's government by Christian emperors. Yet Ammianus would not have been the first man nor the last to have had to reconcile himself to disappointment, and to have lived uncomfortably with the failure of his ideals. Whether he succeeded or failed, Julian challenged comparison with the past; and in this challenge, I have argued, lies the genesis, and in all essentials the evolution, of Ammianus' history.

Notes

1.   E. Gibbon, *Decline and Fall of the Roman Empire*, Chap. 26 (ed. J. B. Bury [London 1897], III, 122).

2.   G. A. Crump, *Ammianus Marcellinus as a military historian* (*Historia*, Einzelschriften 27, Wiesbaden 1975), 4f.

3.   R. Browning, 'History' in E. J. Kenney (ed.), *Cambridge History of Classical Literature*, II (Cambridge 1982), 749.

4.   Gibbon, *op. cit.*, Chap. 30 at end (ed. Bury, III, 284).

5.   See J. Matthews, *Western Aristocracies and Imperial Court, AD 364–425* (Oxford 1975), 102–7.

6.   A.H.M. Jones, *The Later Roman Empire: a Social, Economic and Administrative Survey* (Oxford 1964), at 636–40 surveys the evidence on *protectores*, observing (638) that 'the directly commissioned *protectores* were often sons of fathers high up in the service', and of Jovian that 'he can hardly have had time to serve in the ranks'.

7.   L. Dilleman, *Haute Mésopotamie Orientale et pays adjacents* (Inst. fr. d'Archéologie de Beyrouth 72, Paris 1962), 110. The source is published by G. Hoffman, *Abhandlungen für die Kunde des Morgenländes* 7, 3 (1880), 22–4.

8.   Jacoby, *FGrH* 88 (IIA, 318–23) gives the evidence on Timagenes.

9.   Crump, *op. cit.*, 36–8 — admitting the wider context deriving from Ammianus' erudition and 'curiositas'.

10.   G. Sabbah, *La méthode d'Ammien Marcellin: Recherches sur la construction du discours historique dans les Res Gestae* (Paris 1978), 27–9.

11.   Libanius' letter to Ammianus (*Ep.* 1063 Foerster), written at the end of 392, seems to me to refer to events at an earlier time; see above, p.36. The date of completion of the history is a disputed subject, but I am struck by the *convergence* of references to later events at and around the year 390, and no later, e.g. 27.6.2 (to 387/8); 21.10.6 (to 388/9), 26.5.14 (to 390). The death of Petronius Probus, *c.*390, is referred to (27.11.2, cf. Symmachus, *Ep.* 3.88, which I believe refers to Probus' death), but not the destruction of the Serapeum at Alexandria (22.16.12 would read very oddly if Ammianus knew it to have been destroyed).

12.   N. J. Austin, *Ammianus on Warfare: an investigation into Ammianus' military knowledge* (Collection Latomus 165, Brussels 1979), 17f. suggests that Ammianus was a member of the 'headquarters staff' with an interest in supplies, but I am not convinced that what Ammianus says on this or any other particular subject goes beyond what a generally interested observer might notice.

13.   With Ammianus compare Aurelius Victor 39.22ff., Eutropius 9.26 and (from Eutropius), Jerome, *Chron.* s.a. 296 (ed. Helm 226). I assume that all reflect the earlier Latin history known as Enmann's *Kaisergeschichte* (in the trade simply as *KG*), written probably under Constantine — which is not to deprive them of their independent judgement of the matter.

14.   See for these circumstances Matthews, *op. cit.*, 238, and in more detail in 'Gallic Supporters of Theodosius', *Latomus* 30 (1971), 1078–87.

15.   Ammianus' expression 'nunc usque albentes ossibus campi', with its allusion to Vergil, *Aeneid* 12.36, may, but need not, suggest autopsy. I would like to think, but can hardly expect to prove, that Ammianus witnessed the funeral at Constantinople in 381 of the Gothic king Athanaric, mentioned at 27.5.10.

16.   Alan Cameron, 'The Roman Friends of Ammianus', *Journal of Roman Studies* 54 (1964), 27f.

17.   Perhaps Eutherius was the source for the vivid scene described at 16.7.2, when the general Marcellus described Julian as 'fitting out more powerful wings for himself', evidently adding a mimed enactment of his metaphor: 'ita enim cum motu quodam corporis loquebatur ingenti'. Eutherius was present at the time, to defend Julian.

18.   Libanius, *Oratio* 18.155f. For Praetextatus as Ammianus' informant for events at

Constantinople, accepted by earlier writers such as Ensslin and Klein, see Sabbah, *op. cit.*, 230f.

19. *ILS* 2948: see Matthews, *op. cit.* (n.5 above), 231 n.3.

20. *Histoire du Bas-Empire* (tr. J. R. Palanque, 1959), I, 215.

21. The theory of an entirely separate work devoted to the early Empire — which would of course radically affect our conception of the scale of the lost 13 books of the *Res Gestae* as we have them — propounded by H. Michael in 1880, has been re-stated with some new arguments by H. T, Rowell, *Ammianus Marcellinus, soldier-historian of the late Roman Empire*, Semple Lectures, Series 1 (Princeton 1967), 276–81. But Ammianus never seems to refer to events of the earlier period as if they were described in an entirely separate work (e.g. 23.6.24, 'per duces Veri Caesaris, ut *ante* rettulimus'), and certain matters were evidently not earlier explained in any great detail, e.g. 15.5.18 (the origins of *adoratio*), 19.11.4 (Diocletian's provinces), 14.11.20 (death of Crispus Caesar), 14.1.8 and 23.5.7 (reigns of Maximinus and Gordian III).

22. Gibbon, *op. cit.*, Chap. 26 n.116 (ed. Bury, III, 122).

The Digressions in the Lost Books of Ammianus Marcellinus

Alanna M. Emmett

In the last fifteen years it has become increasingly in vogue to emphasise the importance of the work of Ammianus Marcellinus.[1] This recent appreciation of Ammianus prompts a re-thinking of what his work was once like in its entirety, when it was applauded by its Roman audience and praised by Libanius in the early 390s.[2]

In the books we now have, Ammianus is a contemporary, even at times an autobio-graphical, historian. For us his work opens at Book 14 with the events of 353, by which time Ammianus was at the centre of events as a *protector domesticus* on the staff of the *magister militum* Ursicinus (14.9.1). It may be that even by the sixth century Ammianus' earlier books were already lost, for the African grammarian Priscian, writing in Constantinople, quotes from the beginning of Book 14[3] and then only in a grammatical context.

Whether the earlier books were lost by chance, or through lack of interest in antiquity, the question of their number and extent has long attracted the attention of scholars. H. Michael in 1880 first propounded the view that there were once two works, of which we possess the last eighteen books of the second.[4] The refutation of this theory in 1888 by Jeep[5] (with the endorsement of Petschenig in 1891)[6] silenced critics until Rowell re-opened the matter in the mid 1960s.[7] Although Syme[8] and others[9] were not subsequently convinced that the lost books number more than thirteen, reconsideration of the lost books led to a general acceptance of the view[10] that Ammianus' work was not a brief epitome which at a given point became more detailed but was probably, like that of Zosimus, one which became more detailed in 'stages' of expansion, marked, it seems likely by prefaces.[11] The renewed attention paid to the lost books has not proved merely a 'futile exercise in philological necromancy',[12] for Gilliam has recently shown that a study of the lost books is not devoid of implications for the study of the *Historia Augusta*.[13] The present study seeks to show that an examination of one aspect of the lost books, namely the probable digressions, can tell us more about the overall unity, scale and plan of Ammianus' work.

The first problem confronting any approach to the lost books is how to ascertain their probable contents. Since Priscian's is the only ancient citation of Ammianus, and there is no firm evidence of any impact made by the earlier books of his work,[14] we can rely only on Ammianus' back-references. Fortunately these are numerous because in his writing Ammianus was conscious of the arrangement of his material and of the overall structure of his work.[15] The diversity of his history, as shown for example by the contrasting person-alities (Gallus/Julian, Constantius/Julian, Valentinian/Valens) and the shifting scenes of military operations (Persia, Gaul, Rhine frontier) make cross-referencing necessary (in his view) to help his readers or audience to follow the narrative.

On at least 140 occasions in the extant books[16]Ammianus alludes in terms such as 'ut dixi' (as I said), 'ut dictum est' (as has been said), 'ut ante relatum est' (as has been related before) or 'ut memoratum est' (as has been told) to a previous account of a person, place or event.[17] The terminology he uses is reminiscent of that of other authors, though Ammianus typically uses a great variety of expressions.[18] Ammianus makes more frequent use of cross-referencing than do many other historians, such as Tacitus, whose subject matter is less diverse and more integrated.[19] Some of Ammianus' back-references use words like 'supra' (above) or 'dudum' (a while ago) to give a general indication of previous location, while others such as 'in Gordianorum actibus' (in the deeds of the Gordians, 14.1.8) are more specific. Sometimes, words like 'saepe' (often) may be inserted to indicate that the subject has been handled before. The length or scope of treatment is sometimes suggested by phrases like 'rettulimus plura' (I have related much about, 14.1.8).

If, however, as Jeep argued strongly,[20] we cannot depend on the accuracy of Ammianus' cross-references, there is no way of building up a picture of the lost books. It is worthwhile, therefore, to examine Jeep's case critically. His procedure is to take the back-references to the extant part of the work and compare the passage to which they refer. Since he claims that there are discrepancies, particularly in relation to the extent of the treatment, he argues that they do not provide a reliable gauge for the scale (in particular) of treatment in the lost books. His prime example is the introduction to the digression on Egypt: 'So then briefly ('strictim'), since the occasion seems to demand it, let us touch on Egyptian matters which I treated at length ('late') in relating the deeds of the emperors Hadrian and Severus, narrating mostly what I had seen' (22.15.1).

Since Ammianus, he argues, sets out to describe the country briefly ('strictim') and ends up with a long digression, the two lost digressions on Egypt in connection with the reigns of Hadrian and Severus need not have been long. Jeep's challenge, generally accepted by Ammianean scholars,[21] requires fundamental re-examination. In the first place, a systematic check of all Ammianus' back-references against the passages to which they refer (if in the extant books) vindicates Ammianus' precision in this matter. Cichocka's recent tabulation of all Ammianus' back-references reassuringly finds not one that is unfulfilled and the forward-references too are handled with care.[22] Ammianus' remarkable accuracy is no mean feat. Nowadays, scholars are provided with tables of contents, indexes, even computerised concordances, all of which provide every facility for checking back to the exact spot where a point was made previously. Anyone who has used microfilm is only too well aware of the disadvantages in going back through a roll: being able to flick over the pages of a book is a great help in checking forwards and backwards. Though an ancient writer made use of notes, he must have had to keep a good deal of his material in his head.[23] Ammianus' cross-references no doubt reflect his overall consciousness of the structure of his work as it was in his mind while writing.

Cichocka's tabulation destroys the mainstay of Jeep's argument, yet there is still need to tackle the point about Ammianus' accuracy in estimating the *scale* of his past treatment. There are several weaknesses in Jeep's argument about scale, which is based primarily on the introduction to the Egyptian digression but which also touches on other references.

First, Jeep[24] does not distinguish between those places where Ammianus is claiming to refer back to a description, or a lengthy explanation (22.15.1; 25.4.23) and those where Ammianus refers back to a completed action such as the despatch of Gaudentius to Africa (22.11.1). He therefore fails to realise that a back-reference may refer to an account of any length, and that it is quite beside the point to note that most of Ammianus' cross-references are to minor, or brief, happenings. The vital conclusion to be made from this observation is that the trivial nature of some of the points Ammianus raised in the lost books indicates a generous scale of treatment of certain episodes. For example, the account of the arrival of the statue of the Great Mother in the reign of Commodus (22.9.6) suggests a treatment comparable at this particular point with that of Herodian,[25] and the placing of a digression on Egypt in the reign of Hadrian suggests that the context was probably the voyage of Antinous down the Nile.

Secondly, we should look more closely at the argument based on the introduction to the Egyptian digression. Jeep notes that, after setting out to describe the country 'strictim', Ammianus concludes his digression with the words: 'After this long departure ('euectus longius') I shall return to the order of my narrative' (22.16.24). It is not at all necessary to conclude, as Jeep does, that Ammianus' criteria for judging length are unreliable.[26] In Ammianus, 'fullness' (indicated by words like 'plene') and 'length' are not necessarily synonymous, and Ammianus demonstrates in his two extant prefaces (15.1.1 and 26.1.1) that he is well aware of this distinction. Moreover, formulaic introductions to digressions occur frequently in Ammianus,[27] and it is to emphasise his concern for the *suitability* of the digression to its particular occasion in depth of treatment and in length that he makes these allusions in the introductions and conclusions. Nor should such mock-deprecating phrases as 'euectus longius' (22.16.24) or 'prolati aliquanto sumus longius quam sperabam' (I have been carried a little further than I anticipated, 22.8.48) make us think that Ammianus is really carried away to the point where he cannot tell a long discussion from a short one. He knew well in general what he meant by brevity — it meant to him, as he shows at 15.1.1, selectivity rather than conciseness: 'tunc enim laudanda est brevitas, cum moras rumpens intempestivas, nihil subtrahit . . .'. Brevity in this context to him was relative: a digression of a few lines might be too long (because, by his standards, it was inappropriate) whereas a longer digression might still fulfill his criterion of brevity.

It is precisely that same concern for selectivity that he exhibits in the longer digressions as he passes from one subject to another (for example 15.11.18). Some readers (like some of Ammianus' contemporaries) may feel that he has not been selective enough (15.1.1) or that he has selected the wrong topics (26.1.1). Nevertheless the indications are clear that Ammianus was in control of his own scale of treatment, as he devised it and carried it through.

To recapitulate, Jeep's discussion sidesteps the major point: it is not necessary to assume that each of the back-references points to a long discussion, but that the relatively trivial nature of some of them indicates the range of topics touched on by Ammianus.

So then, the re-examination of Ammianus' back-references affirms their reliability, and reveals Ammianus' attitude to his work. He uses them not so much to refer to broad subject areas as to help the reader (or listener)[28] keep track of his theme or to identify a place or person previously mentioned, thereby taking up the thread of the narrative after a digression. It may be concluded, therefore, that the back-references do give some indication of scale of treatment, either explicitly or by referring to specific points or individuals.

With the ground thus cleared, it is possible to open up the question of the role of the possible digressions in the lost books, a question which has not been systematically tackled.[29]

In the extant part of the work Ammianus frequently discourses upon a variety of topics, sometimes first announcing a departure from his theme, sometimes not. In doing so he was following his Greek and Latin predecessors, Greek in particular; for digressions had been an expected feature of historiography from the time of Herodotus and were to continue in the early Byzantine historians like Olympiodorus, Procopius and Agathias. Possibly they were designed particularly to appeal to those who heard the work recited, but we see from Lucian *How to Write History* that their inclusion was taken for granted. In Ammianus, the digressions may supply information, explanation or dramatic background. Often they are strategically placed to highlight central parts of the work, such as Julian's Gallic or Persian campaigns, or to form a transition from one area to another. A digression arises out of, but is not actually part of, the immediate chronological narrative. So it is that we find in Ammianus various techniques of inserting digressions — introductory formulas, the use of a distinguishing word like 'excursus' (departure) or the use of various syntactic devices.[30] These enable us to identify what is a digression in Ammianus' eyes: not just an irrelevancy, which a modern writer would consign to a footnote, but a distinctive feature of the work, allowing description of people, places, the supernatural, flora, fauna, etc. Digressions have a further value to the modern scholar, in that they can reveal the ancient historian's own opinions as moulded by his life and background.[31] In them too, the writer can cater to the interests (as he saw them) of his readers, and thus reveal something of his own day.

In the references Ammianus made to the now lost books,[32] he refers to many subjects which seem very likely, to judge from their nature and from comparisons with the extant part of the work, to have formed a digression or else a part thereof. Examples are Egypt (22.15.1), the Saracens (14.4.2 and 31.16.5) and Mesopotamia (14.7.21) where the context suggests a description in the style of the ones we possess. It is, furthermore, hard to see how such passages could have been other than a digression from the narration.[33] The present enquiry will now examine these and other examples in order to see what light they throw on the lost books, and therefore on Ammianus' work as a whole.

Possible placement of the digressions

On examining back-references in the extant part to what are probably, to judge from their subject matter, digressions in the lost part, we find that in some cases these probable digressions can be assigned to a specific context, in others not. Arranged chronologically, those topics which can be placed in a specific part are: Egypt (Hadrian's reign) 22.15.1; the Saracens (Marcus Aurelius' reign) 14.4.2; statue of Apollo (Verus' reign) 23.6.24;[34] statue of Great Mother (Commodus' reign) 22.9.6 — where it is particularly noteworthy that Ammianus specifically states that this account was definitely a digression: 'cuius super aduentu in Italiam pauca . . . in actibus Commodi principis digessimus *per excessum*' (I have said by way of a digression a few things about its arrival in Italy during my account of the deeds of the emperor Commodus); Egypt again (Severus' reign) 22.15.1; origin of the war with the Persians (Constantine's reign) 25.4.23; Britain (Constans' reign) 27.8.4; the *arcani* (Constans' reign) 28.3.8; and maybe[35] several anecdotal characterisations of Constantius II, 16.10.12 and 21.16.7.

In other cases the context is uncertain, though there can be reasonable hypotheses linking possible digressions with other parts of the work, extant or not. Thus de Jonge proposes that the remarks about the hunting of Hyrcanian tigers may possibly have been made in connection with the digression on Mesopotamia.[36] It seems likely that the founders of Icosium (29.5.16) were described in the account of Africa, as were those of Caesarea in

Mauretania of which Ammianus says in an adjacent passage (29.5.18) 'Cuius itidem originem in Africae situ *digessimus plene*' (I gave a full acount of its founding in my geographical description of Africa). Similarly, Ammianus strongly implies that his description of Mesopotamia included Osrhoene. At 14.7.21 he declines to repeat a description of Mesopotamia 'iam digesta, cum bella Parthica narrarentur' (already handled when the Persian wars were narrated) while the back-reference at 14.8.7 'ut dictum est' (as has been said) when Osrhoene is mentioned links it back to the passage at 14.7.21. Rowell postulates that the lack of indication as to which Persian wars occasioned the description of Mesopotamia, implies that a recent campaign — that of Constantius — is meant.[37] However, it seems that Ammianus did not reserve the vague reference for recent occasions and the more specific ones for those further removed in time, for he is specific when he refers back to his account of Britain given in connection with Constans' reign (27.8.4).

In an ingenious argument, Michael suggests that a lengthy obituary, like that of Valentinian, may have been given to Constantine.[38] At 30.7.1, where Ammianus is dealing with the death of the founder of a dynasty, he opens the obituary of Valentinian with the words 'replicare nunc est opportunum, ut aliquotiens fecimus, et ab ortu primogenio patris huius principis actus eius discurrere per epilogos breves' (It is now suitable to turn back as we have often done and in a brief obituary run through the deeds of this emperor right from the birth of his father). It was not necessary to run through the father's deeds for Valens or Constantius, since they would be known to the reader of the work. Michael may not be right in assuming that Constantius Chlorus did not feature largely in Ammianus: nevertheless, whether or not Constantine is a case in point, if Ammianus' remark about his frequent practice refers to the whole sentence it seems that at least for the founders of important dynasties, obituaries going back to the father's generation were supplied. Several possible candidates from the second and third centuries such as Constantius Chlorus or Septimius Severus may have fallen into this category. There are many and varied references to possible digressions for which a probable context cannot be established: the names of the Persian kingdom were explained on more than one occasion (23.6.2); the 'armatura' of the Persians (23.6.83) was often described; while the white birds of Leuce (22.8.35), the Saracens on more than one occasion (14.4.2 and 31.16.5), Mesopotamia (14.7.21 cf. 14.8.7) and the vices of the Roman people (28.4.6) were outlined at points in the work.

Even allowing for possible amalgamations of subject matter, and for the reasonable assumption that not all of these discussions were necessarily long, we can see that a wide variety of material was probably contained in Ammianus' lost digressions. There may well have been others also to which he does not refer.

Distribution of the digressions

These digressions must have been present throughout the work, since one on Egypt is referred to in the reign of Hadrian (22.15.1), and we know Ammianus began from Nerva's reign (31.16.9). Digressions of one kind or another were sprinkled through the account of the second and early third centuries (reigns of Marcus, Verus, Commodus, and Severus).

More than half of the specifically located references fall in the period from Constantine onwards. That is not surprising, for it is natural for Ammianus to have in mind what he has most recently dealt with, and to expect this of his readers or hearers also. Most of the back-references in the extant part are to fairly recent passages and most, too, fall within a single section of the work.[39]

A further observation can be made on the distribution of probable lost digressions: some are repeated possibly several times, since Ammianus' use of words meaning 'often', such as 'saepe' or 'aliquotiens', suggests at least twice and probably more. Those topics which he repeated are the names of the Persian kingdom (23.6.2); the Saracens (14.4.2 and 31.16.5); the vices of the Roman people (28.6.4) and Egypt (22.15.1). Repetition as such did not bother Ammianus, unless it was likely to prove boring to his readers, either because the subject was not interesting enough in itself, or because he had dealt with it too recently.[40] Egypt was a fascinating subject, and in addition to what he had read of it Ammianus could write of it at first-hand. The Saracens must have interested him greatly for he tells us (31.16.5) that on their origins and customs 'diversis in locis rettulimus plura' (I have given much information in a variety of places). Ammianus is happy to digress twice in the extant part on the vices of the Roman senate and people, although he had expressed his opinion before (28.4.6). On the other hand, Mesopotamia and Africa are not repeated, possibly partly for the reasons given above, and partly because a digression on them would not suit Ammianus' plan at that point. Ammianus' concern for suitability in the placement of digressions is revealed at 14.7.21 where he regards it as suitable to write about the eastern provinces (in which Gallus was causing havoc) but not about Egypt, which it was necessary to postpone. We find in Book 22 that he wanted to adorn an account of Julian's request for an Apis bull to sacrifice with another account of Egypt. In other words, at Book 14, he does not want a very long digression. It seems that as in the extant part, so probably in the lost part of his work, Ammianus was prepared to write more than once about a topic that interested him.

Subject matter

It appears that the probable digressions in the lost part contained a range of subjects like that found in the extant part. To some extent, the subject classification of digressions, like their original definition, is subjective. Nevertheless, Ammianus' extant digressions may reasonably be shown to fall into several categories of subject matter (not all of which are completely exclusive) namely: digressions on geography/ethnography with which digressions on flora and fauna may on occasion be associated, digressions on science and natural phenomena, characterisations, obituaries or moral judgments, digressions on antiquities or monuments, military or technical digressions, miscellaneous explanatory digressions, digressions on historical method and digressions on religion or the supernatural.

The most numerous digressions in the extant parts are those on geography/ethnography, of which there are sixteen in all. Some are purely ethnographical such as those on the Huns, Alans and Saracens, some are shortish and topographical, for example the pass of Succi, while the longer ones such as those on Gaul and Persia, in Herodotean fashion, encompass accounts of people, places, animals, plants, previous history and anything unusual about the region. This group was clearly well represented in the lost books, for we find references to the Saracens (frequently), Egypt (twice), Britain, Africa and Mesopotamia. Possibly discussions of fauna like white birds (22.8.35) or tigers (23.6.50) formed part of a longer digression, though such descriptions (like the ones of lions at 18.7.5) can stand on their own. There are many reasons why Ammianus should have digressed frequently on geography and ethnography throughout his work. Historiographical precedent (Herodotus in particular) is a significant influence. In this type of digression Ammianus could add his own experiences, as he did in the lost digressions on Egypt, to what he had learned from books. He could use this type of digression to set the stage for, and highlight, campaigns he wished to emphasise (notably those of Julian in Gaul and Persia).

The next most popular category is that of scientific subjects, including natural phenomena, a type of 'learned' excursus in which Ammianus displays his erudition, perhaps more in a didactic spirit than actually to explain the narrative. We can imagine that the disquisition on the ebb and flow of the tides (27.8.4) may have resembled in type those in the extant part on nocturnal visions, earthquakes, eclipses, rainbows, falling stars, comets and the bissextile day. These disquisitions tend to be bookish and to have authorities mentioned frequently[41] — here Ammianus can display an almost antiquarian interest.

Characterisations and obituaries are frequent in Ammianus, with most interest centring on the person of Augustus. There are nine obituaries in the extant part: all the Augusti, all of whom have long or longish obituaries: the Caesar Gallus; two usurpers Silvanus and Procopius; and Barbatio who was killed under suspicion of plotting against Constantius. Ammianus certainly started this practice in the lost part of the work and, as was suggested above[42], may have given special attention to the first emperor of a dynasty, for only in this case would it be appropriate to run through his father's deeds as well.

In addition to the obituaries, Ammianus often gives characterisations (often, though not exclusively, of the emperors) in passing, sometimes in an anecdotal manner and usually with a moral purpose. Julian receives this treatment on a grand scale (16.1.2–5). Ammianus uses this technique to pass judgment frequently on Valentinian (for example 27.7.4, 7.9 and 9.4–5). Once again, from the back-references we can see that Ammianus probably did the same in the lost books — for Constantius II, at least — since he refers back twice to earlier comments on Constantius' attitudes and habits (16.10.12 and 21.15.7).[43]

Political/social digressions with moralising overtones are found often in the extant part. Most notable are the two digressions on the vices of the Romans (14.6 and 28.4), the one on the shortcomings of the legal profession at Antioch (30.4.3–22), and the remarks on the simplicity of provincial bishops (27.3.14–15). There are some marked similarities between the two 'Roman' digressions,[44] and clearly some personal involvement of Ammianus is reflected. There seems no reason to doubt the implication of 28.4.6, 'ut aliquotiens per locorum copia fecimus' (as we have often done according to the supply of topics),[45] that he gave vent to his feelings on quite a few occasions. No doubt both from his reading and his personal observation he would have had plenty to say; and it seems that some Romans at least did not appreciate such erudite foreigners as Ammianus (14.6.12).

In the extant part we find disquisitions on antiquities and monuments such as obelisks (17.4.2–11). These, too, were found in the earlier books, for example the arrival at Rome of the statue of the Great Mother (definitely in a digression, 22.9.6).

It is no surprise to find Ammianus, the soldier, writing on military topics such as siege machinery (23.4.1–15). We can well believe that he frequently described the 'armatura' of the Persians,[46] of which he would have had first-hand knowledge.

Many of Ammianus' digressions have an explanatory function, which can serve as a springboard for a discussion on almost any topic at all. The digression on Roman vices in 14.6 arises out of Ammianus' desire to explain why the references in his work to the Eternal City are now so trivial. His lost discussion of the *arcani* who were probably secret agents (28.3.8) and of the way the lies of Metrodorus fanned the Persian war in the time of Constantine (25.4.23), were probably of the explanatory type.

So then, of the types of digression mentioned above (p.47) all those mentioned as being in the lost part can be paralleled in the extant parts, and only two types (the discussions of historical method and digressions on religion) found in the extant part are not mentioned in the back-references, and it is in any case open to question whether the remarks about the statue of the Great Mother and of Apollo Comaeus (if the latter is accepted) were antiquarian or religious — or both. Nevertheless it may perhaps be suggestive that in the extant part all the digressions on religion (apart from Nemesis and its workings) are found in the central part of the work (Books 19–25) and are connected with Julian. They arise either out of Julian's life, or from some aspect of Constantius' where he is in conflict with, or in contrast to, Julian. It has been suggested that writing about religious topics became more difficult when the last section was being composed.[47] The distribution of the religious digressions suggests the interesting hypothesis that the books concerned with Julian provided the occasion for Ammianus to express his religious views. It is not unlikely that this may have been so if we consider the major role played by Julian in Ammianus' conception of his work.

———————————

Much of the foregoing is, of necessity, tentative, yet certain conclusions (tentative in turn, to varying degrees) can be drawn about the work as it once existed in its entirety. Since digressions, on topics similar to those found in the account of mid-fourth century events, clearly occurred in Ammianus' account of the second, third and early fourth centuries, it can be seen that in this respect there was a degree of homogeneity in the work. It is in the digressions that a historian can (in Syme's words) 'confirm his autonomy, reveal his predilections and permit an approach to his character and opinions'.[48]

So it can be seen that Ammianus' own imprint was left throughout the work. In other words on these, as on other grounds,[49] it can be argued that his work was not — at least from the reign of Hadrian on — a *bare* epitome. The digressions reflect Ammianus' own life and background, and his desire both to interest and educate his public. It seems that the vehicles (that is the digressions) by which he chose to express his aims remained fairly constant.

It would be a striking conclusion to this study if the evidence presented could be used to answer the question which the past hundred years of Ammianean scholarship has not succeeded in settling: one work or two? The whole controversy cannot be outlined here[50] but though it must be admitted the weight of evidence falls heavily in favour of one work the ghost of two works cannot yet be laid to rest.[51]

Taking all of Ammianus' back-references at a conservative estimate, one can envisage as the most likely picture one work which was designed to emphasise Julian but which began where Tacitus (and for that matter Suetonius) left off and which was sufficiently detailed to allow a description of Egypt during Hadrian's reign, the account of the arrival of a statue during Commodus' reign, and so on. By such vague words as 'saepe' and 'aliquotiens', Ammianus may mean that he discussed a given topic on only two occasions such as when he alludes to several obituaries or to frequent accounts of the names of the Persian kingdom, of Persian weaponry, of Saracen customs and of Roman vices. Yet the possibility still exists that Ammianus meant that these subjects were discussed three or more times, and a faint doubt lingers whether thirteen lost books would then have sufficed.

What is, however, clear from the study of the topics and distribution of the probable lost digressions is that Ammianus from the beginning made frequent use of digressions to instruct, to entertain, to explain and to express his views. The work was enriched throughout by his own distinctive ideas.

Notes

1. E. A. Thompson, *The Historical Work of Ammianus Marcellinus* (Cambridge 1947) opened with a lament for the comparative neglect of Ammianus. Since 1967 in particular there have been numerous works on him in English, French, German, Polish, Spanish and Italian. See A. M. Emmett 'Three Recent Interpretations of Ammianus Marcellinus', *Prudentia* 2 (1970), 19–27; and the bibliography in G. Sabbah, *La méthode d'Ammien Marcellin. Recherches sur la construction du discours historique dans les Res Gestae* (Paris 1978). In English the 1970s saw the significant works of Blockley, Austin and Crump (referred to in Sabbah).

2. Libanius, *Ep.* 1063 Foerster.

3. Cited in Thompson, *op. cit.*, 19.

4. H. Michael, *Die verlorenen Bücher des Ammianus Marcellinus* (Progr. Breslau 1880). He was followed by J. Gimazane, *Ammien Marcellin. Sa vie et son oeuvre* (Toulouse 1889) and A. Enmann, 'Eine verlorene Geschichte der römischen Kaiser und das Buch *de viris illustribus urbis Romae*', *Philologus* suppl. 4 (1884), 404–5.

5. L. Jeep, 'Die verlorenen Bücher des Ammianus Marcellinus', *Rheinisches Museum* 43 (1888), 60–72.

6. M. Petschenig, 'Bericht über die Literatur zu späteren römischen Geschichtsschriebern bis einschl. 1890', *Bursians Jahresberichte* 72 (1891), 1–19.

7. H. T. Rowell, *Ammianus Marcellinus, Soldier – Historian of the Late Roman Empire*, reprinted in *Lectures in Memory of Louise Taft Semple*, Ser. 1 (Princeton 1967), esp. 276–81 and *id.*, 'The first mention of Rome in Ammianus' extant books and the nature of the *History*', *Mélanges Carcopino* (Paris 1966), 839–48.

8. R. Syme, *Ammianus and the Historia Augusta* (Oxford 1968), 8–9.

9. R. C. Blockley, *Ammianus Marcellinus. A study of his historiography and political thought* (Brussels 1975), 12–15, with the approval of Sabbah, *op. cit.*, 2.

10. Some suggestions on the layout and possible character of the lost books were made by G. B. Pighi, *Ammiani Marcellini rerum gestarum capita selecta* (Neuchâtel 1948), viii–ix.

11. 15.1.1 and 26.1.1 for the extant part.

12. J. F. Gilliam, 'Ammianus and the Historia Augusta: the lost books and the period 117–285', in *Historia–Augusta–Colloquium 1970* (Bonn 1972), 125.

13. *ibid.*, 146–7.

14. It has been suggested that the lost books may have been sources for works we now have. T. D. Barnes, 'The Lost Kaisergeschichte and the Latin Historical Tradition', in *Historia–Augusta–Colloquium 1968/9* (Bonn 1970), 23, quotes the suggestion of E. Patzig, *Byzantinische Zeitschrift* 7 (1898), 572ff. that the first part of the *Anonymus Valesianus* depends on the lost books of Ammianus. Mommsen in his edition of Jordanes' *Romana et Getica* (Berlin 1882), xxxiii (cf. xliii) has noted the passages where the lost books seem to have been used by Jordanes/Cassiodorus although Kappelmacher, *RE* 9.2, col. 1920–1 doubted that Jordanes used Ammianus directly.

15. See references in A. M. Emmett, 'Introductions and Conclusions to Digressions in Ammianus Marcellinus', *Museum Philologum Londiniense* 5 (1981), 24.

16. Most are listed by Helena Cichocka, 'O Powtórzeniach w "Res Gestae" Ammiana Marcellina', *Eos* 64 (1976), 231–8. (I am grateful to Mr W. Nadolny for a translation

of this article). To this list should be added 14.9.4 (referring to 14.7.18); 14.11.23 (referring to 14.7.7−8); 16.2.1 (referring to 16.1.1); 20.3.9 (referring to 20.3.8); 21.8.1 (referring to 21.5). It is difficult to fix a precise number because of certain textual difficulties, for example at 22.8.35 and 14.11.20.

17. Usually they are found in the following contexts: (a) those arising out of the arrangement of material, particularly the insertion of digressions; (b) those arising out of the need to depart from chronological treatment, for instance in giving the subsequent history of an individual; (c) those arising out of explanations, particularly in battle scenes.

18. Ammianus uses broadly similar formulas to those of Sallust or Tacitus, but we find greater variety in Ammianus' formulas. This reflects the *variatio* that is a feature of Ammianus' style generally. See H. Hagendahl, 'De abundantia sermonis Ammianei', *Eranos* 22 (1924), 161−216. An assessment of the ways Sallust and Tacitus influenced Ammianus is given by P. M. Camus, *Ammien Marcellin* (Paris 1967), 71. Greek models, going back to Herodotus, profoundly influenced Ammianus in the use of such formulas.

19. Tacitus, *Annals* has around 45 back-references (omitting dubious cases) in 398 OCT pages; Ammianus has around 140 in 611 Teubner pages.

20. *op. cit.*, esp. 60−7. These criticisms and the consequent possible unreliability of Ammianus' references to the lost books are in the main accepted by Blockley *op. cit.*, 13. (He does not assume that the lost books contained digressions of any length.)

21. See p.42 above.

22. Cichocka, *op. cit.*, 218−21. The only promises not fulfilled are 22.8.35 which should probably be a back-reference according to Gardthausen's text of Ammianus (1874−5) and 28.1.57. Chifflet, as cited in Wagner-Erfurdt's edition (1808), postulated a lost book after Book 30, but a far more likely explanation lies in the constraints Ammianus may have been working under in the last part of his history, especially in connection with the death of the elder Theodosius. See Thompson, *op. cit.*, 92ff.

23. Cf. the study of Plutarch's memory made by P. Stadter, *Plutarch's Historical Methods. An analysis of the Mulierum Virtutes* (Cambridge, Mass. 1965).

24. *op. cit.*, 66−7.

25. J. Gimazane, *op. cit.*, 139, suggests Herodian 1.10−11 as the likely source of Ammianus' (lost) digression, and in particular draws attention to the origin of the name of Pessinus. Herodian, however, since he was not writing for a Roman audience (1.11.5) does not mention the verses on the role of Scipio Nasica, which Ammianus says (22.9.6) were included in his account. Possibly he supplemented Herodian's account from a Roman source.

26. *op. cit.*, 61−2. If Jeep's argument proves anything about Ammianus' criteria for judging length, it proves that Ammianus erred on the side of underestimation.

27. Emmett, *op. cit.*, [n.15 above], 16. These formulas are not meaningless, for Ammianus frequently reminds himself not to add so much detail that readers will become bored (15.9.7; 21.1.14). On brevity as an ideal of style, see E. R. Curtius, *European Literature and the Latin Middle Ages*, tr. W. R. Trask (New York 1953), 487−9.

28. Libanius' letter (n.2 above) refers to Ammianus' successful recitations of his work at Rome.

29. Gimazane, *op. cit.*, 139ff., in following up Michael's theory does make several suggestions about lost digressions in connection with his theory that Ammianus used Dio, Herodian and Dexippus as sources for the second and third centuries.

30.   Emmett, *op. cit.*, [n.15 above], 28–30.

31.   See below, n.48.

32.   Enumerated by Michael, *op. cit.*, 16; Gimazane, *op. cit.*, Appendix B; Gardthausen's Teubner edition 1.1–4. None of these has collected all relevant passages, and indeed there are several places where Ammianus mentions a topic in a way which assumes the reader's familiarity with it, but without actually stating that he has dealt with it. Any list must therefore contain an element of subjectivity; hence in the following list passages which seem to me to assume though not explicitly assert a past treatment are asterisked, while those where there is a problem of text or interpretation are preceded by a question mark.

    Book 14:   1.8, 4.2, *6.2, 7.7, 7.21, 8.7, 10.2, ?11.20.
    Book 15:   5.16, *5.33, 6.4.
    Book 16:   10.12, 10.16, 6.2.
    Book 18:   *5.7, 9.3.
    Book 19:   2.3, *2.8, *9.9.
    Book 20:   1.1, 6.5, *7.1.
    Book 21:   *8.1 (Vetranio), 8.1 (Jovius), ?16.10.
    Book 22:   ?8.35, 9.6, 13.3, 15.1.
    Book 23:   5.7, 6.2, *6.24, 6.50, ?6.83.
    Book 25:   4.23, 8.5, *8.13.
    Book 27:   8.4.
    Book 28:   *1.1, 3.8, *4.6.
    Book 29:   *1.17, 5.16, 5.18, 6.1.
    Book 30:   7.1.
    Book 31:   *11.3, 16.5.

33.   Since where similar passages of geographic or ethnographic description occur in the extant part they are generally marked out as digressions by Ammianus who in this respect is following long Graeco-Roman historiographical precedent.

34.   A doubtful reference. It is not certain, despite the arguments of Gimazane (*op. cit.*, 104) that Ammianus gave a theological discussion at this point, whether or not the account of the statue did form part of Ammianus' account of the sacking of Seleucia.

35.   The practice of introducing character comments into the historical narrative is traced by I. Bruns, *Die Persönlichkeit in der Geschichtsschreibung der Alten* (Berlin 1898), ch.1. The influence of biography (Greek and Latin) in the imperial period bolstered the practice. Ammianus, outside his obituaries, often remarks on personal characteristics, with or without moral judgements, in the extant part of his work (for example Eutherius, 16.7.4–10, a passage in which Ammianus acknowledges he has been digressing). However not all remarks in the extant part about character and habits do occur in digressions, but given the centrality of Constantius' character in Ammianus, and the way Constantius is contrasted with Julian, who does receive special treatment from Ammianus (16.1.2–5), it is not unreasonable to suppose that Ammianus made at times more than passing reference to Constantius' behaviour, particularly as he recalls it to us.

36.   P. de Jonge, *Sprachlicher und historischer Kommentar zu Ammianus Marcellinus* vol. 2 (Groningen 1939), 51.

37.   H. T. Rowell in *Mélanges Carcopino*, 843–4.

38.   *op. cit.*, 16.

39.   This can be seen from the tabulation provided by Cichocka, *op. cit.* On the effect of

53

the division of Ammianus' work into sections, see W. Hartke, *Römische Kinderkaiser* (Berlin 1951), 70–1.

40. Ammianus spells this out at 27.8.4 with a reference to Homer's reluctance to repeat his tale of Ulysses among the Phaeacians, on the grounds that the repetition was ἐχϑρός (burdensome). Ammianus' word 'difficultas' should be understood in its context, and so translated 'wearisome' not 'difficult' (Loeb). The task of describing Britain could hardly be too difficult if he had already done it once.

41. Roughly three-quarters of Ammianus' citations of authorities are found in the digressions; they are relatively uncommon in the narrative (Thompson, *op. cit.*, 21–2).

42. p.46

43. See above, p.45.

44. For comparisons (and possible development in Ammianus' view of the Romans) see Hartke, *op. cit.*, 62–5; F. Paschoud, *Roma Aeterna* (Rome 1967), 60–2; R. Pack, 'The Roman Digressions of Ammianus Marcellinus', *Transactions of the American Philological Association* 84 (1953), 181–9.

45. See Loeb note *ad loc.* re the translation.

46. There are two problems of interpretation here. One is the translation of 'armatura' which can mean armament or exercise of arms (*Oxford Latin Dictionary*). The second is the text: 'formo' (meaning describe) as Clark, Rolfe and Seyfarth prefer in their editions is preferable to the emendation 'formido' (fear) found in Gardthausen.

47. Thompson, *op. cit.*, 116.

48. *American Journal of Philology* 79 (1958), 18.

49. Especially as argued by Syme (n.8 above) and Pighi (n.10 above).

50. See works cited in nn.5–10 above.

51. Rowell's case has won a firm endorsement from Alan Cameron, *Claudian: Poetry and Propaganda at the Court of Honorius* (Oxford 1970), 359 n.2.

Autobiography and History:
Some Later Roman Historians and their Veracity

N.J. Austin

The purpose of this paper is to attempt to find evidence supporting a general thesis along the lines of a progression that moves from a historian's personal experience to his production of an eyewitness account containing special and unique details, all in a combination which suggests that the information and assessment are as accurate as they can be.

In an article on Ammianus written twenty years ago, Chalmers proposed a generalisation about the limited breadth of vision a soldier serving in the army is liable to acquire. It is worth quoting the relevant paragraph in full:

> Personal participation in a military campaign is in many ways valuable to the historian of that campaign, but few serving soldiers are enabled to obtain the overall picture which must be presented by a work of military history. Ammianus might well have felt that he could profit from the use of a narrative which stemmed from a civilian in close contact with the commander and his staff.[1]

I have elsewhere contended that this is not so in Ammianus' case, where it seems reasonably certain that he formed part of a headquarters staff during the whole of his military career, and was closely involved in intelligence work and operational planning.[2] A fairly close parallel exists with Procopius' career as Belisarius' secretary-cum-staff-adviser, though it is clear that Procopius did not have to undertake such obviously military duties as Ammianus. What I am suggesting therefore is that both historians, precisely *because of* (not, as Chalmers implied, *in spite of*) their positions in military headquarters, were able to acquire a wide grasp of military affairs. This is not only by reason of their ability to get at first-hand reports, to attend policy and planning discussions, and to talk subsequently with figures involved in particular actions, but from autopsy and often personal involvement in the events they describe.

Two civilians may also be adduced here, because their careers also involved close personal participation in historical events (albeit of a rather less military nature). Olympiodorus of Thebes called himself a poet, but carried out important diplomatic work for the East Roman government in the early part of the fifth century, and later travelled as a tourist in some quite remote areas of Egypt; he had been involved in the cultural scene in Athens in the 390s and was again to be later involved in East—West diplomacy. Priscus of Panium's avocation is uncertain, but from his work it emerges that he too participated in delicate diplomatic negotiations in the middle of the fifth century, and later occupied some fairly senior advisory posts under leading figures.

Now all four writers have few inhibitions about bringing their own experience into their general histories, particularly where that history is being written with any degree of fullness;

thus I shall exclude autobiographical material in the *breviarium* and epitome — Aurelius Victor, Eutropius, Festus and others.

What is to be discussed in this paper then is how far the autobiographical element in the work of these historians contributes to the quality of their historiography, and, therefore, the veracity of their accounts, and as a by-product, whether analytic techniques derived from working on one of them can be applied to others.

There are three types of autobiographical material to be found in these historians, if one must attempt a classification (but clearly in dealing with literary works where a great deal of artistic effort has been applied to their composition, such classifications must be fairly loose) — viz, (1) personal material with no significant influence on the course of action, (2) eye-witness accounts, (3) historian as protagonist or active participant.

The least important of our categories, and possibly the most difficult to define, is that which includes *personal material with no significant influence on the course of the action*, such as the historian's individual activity which gives rise to personal anecdotes. Ammianus provides particularly good illustrations for this category in the account of his running around in the desert between Nisibis and Amudis in a fragmented group with Ursicinus trying to respond to the confused situation created by different phases of the Persian invasion of 359 (18.6.1ff.). In no way could this be said to be contributing anything to the history of the year, but it does furnish an excellent dramatic account of the effects of chaotic conditions on an individual, and so it provides invaluable material on background conditions presented in an exciting and interesting way. Many of Procopius' eyewitness episodes fall easily into this category too, in that they represent a useful and vivid method of providing background conditions. Look, for example, at his detailed descriptions of the effects of famine on the local inhabitants of Picenum, an account which underlines the great hardships inflicted on civilians during a war in which they may have had no real interest (*Wars* 6.20.22ff.); or at his story of the child being suckled by the goat at Urbisalia in the same region (*Wars* 6.17.1ff.). Both of these episodes are not mainstream history, but have considerable value as supporting material. In a slightly different category, but equally revealing, is Procopius' own dramatic escape with Solomon from an assassination attempt during the Stotzas mutiny of 536 in North Africa (*Wars* 4.14.37–42). It comes at the end of a long section explaining the North African situation, and it contains large amounts of useful detail on the background to the confusing conditions created by the mutiny as well as personal comment and discussion on them.

I must include in this category Olympiodorus' parrot (frg.36) which appears to have had remarkable talents, and accompanied its owner over a twenty-year period. Undoubtedly it provided him with a reputation for colourful eccentricity. More seriously though, he shows all the marks of the acute observer in noticing things like the high standard in archery achieved by leading Hun chieftains. One is further impressed by him because unlike his predecessors he is quite willing to use the exact terminology for Roman officials and Hun dignitaries (for example, ῥήξ, frg.18; μαγίστερ ὀφφικίων, frg.8), let alone his forceful and independent view of politics and religious controversy.[3]

The next category up the scale is much more important historically and historiograph-ically: that of *participation in the events described, in the role of eyewitness of significant action*. Both historians were admirably situated for this role in that both were members of headquarters staffs at important stages of their careers — Ammianus was a *protector domesticus* with Ursicinus in the East and in Gaul (15.5.22), and later in some similar capacity under Julian, and Procopius was Belisarius' ξύμβουλος or πάρεδρος between 527 and 541 (*Wars* 1.12.24; 3.14.3; etc); both therefore had access to discussions, personnel and documents.

Ammianus' largest contribution under this category is of course the Persian Expedition, as sombre an episode as anything in his work, even including perhaps Book 31. Ammianus' role in the Persian Expedition I have examined elsewhere, concluding that because of his considerable experience of Mesopotamia and the desert country he was in some way connected with the supply side of operations. This emerges from his taking part in a reconnaissance sweep with Julian himself when the army had left Circesium on the Euphrates (23.5.4; cf. 19.8.5), but after this his role is much reduced, and we are left with no more than the strong impression that supplies were included in his duties.[4] But the eyewitness details in the account are so pervasive that it is impossible to avoid the conclusion that it was a headquarters post that he occupied. The matter of his sources in connection with the Persian Expedition needs discussion and will be treated later.

A second example of Ammianus as an important eyewitness concerns the siege of Amida in 359 (18.9.1ff.; 19.1.1–9.2). There are a number of indications that Ammianus was in fact something more than a headquarters observer during the siege: the siting of the ballistae that finished off the seventy Persians who managed to seize a tower on the walls by infiltration, shows a particular interest in a specific operation (more so than in other episodes), as does the raid from the town by Gallic legionaries on the Persian encampment where the King himself was. Both these incidents show a degree of personal involvement beyond the mere sitting-in on the difficult discussions and briefings of the garrison commander. Ammianus' escape from Amida during its storming and his subsequent adventures return us to the first category.

In this same area Procopius has some of his most interesting material. The year-long siege of Rome in 537–8 is certainly one of the high-points (*Wars* 5.18.34–6.10.20); it is recounted with considerable clarity, good eyewitness detail and marked human-interest evidence, and it includes one of his very rare statements on his methods of evidence selection (*Wars* 6.2.37; this will be further discussed). Again, his own role is usually not much more than that of eyewitness reporter. Although once he did move to Naples to organise troop reinforcements and supplies, his new role was only of temporary significance (6.4.19–20). In Rome, however, Procopius during the siege demonstrates amazingly well the results of being an eyewitness. There is a spendid array of detail that would only exist in an account of an eyewitness, for example the changing every fortnight of the keys to the gates (5.25.15), the use of guard dogs outside the walls at night (5.25.17), the fact that the so-called Broken Wall was never an area for any kind of military action (5.23.3–8), among many others. But reinforcing this is a substantial amount of material that could only have come to him as a headquarters man: the extraordinary stories of individual exploits (the Goth and Roman in a hole, 6.1.11–9), Chorsamantis and his shin wound (6.1.26–34), the medical detail (Traianos' arrow wound in the face, which incidentally demonstrates Procopius' continuing contact with his former colleagues after leaving Italy and Belisarius' service, 6.5.24–7), and the documentary evidence (Belisarius' letter to Justinian 5.24.1–17), the armistice dialogue between Belisarius and the Goths (6.6.3–36). And reinforcing this again, the detailed and knowledgeable reflections on actions and events usually introduced by οἶμαι, often putting his own point of view which is by no means that of the headquarters or of Belisarius himself (for example, *Wars* 3.19.26; 5.26.19; 5.29.31). As an observer Procopius also had the good fortune to be in on a number of other important historical occurrences. The Nika riots of 532 and the plague at Constantinople are prominent in this respect.

Being an eyewitness of such important actions allows the historian to give a relatively unbiased assessment of events, one would suppose. In Ammianus' case this is not necessarily so, since the whole account of Julian's reign is overlaid with a veneer of panegyric — though to be fair to Ammianus, criticism of some aspects of Julian's conduct of affairs do occasionally break through. I think, however, that in spite of being in Julian's headquarters and presumably being able to hear the Emperor's strategy carefully discussed on numerous occasions, Ammianus does not fully understand Julian's aims, nor does he appreciate or even approve of the methods adopted to achieve these aims. Confusions of standpoint therefore arise in the narrative, particularly in the account of the events leading up to the burning of the ships outside Ctesiphon; a situation not improved by a lacunose text at this point. Ammianus, it seems, has two viewpoints laid side-by-side in the account: one an official headquarters version, relatively unemotive, explaining the reasons for Julian's controversial if pre-planned decisions; the other the view of those not in on those decisions, and so, highly critical, emotive and overlaid with Ammianus' pessimism and foreboding of disaster. Here, then, being a participant eyewitness suggests limitations of both vision and impartiality.[5]

Priscus' splendidly detailed account of his participation in a high level mission to the 'Court' of Attila the Hun in 448 comes into this category. At the beginning of the episode, Priscus (and the delegation leader Maximinus) were unaware that the mission was being conducted on two levels: an overt level of bearing a formal letter to Attila from Theodosius II, requesting him to keep out of Roman territory across the Danube because this would be an infringement of the treaty of 441/2; and a covert level involving some of the members persuading the chieftain Edeco to assassinate Attila. Only later did Priscus find out the facts, perhaps from the interpreter Bigilas who was supposed to be organising the Roman side of the assassination.

While involved with this embassy, Priscus paid extremely careful attention to his surroundings and to the activities and protocol of the Hun Court; there are details of the journey, not unexpectedly; he was fascinated by the decoration of Attila's house, and the treatment the Hun accorded to his sons; he was impressed by Attila's strikingly ugly appearance and in particular by his formidable charisma.

The whole account is of course invaluable for the history of this period and especially of the Huns, but what makes it such a remarkable story is the almost hour-by-hour description of the events, which can only have come from very detailed notes kept on the spot by Priscus, with some later supplementation from people like Bigilas. Furthermore, the rich colouring of realism is strongly supported by the details of the personal reactions of the negotiating team to outside events and to meetings with the Huns as well as by their confidential discussions among each other afterwards.

Our third category is that of the *historian being a protagonist or active participant in actions that have a direct and positive relevance to the history of the whole period*. Both Ammianus and Procopius have good claims in this area.

Ammianus is involved in two such situations, the first of which is the suppression of the usurper Silvanus in 358 (15.5.1ff.). The suppression of Silvanus was important for the welfare of the Empire as seen by Constantius, but required an avoidance at all costs of more civil war: so whatever the moralities of the situation, the small group under Ursicinus that went out to do the job required great personal courage. A strong flavour of veracity is brought into the narrative by the array of convincing eyewitness details: the rumours that preceded Ursicinus' arrival in Cologne, the search for 'cauti ministri' to do the deed, the obscurity of the soldiers found to suborn the Cornuti and the Bracchiati, the time and circumstances of the assassination of Silvanus — these details are given a further tinge of realism by Ammianus' admission that he was afraid of failure and therefore of death, no doubt in an unpleasant form at the hands of the inflamed supporters of Silvanus. Such feelings of fear are common in intelligent soldiers before difficult and demanding missions. The whole story of the usurpation reads just like a detective-cum-spy story, brilliantly if sombrely composed.[6]

Ammianus' second role as a protagonist centres around his account of his mission into Corduene to check the size and movement patterns of the new Persian invasion (18.6.20–3; 7.1.2). Clearly his duties must be seen to fit in with the whole intelligence effort that he so carefully describes for this campaign, but his own contribution to that effort is important. Ammianus had a contact across the frontier in an important position: the satrap Jovinianus, who because he knew Ammianus, was willing to compromise the usual Persian virtue of *silentium* and allow the Roman into Persian territory to reach his vantage point. (A very interesting use of the personal touch, and also one that invites considerable further specu- lation into Ammianus' background at Antioch.) Ammianus shows how back in Amida he fits into the growing intelligence picture of the Persians' invasion and indicates how his information is collated with that from other sources and modifies it. Again this episode contains a wealth of small eyewitness detail: the centurion, the private meeting and its discussion, the silent companion, the two days of waiting, the vast panorama, the single bridge over the Zab — the narrative is written up with knowledge and insight and drama; it reads like the spy story that it is.

On Procopius' side, probably his most important participatory episode is his intelligence- gathering mission to Syracuse at the beginning of the Vandal campaign (*Wars* 3.14.1–15). Procopius represents Belisarius as at a loss to know quite how to proceed from the North Sicilian anchorage at Caucana because of a general lack of relevant information. Procopius is therefore sent off to Syracuse to find out the answers to a set of questions that for some- one at a loss as to what to do are remarkably pointed and specific. Of course, Procopius is overstating his role at a moment of high drama, since Belisarius' information about the Vandals generally would have been quite adequate because it was derived from obviously regular trading contacts with Carthage by Sicilian-based commercial interests.[7] Procopius' own role was to supplement this wide and generalised information with specifics: it is interesting to see that he too used the trader contact-man and his slave who had just been to Carthage. The assignment given to Procopius may not have been particularly dangerous, but it was an important one because recent information was required and a senior man was needed to deal with it. It acquires its interest and a strong tinge of veracity from the deliber- ateness of Procopius' kidnapping of his friend's slave and the rather superfluous mollifying words shouted out to the bemused owner by Procopius as he sailed out of the harbour. This is eyewitness stuff, as is the element of coincidence and luck in the story, on which so many true-life versions of such stories depend.

Olympiodorus fits well into this category. In about 412, he went from the Court at Ravenna across the Adriatic on a pseudo-diplomatic mission to a group of Huns living in what seems to be the area of modern Hungary. We have no details as to what the purpose of the mission may have been, but, it seems by an amazing series of coincidences, this highly-trusted envoy arrived at the encampment of the Hun chieftain Donatus, when the sudden murder of the chieftain ensued. Fortunately gifts, carried by the envoy from the Emperor Honorius, were immediately available to placate the Hun king Charaton who had been incensed by the murder (frg.18). Here, clearly, the actions of the historian can be seen having an effect on current events.

It is now time to discuss the reasons for the inclusion of this autobiographical material, and for the way in which it is treated. Clearly, Ammianus and Procopius, as part of their methodology, find it necessary to include it even when its direct relevance to the course of the narrative appears marginal. I think that some discussion of their respective methods of assembling their material provides a pointer, though by no means all the answers.

There are two methodological prefaces in Ammianus' extant work, the opening remarks of Books 15 and 26. In the earlier one, he makes the claim that he has either seen the events he describes (the aspect we are most interested in) or else by close questioning of participants has been able to assemble the information he wanted. He says this information is to be treated *limatius*, which I take to mean 'with considerable care and polish in both style of presentation and content': clearly such shaping must imply selectivity. The second passage is even more explicit about the selection process – trivial matters are *praeceptis historiae dissonantia*, and therefore not worthy of record in a larger-scale analysis of events and movement affecting the whole Empire. Clearly, the autobiographical sections have gone through the selection process before their inclusion, and the fact that they are there signifies their importance to the author.

In the preface to Book 1, Procopius makes important claims about being an eyewitness to events – claims which are more explicit than Ammianus' and which have attracted considerable attention from Procopian scholars. They deserve close scrutiny. Truth, Procopius asserts, is the most appropriate quality of history (a claim made by many ancient writers, and therefore a commonplace). But contextually with this is a definition of what it entails – it involves the nonconcealment of $\tau \grave{\alpha} \ \mu o \chi \vartheta \eta \rho \acute{\alpha}$, the embarrassing detail of an incident, moral lapses, any kind of failure; and these $\mu o \chi \vartheta \eta \rho \acute{\alpha}$ he has not concealed even in the case of very close associates, for example the criticisms of Belisarius. Closely associated with truth, is accuracy of assessment in writing up the material at his disposal. Truth, non-concealment and accurate assessment: implicit is a degree of subjectivity in the choice of material and the way in which it is handled. Procopius states that he was present at nearly all the events he describes (certainly for the first six books), and this underlies his attempt to reach the truth: but by implication, in connection with the events for which he was not an eyewitness, the truth may have to be somewhat circumscribed and could be dependent on factors outside his control. This is important for discussions about his veracity.[8] It is, though, a pity that unlike Ammianus he does not discuss his principles of selection but leaves them to be deduced from the work as a whole. There is a small exception to this generalisation, at *Wars* 6.2.37, where he writes of the siege of Rome that while other engagements took place, they were not worthy of being written up.

Let us return to the historians' narratives and see these principles in practice. In the case, then, of our category which covered the active participation of the historian in events that are directly related to the history of the period, there is no problem, since the episodes contain their own justification for inclusion on the grounds of their importance. Silvanus represented a threat, yet another serious threat so soon after the Magnentius/Decentius/Vetranio events of the previous few years. In imperial thinking, another civil war must be avoided as far as possible, so the risky enterprise of sending what is in effect an assassination team is attempted as an opening shot. It worked. Ammianus treats the incident as morally neutral (his duty?), but gives it tremendous impact by describing his own feelings of fear and uncertainty and insecurity, which are given a developed treatment reminiscent of a novel-like presentation. Ammianus' Corduene exploits do not have a very important fear element (they are part of an important assignment), but they do have a peculiarly interesting personal flavour, in that the author is an individual almost alone in the presence of geographical phenomena that are overawing (unmarked paths in very rough country, enormous views from his high eyrie), and in the presence of vast hostile forces over which he has no control (the laconic contacts with the satrap, the sight of Persians everywhere).[9] Here again this sense of isolation is powerfully and persuasively developed to make the personal element and the external a combination that cannot be separated within the episodes without their losing their fullness and sense of conviction.

The same fullness of treatment is accorded by Procopius to his Syracuse mission. This is justified because what he was doing was important in the context of the advanced preparations for an invasion. The carefully explained relationships between the individuals in the episode and their relative contributions to the overall needs of the expedition mean that Procopius is ensuring that full attention will be paid to the significance of the episode. However, his pride in his own achievement is just a little overblown in the wider context of the movement of the Byzantines into North Africa, because Procopius' mission is confirmatory not exploratory. The fullness, however, allows this episode too to stand as a self-contained entity.

Fullness of presentation applies with equal force to experiences in which the historian participated but not as a protagonist. In Ammianus' case, Amida and the Persian Expedition are both highpoints in the history to an extent that the protagonist sections could never aspire to, and are important in their own right and are therefore given the full treatment. Amida may have been a defeat for Roman arms; but only after two and a half months of withstanding a massive pounding from Persian forces under the King himself did it fall by storm. The loss of the place had serious repercussions externally during 360 and 361, as well as internally, distracting Constantius, as it did, from the machinations of Julian in the West, and also affecting Ammianus himself. Because of Ursicinus' strong reaction to the enquiry set up to investigate the fall of Amida, he was prematurely retired and Ammianus was plunged into obscurity (20.2.1–5). But in spite of this the account of the siege is not sombre or depressed, but vivid and interesting and incidents in the conduct of the siege are given full and detailed examination: not all of them of course, but those that are important and add to the experience of the siege. These features are distinctive, and because they are full of the eyewitness details that any other account would lack (that is, down to very small details), the trustworthiness of the account is given credibility in the eyes of its audience.

Even more than Amida, the Persian Expedition possesses the fullness of treatment that we are looking for. This episode could stand on its own as a monograph, with the theme of greatness in a leader extinguished by internal and external causes. But Ammianus' own role in reporting the Persian Expedition is important in that it is written to establish authenticity, to demonstrate that the eyewitness can step back and see the greatness of his theme and yet be integral with its workings. Ammianus sustains this exposition longer in this part than in any other. The means used by Ammianus to sustain the feeling of involved participation over such a lengthy span of writing is to use a string of eyewitness details that no other source writing on the Persian Expedition can possibly match. These details carry enormous conviction with them because of their individual smallness but cumulative authority, showing that the view of the Persian Expedition given by Ammianus must ultimately be more credible than others.

Much discussion has taken place over the matter of Ammianus' sources for the Persian Expedition. It is of course clear from a number of passages that he was actively involved in some incidents, and passively in a larger number, so the fact of eyewitness detail becoming omnipresent is one that has to be taken into account at all times in evaluating his use of literary sources. Barnes discusses the well-known correspondences between Ammianus and Zosimus which are so marked that use of the same literary source must be accepted.[10] Zosimus is a close abbreviator of Eunapius of Sardis, though on one occasion with inexplicable misrepresentations of his archetype. Barnes has demonstrated convincingly that the first edition of Eunapius' history was published about 380, shortly after Adrianople, and that the work was therefore easily available for Ammianus when his history was being prepared, say early in the 390s. There can be no doubt that Ammianus consulted Eunapius as one of the sources that he used.

It is, however, not all that important in an analysis of Ammianus' methods: what must be equally strongly stated is the fact that the similarities in the two accounts of the Persian Expedition are due to both Ammianus and Eunapius agreeing on the facts — Ammianus was present as an eyewitness of much. Eunapius was not, so derived his material from individuals who were. The similarities and indeed verbal echoes must therefore mean approval by the eyewitness of the facts as stated by the earlier writer. The divergences may therefore have to be regarded as tacit corrections or shifts of emphasis in the account. This means that the bald statement: 'Ammianus drew heavily on Eunapius' account' of the *Oxford Classical Dictionary* (2nd edn 1970), is unrealistically simplistic and denies the value of Ammianus' own methods of enquiry so clearly stated at the beginning of Book 15. It is here that the autobiographical element is seen at its most convincing — without the ability to concentrate on fact as directly experienced by a historian, history instantly becomes second-hand, creating a possible further barrier against the truth. In an absolute sense, Eunapius has less claim than Ammianus to be the purveyor of truth.

Hindsight and post-eventum reasoning play an important part in Ammianus' interpretation of the Persian Expedition. Julian's death did not signify a defeat for Roman arms: the army left Persia undefeated, if under a cloud of a negotiated settlement; losses had not been excessive; it had been the last attempt of Rome to expand the boundaries of the Empire. Ammianus, writing years later, can see that no similar enterprise can be mounted with the resources available in the post-Adrianople era; and this view was reinforced by the Eunapian view that the Roman world had taken a pounding to the point of ruination — the death of Julian, the withdrawal from Persia, and the battle of Adrianople are all moral setbacks to the Empire from which recovery will be difficult. But the facts of the Persian Expedition, that it was not a total failure, emerge from Ammianus' handling of the story: once the overlay of his gloomy interpretation is stripped away, it is clear that he was out of sympathy with its aims and may not have fully understood them. But the details which give authenticity and fullness to the account are there, and make it, then, clearer and more convincing.

There are close parallel features in Procopius' account of the siege of Rome, except that there is no atmosphere of doom and only minimal criticism. It too is a sustained piece of writing, with many elements of panegyric regarding Belisarius and in fact generally raising him head and shoulders above other figures. As part of the means to sustain the atmosphere of success Procopius too uses the eyewitness detail, the accurate use of conversation, document and archive, and human interest in a way that is remarkably convincing and plausible: it is the sheer cumulative weight of these materials that must push the credibility of the account into his audience's consciousness. There are of course areas that arouse scepticism, for example the arrival of Martinus and Valerianus with their troops only twenty-three days after Justinian had been requested by Belisarius to send· them orders to join him in Italy when they had been wintering in Aitolia and Akarnania (*Wars* 5.24.18–21; cf. 3.11.24) – either an order had been sent considerably in advance of the moment attributed to it by Procopius, and Justinian's follow-up was confirmatory, or else they were already packed and moving. Similarly the information on Gothic tactical weaknesses in battle that Procopius gives to Belisarius, and reportedly only discovered by Belisarius at the first engagement (*Wars* 5.27.25–8), clearly cannot be so, but is only conveniently used by Procopius as the occasion for passing on and developing the 'thoughts of General Belisarius'. Alternatively, it could be material that Belisarius used to discuss on occasion and used by him to illustrate features of this first engagement, in which case it shows a minor inaccuracy or lack of comprehension by Procopius.

One area where one would expect considerable eyewitness material in Procopius is in the account of the Nika riots in Constantinople in 532 where Belisarius played a leading role in their rather brutal suppression (*Wars* 1.24.1–58). The problem is that the information in the story is unsatisfactory and clearly incomplete, for example the presence of Narses as a leading co-commander with Belisarius and Mundo is not mentioned at all. It seems pretty clear that Procopius did not form part of the Court-centred planning entourage which discussed the means of ending the disturbances. This would explain why there are no eyewitness details, but only the main important pieces of information. There is however a further indication. There is no use of the first person and even more marked, no personal comments and no form of personalised analysis, as revealed by οἶμαι in other eyewitness areas, apart from a single very generalised condemnation of the activities of the Blues and Greens. When set against the very detailed analytic treatment of the plague in Constantinople not long afterwards, where there is a lot of eyewitness medical accuracy (*Wars* 2.22.1–39; 23.1–21), it seems almost as if Procopius was not in fact present in Constantinople at all at this point, and derived his information from participants. So in this case, we may have evolved some kind of controlling criterion for the treatment of such evidence.

The fragments of Priscus do not allow any comment to be made about his methodology in general, but the very detail of the account of the mission to Attila has a fullness and a personal commitment that are present all the way through, self-consistent, and which constitute material designed to underline the substantive veracity of the account. Of course, there is bias in the presentation of the material – one cannot ignore the implicit (and misguided) criticism of the East Roman government for not facing Attila squarely in the battlefield; and in the individual case of the Greek-speaking slave/ex-trader captured at Naissus whom Priscus met, his frigid, sterile and unconvincing defence of the legal and social status quo in the Empire is hard to take. But a stream of facts emerges from the story, logically connected and consistent, the result of careful and perceptive personal observation, and so they carry conviction. The fragments that do not have the eyewitness element are in a way less immediately convincing and need to be assessed differently.

Finally we come to look at the episodes that are autobiographical but by no means contribute to the main history as a whole. In this area I think it is clear that the criteria for their inclusion are different from that of the others', and perhaps here we have to look at the kind of person the authors are. It was remarked earlier that this kind of material provides first of all a dramatic personal account of a series of exciting incidents, and second, an insight into the background conditions for those events. The first is definable almost as picaresque novel; most of the events read like an adventure story, which of course they are, with comment by the author. In Ammianus' case, each incident in the Amudis–Nisibis–Amida run-around (18.6.8–17) is a fascinating little vignette of what can happen to an individual when the world of order collapses and what can happen to a small group when faced with a hostile environment – it is harsh and brutal and the watchword is survival of the fittest. Look at the conditions of desert warfare, the quick interrogation scene at Meiacarire, the picking-up of that eight-year old boy outside Amida – all these show some-thing of the personality of the author. Such insight into his character leads us to look at the depiction of the background conditions which these incidents reveal. The collapse of a frontier system to a power like Persia leads to chaos for soldier and civilian. Ursicinus attempted to establish a second line of defence along the Euphrates by installing defence points on the banks and breaking down the bridges along the projection of the invasion line taken by the Persians; but civilians had their crops totally destroyed and were herded off their farms into strongpoints to deny the invaders any supplies. What saved the Roman provinces further west was of course the unexpectedly high flood levels of the Euphrates and the long siege of Amida. These facts Ammianus does not discuss because the story of his own experience and active roles are much more important. The more sober analytic history is pushed into the background. So the purpose of this kind of material is to entertain and enliven: what lies behind the surface is useful for understanding the conditions that exist in circumstances of confusion and disorganisation stemming from widespread invasion; not essential, but valuable.

In Procopius' case, his own contribution in this area is almost negligible, because as a rule Procopius does not have many exciting adventures. The difference from Ammianus centres around his use of first-person supportive material. It is not quite autobiographic but it indicates the fact that he is making use of his location to indulge curiosity in the course of his investigations. By this I mean things like the vision he had had before the North African Expedition left Constantinople and which augured well for its success (*Wars* 3.12.3–5). Then again there is his symbolic interpretation of the unexpected finding of water just after the actual landing in North Africa (*Wars* 3.15.35). His (unfounded) feelings of alarm during an engagement at Decimum outside Carthage and the associated reflections are similar (*Wars* 3.18.2; 19.25–9). More valuable in this area, I think, are the deliberate injections of his persona into background information: his knowledge of early Vandal history came from his own contacts and personal experience with Vandals ('I heard this discussed in this way from the Vandals': *Wars* 3.3.34); his information on the Moors was given him by Solomon's ally Ortaias himself (*Wars* 4.13–29); he heard the story of the brazen bull and the Tuscan prophecy about the capture of Rome by a eunuch from a senator (*Wars* 8.21.10 – clearly he was in Rome for a second time on another visit late in the Gothic War), among a number of others. His scepticism too with regard to some of the information he is given (a Herodotean touch) fits into this category (for example *Wars* 5.9.2). There is no essential historiographical or autobiographical need for Procopius to put himself forward in this way — he does so primarily for the purpose of underlining the accuracy of the information he is transmitting: it adds to its interest, and allows the use of often marginally relevant material to enliven the narrative and shift its pacing.

What then is the role of autobiography in history? Why are such passages there? It is surely because if we are to take the works of the historians seriously as they clearly intend us to do, the inclusion of material that may on occasion be assessed as trivial is important because it stamps that material as peculiarly belonging to the author. It cannot be found in works that derive from theirs or are later than theirs, for example Zosimus does not have any significant or even insignificant eyewitness detail of this type. The purpose then is this: by marking out their presence at the events they describe, these authors establish a claim to have their perception of the events taken seriously. It is not only an aspect of the literary taste of the period but also a kind of *sphragis* of authenticity in the construction of their histories.

Notes

1. W. R. Chalmers, 'Eunapius, Ammianus Marcellinus and Zosimus on Julian's Persian Expedition', *Classical Quarterly* 10 (1960), 152–60.

2. N. J. Austin, *Ammianus on Warfare*, Collection Latomus 165 (Brussels 1979), 19ff.

3. J. Matthews, 'Olympiodorus of Thebes', *Journal of Roman Studies* 60 (1970), 79–97.

4. L. Dilleman, 'Ammien Marcellin et les pays de l'Euphrate et du Tigre', *Syria* 38 (1961), 87–155; W. R. Chalmers, 'An alleged doublet in Ammianus Marcellinus', *Rheinisches Museum* 102 (1959), 183–9; Austin, *op. cit.*, 15, 17f.

5. Austin, *op. cit.*, 97–101.

6. E. A. Thompson, *The Historical Work of Ammianus Marcellinus* (Cambridge 1947), 44ff.; Austin, *op. cit.*, 48–51.

7. B. Rubin, 'Procopios von Kaisareia', *RE* Supplementband 23, 1 (1957), 411. Rubin is, however, extremely sceptical about the role of coincidence and luck in Procopius' version: I am less so.

8. Two attacks on non-eyewitness veracity can be adduced. G. Downey, 'The Persian Campaign in Syria in A.D. 540', *Speculum* 28 (1953), 340–48, indicates that Procopius is willing to suppress the truth on occasions when it is inconvenient (here, Germanus' financial transactions in Antioch, *Wars* 2.6–10, to be compared with Malalas 480.1–5 (Dindorf); the non-existence of a large rock anywhere in the town walls; the fact of Germanus' leaving early, before the negotiations with Chrosroes were completed; and the fact of there being too few Roman troops available for defence — only 6,000 could get there, since the rest of those normally available were away in Italy with Belisarius). Carelessness must be part of the reason — but note that Procopius was in no way an eyewitness. The second case: B. S. Bachrach, 'Procopius, Agathias and the Frankish Military', *Speculum* 45 (1970), 435–41 is very critical of Procopius' account of Frankish weaponry at *Wars* 6.25.3–4, since it fails to mention their barbed spear the *ango*, asserts the presence in battle of 100,000 Franks, and is generally short on detail.

Here, however, is a passage dealing with events that Procopius is not an eyewitness of, having to rely on reports to Belisarius made by Roman troops defeated by the Franks, *Wars* 6.25.15 — but Procopius is quite clearly giving a short, incomplete and impressionistic account since the Franks play no more than a very distant and marginal role in the *Wars*. Important and detailed support for an aspect of Procopius' veracity comes from K. Hannestad, 'Les forces militaires d'après la guerre gothique de Procope', *Classica et Mediaevalia* 21 (1960), 136—83 where the pertinent military statistics are analysed and found credible and coherent. It is instructive to note that where events of which he is not an eyewitness are concerned, he is often extremely sceptical or guarded where the material looks exaggerated, for example *Wars* 4.12.25; 5.9.2.

9.   For Ammianus' isolation as a phenomenon of his psychology, see R. C. Blockley, *Ammianus Marcellinus: a study of his historiography and political thought*, Collection Latomus 141 (Brussels 1975), 155—6.

10. T. D. Barnes, *The Sources of the Historia Augusta*, Collection Latomus 155 (Brussels 1978), 114—23, now sharply criticised by F. Paschoud ('Quand parut la première édition de l'histoire d'Eunape?', *Bonn—Historia—Augusta Colloquium 1977/8* (1980), 149—62) and incidentally by R. Goulet ('La vie et les oeuvres d'Eunape de Sardes', *Journal of Hellenic Studies* 100 (1980), 60—92 [not before 396]). Ammianus' account may thus be rehabilitated as the most accurate and worthwhile.

Patterns of Communication and Movement in Ammianus and Gregory of Tours

R.F. Newbold

Study of patterns of human communication and movement that are present in the work of an intelligent and reasonably well-informed observer can reveal much about the concentration and dispersal of power in the observer's society; about the nature, direction and strength of the various currents of energy that animate that particular society. The significance of such revelations is greatly enhanced if they can be compared with the perceptions of comparable observers of the same society (in so far as it can be said to have remained 'the same' — at least they are products of a recognisably continuous cultural milieu) from different periods. Even allowing for the limitations, subjectivity and idiosyncrasies of individual observers' perceptions, these can still provide useful indicators as to how the society is evolving and the routes along which information and influence are flowing.

The purpose of this paper is, firstly, to use the evidence of Ammianus and of Gregory of Tours to study the patterns of movement and communication in the Roman Empire of the fourth century and in sixth-century Merovingian Gaul; secondly, and as a product of the comparative method we have employed, to see how their perceptions differ from those of writers from earlier eras.

By plotting references to spatial movement and by noting the social status of those involved in movements, one can construct an 'energy field' that reveals the geographical areas, the motives for travel and the social group most salient in the minds of different authors. This can be done by charting whether, where and whence people move themselves or others, and by recording how and for what reason movements are made. For example, do people move slowly or quickly, by foot or by horse, to meet someone or to escape from him? Are movements away from or towards the centre(s) of power? How extensive are movements and who moves or is moved most and least? The data generated by such analysis cast light upon contemporary perceptions of the environment and loci of concern. Matters such as the state of technology and the availability of material resources may be illuminated.

Method
Our method has been to take a sample from Ammianus and Gregory, to put questions to the material and to compare the statistical data generated with identically-sized samples from two earlier times, viz. Livy and Tacitus. Clearly, in determining the size, nature and number of the samples several tradeoffs have to be made so as to achieve significant and soundly-based conclusions without extravagant effort. With Ammianus 1500 lines of Loeb text seems to provide sufficient material to produce meaningful results. Heterogeneity was assured by composing the sample from nine books, the sample being the first 166 2/3 lines of alternate books from 14 to 30.[1] Identically-sized and similarly composed samples were assembled from the three other authors,[2] who are all widely acknowledged as historians of some

66

sensitivity, vision, originality and comprehensiveness rather than mere compilers, annalists or epitomators.

The first question put to each of the assembled samples was: how many references are there to someone moving (or causing to move) an object or person across space (Directed Movement)?[3] Clearly, capacity to direct movement is one of the most basic indices of power. The next question to be asked was: how often do persons move themselves across space (Autonomous Movement)?[4] Obviously there can only be a rough distinction between Directed and Autonomous Movement, for even though an author may simply say that someone 'went' rather than 'was sent', that someone might not be exercising much personal discretion in determining the goal or timing or manner of his movement. Nevertheless if an author consistently prefers to accent autonomy rather than direction and say that someone went rather than was sent it is probably not unrelated to his perception of the modes and patterns of movement and communication in his society.

Having gathered all the references to Directed Movement, the next step in trying to discern where the centres of power lay, and how far they extended, and in trying to understand the pattern of transmission, was to ask: who sent what or whom, whence, whither and why? The grouping of transmitters, sources, goals and motivation is revealed under *Results*, below. Similarly, the data on Autonomous Movement was put onto grids and maps to reveal who went whither, whence, how and why. Results of all this analysis suggested further questions, and these are dealt with below.

Results and Discussion

A. i. The number of separate references to Directed Movement in the respective samples were as follows: Livy 83, Tacitus 71, Ammianus 74, Gregory 86. The cognate activity of giving and handing over[5] yielded scores of 12, 3, 3 and 12 respectively and if combined with the former set of figures provides totals of: Livy 95, Tacitus 74, Ammianus 77, Gregory 98.

ii. The number of references to Autonomous Movement were as follows: the meaning of the sub-categories is provided in note 4 (below, p.78).

	Livy	Tacitus	Ammianus	Gregory
a	86	60	89	126
b	9	10	19	1
c	8	4	16	4
d	10	2	9	3
Total	**113**	**76**	**133**	**134**

Before giving details on the who, where, why, etc. of the above movements a few preliminary observations on the figures and some further questions they raise might be timely. The totals of the various authors for (i) are not strikingly different from each other, although they fall into two pairs, the two histories of the pre- and post-imperial rule and narrowed horizons, Livy and Gregory, forming one pair and the two historians of large Empire, the other. This may simply be coincidental. On the other hand, direction and giving is a form of communication and smaller horizons may encourage more of it. A related form of activity can be mentioned here, namely placing, setting down, burying and generally arranging in space: the statistics from the sample reflect the above figures for Directed Movement fairly neatly: Livy 20, Tacitus 11, Ammianus 9, Gregory 14, so that if added to the existing totals they tend to reinforce the distinctiveness of the pairings, so that we get 115, 85, 86 and 112 respectively as the overall totals. This supports the idea that less expansive areas permit more frequent controlling activity.

As for Autonomous Movement ii., several features stand out. While Tacitus has by a narrow margin the smallest number of Directed Movements, he has easily the smallest number of Autonomous Movements. Taking the two totals together, this signifies that, comparatively speaking, staticity rather than mobility prevails in Tacitus: especially uncommon compared with Livy and Ammianus is rapid movement in Tacitus (c and d). This is partially due to less prominence being given to military affairs. The same explanation would apply to Gregory, and in Gregory's case there is a lack of style and artistry, that is satisfied with simple 'went', etc. to denote movement. In Ammianus, then, there is emphasis on the rapidity of movement, but in Gregory, particularly if one adds his total for i. to his total for ii., there is a greater picture of human movement in general. A further set of figures reinforces this impression: if one asks, how often do people engage in autonomous muscular activity, making contact with some object or aspect of the environment, such as wrestling, rioting, grabbing, digging, etc., we find that, in the sample Gregory has 31 references compared with Livy 17, Tacitus 13 and Ammianus 8.[6] The comparatively low score of Ammianus in this form of activity is interesting. In so far as movement across space, particularly energetic, rapid, purposeful movement requires muscular exertion and offers psychic relief, Ammianus' world is populated by characters who act in this way rather than in the more intimate modes of muscular exertion.[7] Furthermore, as speed increases, so does tunnel vision, that is, the peripheral vision which helps to keep a person in immediate contact with the environment diminishes. The reader is reminded of the incidence of rapid movement in Ammianus.

The suspicion that Ammianus' preferred mode of reported activity appeals because of the greater impersonality and detachment which it permits may be reinforced by some additional data. The number of references in the Ammianus sample to instances of spontaneous, non-human movement by the environment (storm, flood, earthquake, etc.) is 17 and exceeds the total for Livy (1), Tacitus (8) and Gregory (8).[8] Yet if Ammianus' environment appears the most unstable it is also the one that is (as if by way of compensation) most imposed upon by activities of an impersonal kind, such as ravaging, destroying, burning or constructing (Ammianus 19 times: cf. Livy 10, Tacitus 14, Gregory 13). That is, there is in Ammianus more interraction of a remote and impersonal nature with and within a perceptually less stable and less human environment.

B. *The social and material groups*
In trying to understand more fully the patterns of Directed Movement it was necessary firstly to arrange the human directors in groups as follows: Ruler (Roman/Etruscan/Latin/Merovingian king, dictator, emperor); Associates (their relatives, courtiers, close associates of the Ruler); Magistrates (civilian magistrates, officials, senators); Commanders (military commanders, officers); Foreign Rulers (foreign rulers, chiefs); Troops (Roman, Gallic or allied troops); Foreign Troops (foreign, enemy, barbarian troops); Foreign

Others (other foreigners including envoys); Priests (priests, bishops, monks); Knights; Crowds; Commoners (plebeians, commoners); Unknown; Uncertain; Miscellaneous (miscellaneous, including slaves). Employing data for analysis on *what* was moved involved extending these groups to include: Letters, messengers (other than envoys); Property, clothing, jewellery, cattle; (articles of) Furniture; Vehicles; Wives, children; Food, supplies; Weapons, standards; Structures, building materials; and Angels.

i. *Who does the directing?*
    Because the total number of references to Directed Movement varies in each author, the figures for separate (groups of) directors become more meaningful if they are also expressed as percentages of the author's total. The three most popular directors are:
    Ammianus: Ruler 24 (32%), Commanders 16 (22%), Foreign Rulers 10 (13%). Total 50 out of 74 (68%). Compare:
    Livy: Magistrates 27 (33%), Foreign Rulers 14 (17%), Rulers 12 (14%). Total 53 out of 83 (64%).
    Tacitus: Rulers 24 (34%), Commanders 11 (15%), Associates 9 (13%). Total 44 out of 71 (62%).
    Gregory: Rulers 17 (20%), Miscellaneous 11 (13%), Priests 9 (10%). Total 37 out of 86 (43%).

ii. *What are the most common reasons for directing movement?*
    The three most popular reasons are:[9]
    Ammianus: to destroy or attack 10; unknown 10; to request, discuss, communicate 9.
    Livy: to banish, remove someone 16; to request, discuss, communicate 14; to destroy, attack 10.
    Tacitus: unknown 8; to rescue, save 8; to attack 7.
    Gregory: to banish, remove 10; unknown 10; miscellaneous 10.

iii. *Who or what is directed?*
    Analysis of who or what is transmitted through the network of communication – the directed traffic – can throw light on the role and resources of the directors as well as on the preoccupation of the authors. In Livy, the four most popular categories are: Rulers 13, Troops 10, Foreign Troops 10 and Foreign Others 9, making up together nearly one half of the total directees. Priests, Knights, Crowds, Unknown, Furniture, and Food never figure in Livy. (In 9 cases out of 13 Rulers are directed by Magistrates, and in 7 cases out of 10 Roman Troops are directed by Magistrates. Foreign Troops and Foreign Others have a range of directors.) Rulers are never directed in Tacitus; nor, like Livy, does he direct Priests and Crowds, Commoners and Unknown. But unlike Livy, he makes no references to Foreign Troops, Weapons or Structures. The most common directees in Tacitus are: Roman Troops 13, Foreign Troops 12, Magistrates 9 and Wives 7. (Magistrates are 5 times directed by Rulers, and Troops 7 times by Rulers.) As in Livy and in Tacitus, Priests, Crowds and Furniture are never directed in Ammianus: as in Livy, Knights are never directed and as in Tacitus, Commoners never. The most common directees in Ammianus are Troops 15 (9 times by Rulers, and 6 times by Commanders), Letters 8 (4 times by Foreign Rulers), Associates 7 (4 times by Rulers).

Although there are some marked differences in the balance between civilian and military, rulers and ruled, Roman and non-Roman, human and inanimate in the traffic patterns of Livy, of Tacitus and of Ammianus, these differences almost pale into insignificance when compared with the pattern that emerges in Gregory. His four most common groups of directees are: Priests 23 (5 directed by God or Angels, 5 by Commoners, 5 by Unknown), Property 14, Commoners 8, and Letters 7. He is alone in having no reference to Magistrates, Foreign Rulers, Vehicles, and his other blanks are Knights (a blank common to all 4 authors in fact), Food and Structures. Other signs of Gregory's narrow, relatively pacific and unfocused world are only 2 for each of the following: Troops, Foreign Troops and Foreign Others, and 6 for Uncertain (uncertain as to the identity of the person *sent*: cf. Livy 2, Tacitus 2, Ammianus 3). Other features which stand out in the overall comparison are Tacitus' 0 for Rulers (compare Livy 13, Ammianus 5, Gregory 5) and Gregory's 0 for Vehicles (Livy 5, Tacitus 3, Ammianus 1). Ammianus has the highest number of Letters sent: 8 (compare Livy 4, Tacitus 6, Gregory 7) but it is worth noting that none stem from Rulers, Magistrates, or Troops: 4 are from Foreign Rulers and 1 each from Associates, Commanders, Unknown and Uncertain.

iv. *What are the sources and goals of Directed Movement?*

In Ammianus it is in and beyond the provinces, not in Rome, Constantinople and Italy, that men act as directors of movement. It is mainly emperors and Roman soldiers who do the directing, and not, predictably, peasants, civilians — but no barbarians or Roman military commanders either. This can best be illustrated by limiting comparison to Tacitus for the moment. Movements can be plotted on a map concentrically arranged with the imperial palace at the centre and then, moving outwards, Rome (or Constantinople), then Italy, then the provinces — divided into East and West, and then the region beyond the frontiers, again divided into East and West. As regards activity in the East beyond the frontiers (Ammianus 15, Tacitus 21), beyond the Western frontiers (Ammianus 6, Tacitus 7), in the eastern provinces (Ammianus 18, Tacitus 14) and in the imperial palace (Ammianus 3, Tacitus 4), there is not much difference between the two authors. But elsewhere, the differences are striking: in the western provinces (Ammianus 19, Tacitus 2), Italy (Ammianus 1, Tacitus 24), Constantinople (Ammianus 5), Rome (Tacitus 22). Also significant is the greater *extent* of direction in Tacitus. A greater proportion of Ammianus' directions are within just one of the geographical areas listed above, or, if they move outwards or inwards to an inner or outer circle, they only cross one boundary in doing so.[10] Moreover, 29 out of Tacitus' 69 radial Directed Movements cross more than one boundary while 17 out of Ammianus' 51 do so. In other words, there is more extensive radial direction in Tacitus, and in Ammianus more lateral or more limited radial movement. This is another mark of decentralisation and of declining power to transmit over long distances.

In plotting Directed Movement (where both source and goal are given) in Livy, forum and senate take the central spot occupied by palace in Tacitus and Ammianus. Then, moving outwards, the circles are: Rome, Latium, Italy and the eastern and western Mediterranean. Sixth-century Gaul is so fragmented and decentralised that Gregory's world rather defies concentric representation. It is not just that Merovingian kingdoms form a patchwork quilt over Gaul but the power of the Church exists alongside the secular power, with its own centre and periphery; and then there is a further dimension — heaven, whence or whither messages or messengers might be sent. Nevertheless, one can draw a central circle to stand for the dwelling of whatever king Gregory mentions, then move outwards to that king's capital, then to his kingdom, then to other kingdoms or Gaul in general, and then to areas beyond Gaul, such as Germany, Spain, Italy or Byzantium.

The world beyond Italy hardly enters into Livy's world of early Rome. Once the Roman government sends Q. Fabius to Gaul from Rome and on 4 occasions persons outside Italy sent forces into Italy but over half of the directions start or end in Italy, almost one third in Rome, nearly one fifth in Latium, with the forum or senate figuring 4 times. By contrast the world beyond Gaul figures 13 times in Gregory's sample. One third of the Directed Movements start and/or end in a particular kingdom and 4 in a capital or palace. Included in Gregory's Directed Movements are 13 which might be termed ecclesiastical, of which half are lateral rather than radial. There is also the third vertical dimension of direction: 3 from heaven to earth, 2 from earth to heaven, plus 2 within heaven itself.

Of Livy's 59 radial movements, 19 cross more than 1 boundary; but only 2 of Gregory's 51 do so (we excluded the heaven/earth transmission). In other words, where 42% of Tacitus' directions have sufficient power behind them to cross more than one boundary or go beyond an area, the proportion for Ammianus is 33%, for Livy 32% (although they are dealing with very different sized geographical areas, this lower proportion is still a reflection on the perceived degree of control that was exercised over the respective areas) and 4% for Gregory's world. Another indication of greater power to direct, to suggest and to effect cohesion in the kingdom is knowledge of frequency of reference to *both* source and goal of the transmission, whatever its extent. This information is available in almost all of Tacitus' references (97%), in 71% of Livy's, just over 68% of Ammianus' and 59% in Gregory.[11] Additionally, it is 11 times uncertain or unknown who transmits in Gregory, 6 times in Ammianus, 4 times in Livy and never in Tacitus.

Potentially as significant as the most common directors and reasons are those that rarely or never direct, particularly when their incidence varies from author to author.

Ammianus:	7 groups never, 2 once, 1 twice.
Tacitus:	7 groups never, 0 once, 1 twice.
Livy:	3 groups never, 1 once, 3 twice.
Gregory:	1 group never, 3 once, 0 twice.

In both Tacitus and Ammianus, Priests, Knights, Crowds and Miscellaneous never direct. (Commoners never direct in Tacitus, but they do so once in Ammianus.) In Livy Priests, Knights and Crowds never direct, while Miscellaneous do so once. In Gregory only Foreign Others never direct, whereas Priests figure 9 times as directors, Knights once, Crowds 4 times, Commoners 6 times, and Miscellaneous a resounding 11 times. The heterogeneity and dispersal of the ability or opportunity to direct in Gregory's world is thus in strong contrast to those of his predecessors. And this sense of heterogeneity and dispersal in Gregory is heightened by consideration of the most popular motives for direction: Miscellaneous and Uncertain are joint first, closely followed by Specific Tasks.[12] Motives for direction are spread fairly evenly among the groups who direct in Livy, Gregory and Tacitus: but in Ammianus there is more clustering; there occurs a narrowing of range of motivation,[13] except in the case of the Ruler. This latter group exceeds any other group in Ammianus and in the other authors as well for range of motivation, portraying a collective character of many facets.

C. Turning now to consider the patterns of Autonomous Movement, we come to less obvious foci of power. Yet the author's perception of where the most common paths of movement and energy lie, and the nature of those paths, as far as they may be defined by the status and purpose of the people who move along them, can provide data that may confirm, elucidate or correct the discernible pattern of Directed Movement.

i. *Where does Autonomous Movement begin and end?*
    114 of Ammianus' references to Autonomous Movement supply the origin of these movements. None originate in Rome or Italy (cf. Tacitus 21 and 17 respectively, from 57 sourced movements), 4 originate from palaces at Antioch and Constantinople (cf. 3 in Tacitus from palaces at Rome), 35 originate in the western provinces (Tacitus 2), 36 occur in the eastern provinces (Tacitus 8), 10 beyond the western frontiers (Tacitus 8) and 29 beyond the eastern frontiers (Tacitus 8), largely due to Julian's Persian campaign falling within our sample. Obvious, then, is the greater activity in the more peripheral areas of the Empire in Ammianus, the comparative centrality of Tacitus' movement, and the preponderance of activity in the east in Tacitus compared with the better balance between east and west in Ammianus. As for who engaged in this movement, the Roman soldier figures most prominently — 21 times — beyond the frontier (both east and west), well in excess of the 7 references to all 3 groups of foreigners there (Tacitus has 2 references to Roman soldiers, 6 to Foreigners beyond the frontiers).

    The comparative porosity of frontiers in Ammianus' time is also suggested by the number of references to Roman soldiers active in the provinces: 20 (compare Tacitus 2) — and the urgency of the problem is further suggested by his references in the provinces to Rulers — 19 (Tacitus 0) and Commanders — 8 (Tacitus 5). Surprisingly perhaps there are only 3 references to foreigners in the provinces and they are all non-combatant (Tacitus 0, but 1 in Rome and 1 in Italy). If in Ammianus the Roman soldier is very much the central figure inside and beyond the provinces, he is very much a peripheral figure in Tacitus, not appearing at all in Tacitus in our sample. In Tacitus, 13 of the 17 Italian references to Autonomous Movement concern Rulers or their Associates (8 and 5 respectively); and in Rome 14 out of 21 (7 and 7 respectively) are so concerned. Beyond the central regions of Rome and Italy, Commanders are more prominent movers in Tacitus than Troops. The number of references in Ammianus to Rulers, Troops, Foreign Rulers, Foreign Troops and Foreign Others moving about suggests a diffusion of power and attention that parallels the geographic diffusion. The increased prominence of the Roman soldier and his adversaries is at the expense of the old élite and leaves the civilian lower orders as unimportant as ever; the Emperor is the military apex.

    As far as goals are concerned, in Tacitus, both in the east and west beyond the frontiers, twice as many goals of movement (compared with sources) are given and much the same is true of Ammianus beyond the eastern frontier (but not beyond the western). There is evidence in Tacitus but not in Ammianus of an expansionary and centrifugal tendency, for the total number of references to goals beyond the frontiers greatly exceeds sources there (29 to 16) and there is marginally less movement towards places in the provinces (6 goals to 8 sources), towards Italy (15 goals to 17 sources) or towards Rome (18 goals to 21 sources).

The different sources of Autonomous Movement in Gregory are more numerous, scattered and widespread than in Livy. More movement originates outside Gaul in Gregory than outside Italy in Livy. In Livy, Rome, the chief source (15 references), is more dominant as a source than Tours, the chief source (10 references) in Gregory: Latium altogether accounts for 11 references in Livy, Picenum 7, Samnium 8 and southern Italy 2. Goals are also more diffused in Gregory: 12 lie outside Gaul, in part a reflection of the kings' need to seek revenue from booty abroad in the absence of a centralised taxation system. Only 3 Livy goals lie outside Italy.

ii. *How precise is the location of sources and goals?*
The number of cases in each sample in which no information is given concerning source and/or goal are as follows:

	Livy	Tacitus	Ammianus	Gregory
Source	6	5	14	18
Goal	3	2	18	8
Total (above A. ii.) **113**		**76**	**133**	**134**

Even allowing for the different proportions of the respective totals that the above figures comprise, there is much more uncertainty about termini in Ammianus and Gregory than in Tacitus, and, somewhat surprisingly in view of the remote times of which he is writing, than in Livy.[14]

iii. *What groups are the most common Autonomous Movers?*[15]
The six most common Autonomous Movers in each author are as follows:

Livy		Tacitus		Ammianus		Gregory	
Foreign Troops	29 (24%)	Associates	22 (27%)	Troops	48 (34%)	Priests	29 (25%)
Troops	23 (19%)	Rulers	15 (18%)	Rulers	28 (20%)	Rulers	27 (23%)
Magistrates	16 (13%)	Troops	12 (15%)	Foreign Others	21 (15%)	Uncertain	12 (10%)
Foreign Rulers	15 (13%)	Commanders	10 (12%)	Foreign Rulers	16 (11%)	Magistrates	9 (8%)
Foreign Others	15 (13%)	Foreign Rulers	7 (9%)	Commanders	10 (7%)	Foreign Troops	9 (8%)
Rulers	15 (13%)	Magistrates	4 (5%)	Uncertain	7 (5%)	Associates	8 (7%)
113 (95%)		**70 (85%)**		**130 (91%)**		**94 (82%)**	
Total out of 119		Total out of 82		Total out of 143		Total out of 115	

Livy and Ammianus have a similar narrow distribution profile in that the six most popular moving groups account for almost all of the total. The spread across social groups in Tacitus and Gregory is slightly wider, with Gregory having the least number of 0, 1 or 2 scores of all the other authors. The figures are eloquent indicators of who were perceived to be the most active movers in the respective societies. The more militarist narratives of Livy and Ammianus centre around Roman troops and their leaders, whether consuls or emperors, and the foreigners they had to deal with. In Tacitus, the focus is on the society's social élite — emperors, associates and senatorial commanders and governors — and their collective movements are largely the result of warfare, ceremonial parading, greetings and interviewing (or being greeted and interviewed — see below). This produces a pattern of deliberate and hence of ordered communication which substands the comparative order in society and which is performed by an élite which understands the rules and conventions. In Gregory the focus is on kings and their associates plus bishops and civilian magistrates, with a notably high proportion of people whose social status is uncertain — either because Gregory did not know, did not care and/or did not hesitate to include such undefined actors in his narrative. In Livy alone one is never uncertain about status, in Tacitus this occurs 3 times. Troops and foreigners figure rarely in Gregory compared with the other three. In Ammianus and Gregory, the greater absolute number of movements by Rulers (yet communicating little — an activity more commonly found amongst Priests in Gregory) may in itself be a form of communication, a holding of dominions together by frequency of presence.[16]

iv. *What are the reasons for Autonomous Movement?*[17]

Livy		Tacitus		Ammianus		Gregory	
Attack	43 (36%)	Attack	18 (22%)	Attack	46 (32%)	Attack	26 (23%)
Escape	26 (22%)	Enter	15 (18%)	Enter	21 (15%)	Uncertain	14 (21%)
Uncertain	13 (11%)	Greet	10 (12%)	Uncertain	19 (13%)	Specific Task	16 (14%)
Miscellaneous	12 (10%)	Specific Task	10 (12%)	Escape	18 (13%)	Communicate	13 (11%)
Communicate	9 (8%)	Interview	9 (11%)	Miscellaneous	17 (12%)	Enter	13 (11%)
Enter	7 (6%)	Miscellaneous	8 (10%)	Specific Task	9 (6%)	Greet	11 (10%)
Greet	5 (4%)	Escape	6 (7%)	Communicate	6 (4%)	Escape	6 (5%)
Specific Task	4 (3%)	Communicate	4 (5%)	Interview	5 (3%)	Miscellaneous	6 (5%)
Interview	0 (0%)	Uncertain	2 (2%)	Greet	2 (1%)	Interview	0 (0%)
	119		**82**		**143**		**115**

Although Attack is the most common reason for movement in all four authors, it occupies one third of the more military-oriented Livy and Ammianus, and less than a quarter of Tacitus and Gregory. In the latter two the category of Escape, which embraces much military activity, is also far less prominent. The diligence with which Tacitus (only 2 Uncertain) documents or attributes motives is notable compared with the other three authors. The most social and ceremonial groups of reasons — Communicating, Interviewing, Greeting — account for a relatively high proportion of Tacitus' reasons (28%) and a low proportion in the two more military historians, especially Ammianus.

The relationship of reasons to Autonomous Movement provides further information on perceived role, status and importance. Livy's grid reveals the greatest degree of clustering: both the spread of movers and of motives are comparatively restricted, or, to put it another way, a comparatively narrow range of social groups move for a comparatively narrow range of reasons. In Tacitus, Roman Emperors and their Associates move for a wide variety of reasons, there being only one category in each case that they do not fill. Interviewing (8 out of 9) and Greeting (8 out of 10) are overwhelming motives of the Roman social élite — Rulers, Associates, Magistrates and Commanders. Rulers in Ammianus account for 2 of his 6 Communications references, and Associates account for 1, plus 2 of the 5 Interview references. The 9 out of 19 Enter references that are accounted for by Rulers in Ammianus is an aspect of their military rather than ceremonial activity; and although Rulers have 5 Miscellaneous scores and 3 Specific Tasks, their range of motivation is not especially varied, including as it does 8 Attack scores. Attack in Tacitus is dispersed amongst Associates and Commanders. The 46 Attack scores are dominated by Troops in Ammianus (26), followed by 9 for Foreign Others. Troops in fact share with Rulers the highest range of motivation, featuring in 7 out of 9 categories and suggesting not only centrality but diversity of function (cf. Tacitus — where Troops figure in only 4 out of 9 categories). Not surprisingly, Uncertainty of motives (6 out of 19) and Miscellany of motives (6 out of 19) are associated most with Foreigners, but Troops score 5. These figures may suggest a major source of communication disorder — the growth of groups moving and acting from unclear, varied or unusual motives.[18]

In Ammianus Rulers have 8 scores for Attack, in Tacitus they have none, a function left largely to Associates and Commanders, and Rulers in Tacitus are generally less mobile (only 4 Enter). Commanders perform 6 out of the 10 Specific Tasks in Tacitus while Rulers do none, whereas Ammianus' Rulers do so 3 times. In Gregory the two most prominent movers, Priests and Rulers, act for every reasaon except Escape, the former group in particular displaying versatility and variety in predominantly civilian functions, including the important liaising one of Greeting (4 of the 11 references) and of Communicating (5 of the 13 references).

Conclusions

Gregory and Livy may have more direction, placing and giving (see p.67) but their canvas is much smaller. The lesser frequency of direction and so on in Tacitus and Ammianus is made up for by the greater distances involved. And Ammianus' high score for controlling the non-human environment (see p.68) attests to a vigour of will and assertion, despite (or because of) a comparatively high awareness of the instability of the environment. One could say of Ammianus and Gregory that their high incidence of Autonomous Movement reflects disorder rather than order, and that it is an attempt to prevent entropy. Much of this movement is carried on by authority figures unable to relax and simply radiate power from a stable centre. And a good deal of movement in Ammianus is of a hurried nature, carried on by non-Romans and stemming from a variety of geographic sources. Much more of the movement in Livy and Gregory is of a very local nature, traversing short distances. In Gregory it has a lot to do with buildings (see n.14). Surprisingly, vehicles are rarely mentioned in Gregory, a sign of a transport system that is more pedestrian and therefore slower and less able to transport heavy traffic over long distances.

Presumably, the main foci of attention are where the main sources of power are assumed to lie. Thus Tacitus' interest in the movements of the upper echelons is a depiction of the flow of power within the grid of imperial society. It is a view from above, with the Empire largely peaceful — emperors do not attack at all, nor are they ever directed anywhere — and when the peace *is* threatened, where the Empire's strength *is* being extended or asserted, it is the Commanders, and not the Troops, who are most important. The input of emperors into activity and movement is still important in Ammianus but Roman troops assume much of the role of Tacitus' higher status carriers in asserting Roman authority, and there is much more input from foreigners. The system is more open, less bounded; and there is more osmosis and two-way traffic. Yet movement by civilian commoners is no more prominent. Emperors or high officials in Ammianus do not communicate much. This may be both cause and symptom of a problem of power and order which may have been overcome partly by sheer frequency and mobility in physical presence. A striking difference between Ammianus and Tacitus is the greater variety of motivation behind the movements of Roman soldiers in Ammianus.[19]

Tacitus' more concentric conception of empire is underlined by the greater frequency of direction over circular boundaries. More of Ammianus' are within a geographical region and this may foreshadow the decentralised, smaller scale world of Gregory — where less energy is available to sustain distant and heavy movement of people, goods and services. The reasons for direction in Ammianus and Tacitus form a fairly similar pattern but there is a decline in certainty from Ammianus to Gregory. Livy's world is as militaristic as Ammianus' but is on a smaller canvas. Tacitus' emperor and élite move about more with the purpose of greeting and interviewing and this does suggest a more fluid flow of information to and from the centre. That is, the system is sustaining itself on good communication. Certainly, in Tacitus there is a strong impression of people secure enough to know what they are doing and transmitting, a security reflected by a narrower range of reasons and motives for action. Soldiers are not the best of communicators and their prominence in both Livy and Ammianus does not make for a balanced and fluent society, but rather for a rigid and besieged one. And people who are trying to escape (as they so often do in Ammianus) are obviously not trying to communicate. The prominence of the group of Foreigners is in itself both a sign and an effect of communication difficulties. This also applies to the activity of soldiers, for their movement lends itself less easily to explanation — not only to Ammianus but to the populations they passed through. The rapidity and breathlessness of movement in Ammianus helps shake the old structure to pieces. Emperors in fourth-century Rome have less faith in coins and representatives as methods of communicating ideals and are themselves too busy with the gathering and evaluation of military intelligence to communicate the legitimacy of their power in other ways.[20] While Roman troops are moved around more by emperors, in Tacitus it is Foreign Rulers who get thus directed and also imperial Associates, Magistrates and Commanders. Needing to be less concerned with military activity and with the survival of the Empire as a whole, Tacitus' emperors thus direct more of their attention to moving and banishing Associates, Magistrates and Commanders.

The decentralisation of Gregory's world shows in various ways — the lack of any dominant centre of origin of movement, the high score for uncertainty over origin of movement together with the greater total number of references to sources and goals, the trivial nature of the directed traffic, the greater attention paid to people of low social status and the rise of Priests (never mentioned by Livy, Tacitus or Ammianus) to a prominence rivalling that of Rulers. In Livy, there is a fairly clear pattern of movement from the centre outwards: the movements are most numerous at the centre and then they thin out. Gregory's awareness of the relics of the Empire may show in his greater awareness of the world outside Gaul as compared with Livy's few references to places outside Italy. Yet for Gregory a limited range of geographical awareness is also suggested through the comparative frequency of his references to structures and to property (movements of plate, for example — an activity which in turn is the result of the collapse of a centralised taxation system[21]) and through the infrequency of his references to natural features. This bias may be a consequence of the Christian investment of significance in general and of holiness in particular upon man-made structures rather than upon natural or geographical features.[22] Tacitus also mentions structures quite frequently. But they are concentrated in Rome, and they do not preclude reference to natural features outside the capital. Furthermore, the nature of the structures mentioned in Tacitus is quite different — camps, public buildings and houses, rather than Gregory's churches, tombs and monasteries.

The contrast of social focus between Gregory and Livy is very marked — bishops and kings on the one hand, Roman and non-Roman troops on the other. The very prominent non-Roman movement in Livy foreshadows Ammianus' militaristic world again, except that it has more of a centre, and that it covers a smaller canvas than in Ammianus. The lack of military emphasis in Gregory goes along with the lesser salience of non-Gauls generally: it is a more inward-looking world, where people look inwards to a variety of scattered local centres. Tacitus' position on the peace/war spectrum is somewhere in the middle but peace is sustained by a focus of power that radiates from one centre — social and geographic. Such centralisation may lead to greater efficiency for a time but it eventually causes a decline of morale among the lower social strata, and this militates against the flow of information which is necessary to sustain centralised authority. The rather frenetic and even more alienating consequences of this are evident in Ammianus, where speed and uncertainty about movements increase in an increasingly unstable environment, and where more and more energy has to be put into the system to prevent entropy.[23]

Tacitus' world, as do those of Livy and of Ammianus, requires fairly precise location of social status, but in Gregory's world this is less important. Hence his greater geographical vagueness, a vagueness which extends even to the reasons for movement. People move without discernible motive and in a low information society perhaps that seems inevitable. It has been argued that it is governments, and not subjects, who want improved communications[24] — and the multiplication of the late Roman communication network[25] may be part of the government's desperate attempt to saturate society with the sheer presence of Rulers and Commanders, and thus to compensate for the deficiencies of morale and of information-dispersal engendered by centuries of centralisation. There is a sinister aspect to knowing (or pretending to know) the reasons for people's movements, part of an interest in social as well as geographical origins, the two being closely connected. The greater prominence of greeting and meeting in Gregory suggests a more relaxed, civilian world which recalls the relative peace of Tacitus', a world where there is more time for pleasantries or ceremonials. This impression coheres with archaeological evidence which suggests that sixth-century Gaul, although a warrior society in many respects, was relatively peaceful.[26]

Notes

1.   I.e. 14.1.1−2.8 (up to *arduis*), 16.1.1−5.4 (*divideret*), 18.1.1−2.19 (*deliquissent*), 20.1.1−4.4 (*paterentur*), 22.1.1−4.8 (*Parthicum*), 24.1.1−2.6 (*vincendi*), 26.1.1−2.9 (*etiam*), 28.1.1−1.23 (*imperatoris*), 30.1.1−2.3 (*extrema*).

2.   Tacitus: the first 136½ lines of Loeb text of the books of the *Annals*, i.e.1.1−6 (*vim*), 2.1−9 (*fratre*), 3.1−10 (*consules*), 4.1−7 (*superfuit*), 6.1−7 (*verentur*), 11.1−8 (*firmatae*), 12.1−10 (*expetendum*), 13.1−8 (*sed*), 14.1−7 (*pereundum*), 15.1−8 (*frumentariae*), 16.1−10 (*eius*). Livy: the first 150 lines of Loeb text of books 1−10, i.e. 1.1.1−5.1 (*Pallantium*), 2.1.1−2.7 (*non*), 3.1.1−2.12 (*meliores*), 4.1.1−2.11 (*illum*), 5.1.1−2.13 (*collegis*), 6.1.1−2.7 (*iussit*), 7.1.1−2.11 (*iuventus*), 8.1.1−2.12 (*responsum*), 9.1.1−2.10 (*sua*), 10.1.1−2.13 (*quibusdam*).

The reasons for confining the sampled material to the narrative of the early Republic were twofold. In view of the scarcity of reliable evidence compared with the Polybius-dominated narrative of the middle Republic Livy has more scope to impose his own conceptions on what energy paths existed in early Rome, conceptions obviously influenced by his perception of the contemporary Augustan structure of imperial power. In this regard he provides useful comparisons with Tacitus and Ammianus. At the same time, he offers another point of contrast in that the operations he describes are largely confined to a limited geographical area. In this respect his material is akin to Gregory's, with the important difference that whereas Gregory is observing a decentralised society while still mindful of the past extent, majesty and duration of Roman power, Livy for his part is writing of a people who have little inkling of the future extent of Roman Mediterranean power and he is himself without experience of the full and prolonged flowering of that power. As for Gregory, there being no Loeb text of Gregory, the first 169 lines of the Latin text of his *Historiae Francorum*, (eds. M. Flacius and I. Casaubon), Books 2−10, were used and the number of lines calculated so as to yield the same number of words as the other samples. Book 1 and the prefaces to Books 2, 3 and 5 were omitted because of their theological content. Therefore: 2.1−3 (*pro*), 3.1−6 (*iactari*), 4.1−6 (*gloriam*), 5.1−4 (*domo*), 6.1−5 (*verumetiam*), 7.1−2 (*domos*), 8 (*adducebatur*), 9.1−6 (*radicibus*), 10.1−2 (*propagaretur*).

3.   Movement can be up or down, in or out, as well as across, and involves dragging, carrying, leading, pushing, lifting, driving, throwing, exiling, sending (for), collecting, routing.

4.   Such movement was categorised in the following ways: (a) simply to go, come, return, enter, exit, arrive, assemble (intransitive), etc.; (b) to go in a certain, more fully described manner: sail, follow, walk, swim, ride, wander, etc.; (c) to go quickly: flee, run, hurry, etc.; (d) to go both quickly and aggressively: to charge, attack, invade.

5.   Not just a physical handing over but a bestowal of material resources by fiat.

6. At this point one might legitimately ask what the figures are for staticity in the various authors (i.e. references to standing, sitting, lying, waiting and remaining still generally) and whether they complement the figures for movement in any way. The answer is that they apparently do not: Livy 13, Tacitus 11, Ammianus 11, Gregory 10. Similarly, figures for keeping *others* still (restrained, confined, etc.): Livy 13, Tacitus 10, Ammianus 10, Gregory 9.

7. See A. Rapaport, *Human Aspects of Urban Form* (Oxford 1977), 193: 'One of the ways in which the various sensory modalities are integrated is through movement, which increases the dimensionality of the information being provided through the senses'.

8. The following figures are probably too small to be significant but they may amount to another arrow flying in the same direction and suggesting a perception of environmental instability. Six times the non-human environment moves, prevents from moving, buffets and generally controls men in Ammianus: cf. Livy 4, Tacitus 2, Gregory 5.

9. From a list of 16 groups of reasons; in addition to those that follow immediately in the text, they are: to influence or to persuade; to arrest, detain; fear, distrust; simply to gain or convey something/someone; to punish (apart from banishing); cruelty, anger; to seek prestige, fame; to observe, gain information; to appoint, install someone; to perform some other specific task (e.g. to skirt the banks of the Euphrates with a cavalry force, to bury a corpse) and miscellaneous (e.g. being assembled to await the arrival of a leader). By 'unknown' is meant that the author gives no clear reason for direction.

10. I.e. a direction from Gaul, say, to Italy goes inward and crosses one boundary; to Rome or the imperial palace it crosses two or three respectively.

11. As far as proportion of references to inward and outward movement is concerned, all four authors are more or less equally balanced.

12. The number of motives rarely or never occurring is fairly even among all four authors.

13. So that, for example, while communicating might be an important motive overall in Ammianus, 5 out of 9 times it comes in the Foreign Rulers box; 6 times out of 10 there is uncertainty about the motives of Roman Commanders.

14. A separate category of Autonomous Movements is 'local' movement, that is, movement where no termini are supplied because the movement is reported as taking place within a structure, area or geographical feature or region, e.g. 'the army marched through Picenum' or 'someone was pursued in a camp'. Incidence is as follows:

Livy	Tacitus	Ammianus	Gregory
36 (32%)	16 (21%)	22 (17%)	23 (17%)

As proportions of the total number of references to movement, there are no startling variations for the figures of Tacitus, Ammianus and Gregory. It is the figure for Livy that stands out; and it suggests how Livy has been able, in part, to avoid the greater apparent vagueness of Ammianus and Gregory concerning termini — he describes movement within an area in such a way that he does not need to supply source and goal. What is also of interest in these references to 'local' movement is that they reveal the different preoccupations of the authors. Thus, apart from one reference in Livy to movement from house to house in Rome, almost all local Autonomous Movement concerns military activities and movement within, along or across natural features such as rivers, regions or passes. The only man-made structures mentioned are camps and ships. References in Tacitus mainly centre around man-made civilian structures such as palace, senate house, altar, theatre, tribunal, tomb: there are 2 references to a river, 1 to Parthia, 1 to the eastern provinces. Ammianus' 'local' references eschew man-made and civilian structures and revolve entirely around geographical features (mountains 5, river 1) and the whole provinces or extensive areas — Germany, Cyprus, Lycaonia, Pamphylia, Gaul. Gregory's 'local' references are overwhelmingly within or around civilian or ecclesiastical structures — mainly towns, churches, tombs and altars, but also several references are made to specific dwellings (4) and 1 to a ship, plus 1 reference to Spain.

Some other points of interest from the Autonomous Movement data: in Livy, structures figure 6 times as a source, twice as a goal; in Tacitus, 4 times as a source, twice as a goal; in Ammianus, never as a source, twice as a goal. Tacitus has 4 references to an imperial palace as a source or goal, as has Ammianus; Livy has 7 references to camps as source or goal, Tacitus 2, Ammianus 6; Tacitus has 9 references to geographical features as goal or source, Ammianus has 24. On structures and movement in Gregory, see P. Brown, *Relics and Social Status in the Age of Gregory of Tours* (Reading 1977), 3, 12 (rp. in P. Brown, *Society and the Holy in Late Antiquity* (London 1982), 222–50).

15. There are two reasons why the totals of which the movements made by each group (expressed as a percentage in the table that follows in the text) do not correspond with the totals for Autonomous Movement that we have been hitherto working with: (i) to study the relationship between Autonomous Movements and the reason that explains the movements, only references which give a reason were included and (ii) frequently, a reference to an Autonomous Movement involves more than one group moving, e.g. a Ruler proceeding with his Associates or Troops.

16. Cf. for instance, the observations of C. Geertz, 'Centers, Kings and Charisma: Reflections on the Symbolism of Power', in J. Ben-David and T. N. Clark, *Culture and its Creators*, (Chicago 1977), 150ff., referring to a rather fragile nineteenth-century Moroccan kingdom or to Elizabethan Tudor England where the ruler had to rely on constant personal appearances in all quarters of his domain to prevent fragmentation and usurpation, instead of being able to stay at the centre and radiate cohesive power and create an impression of 'divine ubiquity' from that centre, using such diverse measures as coins and personal representatives to achieve this effect. R. MacMullen's useful study of imperial movement in the Empire, 'Two notes on imperial properties', *Athenaeum* 54 (1976), 19ff., speaks of the needs which 'slowly transformed the throne into a sedan-chair as the emperor changed from a single fixed and central figure into the co-rulers peripatetic in the later period' (27), and the movements' 'early medieval quality' (36).

17. If 2 groups have the same reason for Autonomous Movement within a single reference, the reason is counted twice. The range of reasons is less extensive for Autonomous Movement than it is for Directed Movement, namely Interview, gain information; Greet, meet; Attack, protect, seize; Communicate, request; the simple wish to Enter, or return; Escape, avoid; perform Specific Tasks; Miscellaneous; Uncertain.

18. See H. D. Duncan, *Symbols in Society* (Oxford 1968), 130ff., on disorder in society originating from disorder in communication.

19. See R. MacMullen, *Soldier and Civilian in the Later Roman Empire* (Cambridge, Mass. 1963), *passim*, on the increasingly diverse functions performed by the Roman soldier in the late Empire.

20. On the prominence of military intelligence collection and evaluation in Ammianus, see N. J. Austin, *Ammianus on Warfare* (Collection Latomus 165) (Brussels 1979), *passim*. But see also W. S. Cooter, *Pre-Industrial Frontiers and Interaction Spheres: Aspects of the Human Ecology of Roman Frontier Regions in N. W. Europe* (Diss. Univ. of Oklahoma 1976), 171ff., on the general poorness of communication between emperor and governors, between centre and periphery in imperial Rome; and R. MacMullen, 'Fourth-Century Bureaucratese', *Traditio* 18 (1962), 346ff.

21. As J. M. Wallace-Hadrill, *The Long-Haired Kings* (London 1962), 67ff. explains.

22. See P. W. English and R. C. Mayfield (eds), *Man, Space and Environment* (London 1972), 69ff.

23. Cf. M. I. Stein, *Stimulating Creativity* vol. 2 (New York 1975), 5ff.

24. See M. McLuhan, *Take Today. The Executive as Dropout* (New York 1972), 27.

25. See H. von Petrikovits, 'Fortifications in the N. W. Roman Empire from the Third to the Fifth Centuries AD', *Journal of Roman Studies* 61 (1971), 178ff.

26. See L. Musset, *The Germanic Invasions* (Glasgow 1975), 130ff., 227ff.

Thucydides and Agathias

Katherine Adshead

The suggestion I have to make is that since our understanding of Thucydides has immeasurably deepened (thanks to de Romilly and her followers)[1] our understanding of Thucydides' imitators, specifically Agathias, may well require revision. At present his imitation (*mimesis* 3.1.4) is crudely understood as the plagiarising, probably from handbooks, of atticising words and phrases; the siege of Plataea, the plague of Athens, the Epitaphios being the preferred quarries for the embellishment of an otherwise tedious (because moralistic) attitude.[2] I would like to suggest, on the contrary, that Agathias' reading of Thucydides was thorough, and certainly included Books 6 and 7 as well as Books 1–3; that, having his illustrious predecessor at his fingertips, he attempted a mimesis of basic methods as well as vocabulary; and that, as J. A. S. Evans in a brief but penetrating paper noted, Agathias did in fact attempt the hitherto inconceivable, namely the writing of history from a Christian standpoint but after the manner of the classical historiographers of the past.[3]

I shall focus on three points: the interrelation of narrative and speeches; the preoccupation with a psychology of action; and the concept of the utility of history, that it should be ὠφέλιμον (profitable) for those who want to know the truth (τὸ σαφὲς σκοπεῖν : Thuc. 1.22.4).

I: The interrelation of narrative and speeches

In Thucydides, the speeches are regularly reflected in the subsequent narrative: indeed they may form part of a complex cycle of narrative–speech–narrative, Hunter's 'erga–logoi–erga' series:[4] thus the thematic concept, be it cognitive (ἐμπειρία, experience), or ethical (πλεονεξία, greed), is developed and reinforced. Brasidas, for instance, forecasts barbarian bravado and disarray and when the narrative comes, sure enough, barbarian bravado and disarray, 'totidem verbis', is what we find.[5]

In Agathias, there is a similar technique and a similar variation of the pattern. Indeed, I suggest that he may be referring to this in the Preface (*proem.* 5) by his phrase ποικιλία παραδειγμάτων 'subtlety of patterns'? 'variatio exemplorum'?

A straightforward instance of one such 'erga–logoi–erga' pattern occurs when Fulcar, general of the Herul contingent in the Roman army, charges full tilt (δρομαῖος) into the Frankish host in a mindless and disorderly attack: his army perishes, himself with them (1.14). The narrative is peppered with the vocabulary of impulse, rashness, disorder (προπετεία, ἀκοσμία, παράλογος, ὁρμή). Narses takes up the theme in his speech (1.16). Fulcar was rash (προπέτης) ('being a barbarian') and tolerated disorder (ἀκοσμία) whereas what is most needed against greater numbers is order (εὐκοσμία) which obviates the need for the irrational (παράλογον).

Narses next exemplifies his points in action. With a small troop of horse he feints a rash attack on a large contingent of Franks and then, still according to plan, pretends to flee (1.21). Forgetful of good order (εὐκοσμία) the Franks rush headlong (χυδήν) forward, only to fall back, irrationally terrified (παραλόγῳ τεθηπότες), when the Romans show their hand. These selected episodes form the main action of Book 1 and in the theme of control and its opposite we have, I think, a Thucydidean type of motif.

A subtler example, also from Book 1, is that of the Gothic envoys who while seeking to rouse the Franks against the Romans, allege that the latter will insist on their moral claim to Italy, 'cloaking their greed with specious pretext' (εὐπρόσωπος αἰτία ἐς προκάλυμμα τῆς πλεονεξίας 1.5). It will be said that Italy is the home of their ancestors (κτήματα τῶν σφετέρων προγόνων), that justice (δίκη) is wholly on their side, in fact that they have a monopoly on piety and moral virtue (δεισιδαίμονες καὶ μόνοι σὺν δικαιοσύνῃ). In fact Narses says nothing like this and in the siege of Luca he shocks his opponents by what even he regards as near-blasphemy, namely pretending to raise the dead (1.13.3, 6). Instead, it is Aligern, the renegade Goth (a nice twist) who resumes this theme (1.20). Aligern has come to doubt the Franks' ultimate intentions. Under the specious cloak of alliance (σκῆψις καὶ προκάλυμμα εὐπρεπές) they will get control of Italy for themselves. Are not the Romans, as ancient owners of the land (τοὺς γοῦν ἐκ παλαιοῦ οἰκήτορας), the people with right (ὅσιον) on their side?

Returning to Thucydides, a frequent variation of the 'logoi–erga' theme is the 'antilogia', the debate, where the following narrative settles which of the 'logoi' was superior. Thus in Thucydides 2.83–92 Phormio's speech and that of the Peloponnesians recommend contrasted conclusions: the battle which follows, of course, leaves us in no doubt that Phormio was right.[6]

Agathias also employs this 'antilogia–erga' pattern. An example is given in Book 3 where, in perhaps the most elaborated passage in the *Histories*, two Colchian leaders debate the advantages and disadvantages of changing from the Roman to the Persian alliance.[7] It is based, inevitably, on the Mitylenean Debate in Thucydides Book 3; Aietes, the first speaker is represented as a demagogue like Cleon (σὺν ὀργῇ προπηδήσας ἐς μέσους ἐδημηγόρει); both speakers charge the other with sophistry; there is an echo, further, of Thucydides 3.81 in Aietes' remark that his opponents conceal indolence behind the pretext of holding fire (ῥαθυμία, ἀπραγμοσύνη). All this is the received content of Agathias' mimesis of his predecessors, but here too may there not be a more organic mimesis? Aietes' first argument (3.9.6) rests on the assumption that the Emperor endorses all subversion (πανουργότατον καὶ ταῖς μεταβολαῖς τῶν ἀεὶ παρόντων ἀεὶ ἡδόμενον). Phortazes takes up this point (3.12.1), namely that the Emperor supports revolutions (καινουργότατος), calling it a childish threat (μορμολύττειν); and his final advice (3.13.10) is that they should appeal to Caesar for justice (ὡς ἂν ἐνδικώτατα μετέλθοι . . .). Whom do the events prove right? Whose was the accurate forecast? Indisputably, Phortazes. Far from encouraging revolution, Justinian immediately (3.14) consents to the accession of the heir apparent Tzathes 'in accordance with ancestral custom and in recognition of the purity of the royal line' (πάτριος νόμος καὶ ἡ ἀνέκαθεν τοῦ βασιλείου γένους ὁμολογία), and a chapter is then devoted to the colourful details of Tzathes' installation (3.15). At the same time a judicial investigation is launched (3.14), this being the path of virtue and justice (ὅσια καὶ δίκαια) and two at least of the culprits are at once arrested. In other words, the two chapters following the debate at once endorse Phortazes and refute Aietes. This may be what Hunter calls (in the case of Thucydides) 'an isolated antilogia – the erga which follow decide immediately between the two logoi'. On the other hand it may be more like what she terms 'a major debate [which] anticipate[s] whole periods',[8] (of time, that is) since I suspect that there are other themes, such as the question of whether the Persians will prove good allies, or whether (unlike Romans) the Persians reserve all their atrocities for the enemy, or the full course of Roman justice which it takes the rest of Book 3 and all of Book 4 to work out.

II: Agathias' 'psychology of action'

Here Agathias is at his most 'Thucydidean' and it is, I think, hard to believe he would have characterised personalities or put dissections of human nature into their mouths in the way that he does without a longlasting acquaintance with Thucydides' way of doing these things. I illustrate this from the first chapter of the first book (1.1) and the last chapter of the last book (5.25) and then from Belisarius' speech (5.17–18).

In 1.1 the *flosculi*[9] are obvious. The Goths seem to be quelled, but in fact this was only the beginning. 'For there will never be an end to wars and suchlike, as long as human nature remains the same' (ἔστ' ἂν ἡ αὐτὴ φύσις ἀνθρώπων ᾖ, which is directly lifted of course from Thucydides 3.82). A little later the same ultimate explanation is offered: avarice, πλεονεξία, and injustice, ἀδικία (in Thucydides it was πλεονεξία and φιλοτιμία). But the more significant phrase, not much remarked on, comes between the two — predeterminism is unthinkable, says Agathias, because it would annihilate man's ability to choose his own goals and chart his own path (τὸ προαιρετὸν καὶ ἑκούσιον). Though the phrase is more Aristotelian than anything else, it directs us to that constant preoccupation with decisions and their translation into acts, which is so marked a feature of Thucydides' writing. So as we leave the ageing Justinian (in 559 A.D.), it is with the comment that now more than ever his forethought and good judgement (προμηθεία καὶ εὐβουλία) were evident, since without going to war, but by intelligence alone (γνώμη), he had achieved his goal (5.25). One might compare Narses telling the troops that they must never rely on their strength (ῥώμη) against the Franks, but on their intelligence (γνώμη) 'so casting aside indolence (ῥαθυμία), and renewing your capacity for daring (τὸ φιλοκίνδυνον)' (2.12); it might be the Corinthians in their famous speech (Thucydides 1.68–71).

In 5.17–18, Belisarius, recalled. from obscurity to confront the Cotrigur Huns, now massing on the outskirts of Constantinople itself, feels it imperative to inject a little realism in the face of his army's excessive confidence. He is not, he says, going to rouse them from fear to confidence (δέος, θαρρεῖν) as is the custom. Rather, in the face of overconfidence (τὸ θρασυνόμενον) the value of discipline (εὐκοσμία) needs stressing — the folly of rashness, the merits of calculation, the hazards of τύχη — then 'solid intelligence' (στέρρα γνώμη)[10] which will compensate for his own old age and their youth also. As it was γνώμη σφαλεῖσα, failure of the intellect, which lay behind their predicament, so carefulness and planning, which are not to be thought cowardice, will bring rational confidence (τὸ δικαίως θαρρεῖν).

This speech is not an adaptation, as it might have been, of (for instance) Pericles' strategy-speech repressing in advance the ardour of the young cavalry (Thucydides 1.140–4). Belisarius' words are perfectly in place in the historical setting. Yet the entire analysis is conditioned by Thucydides' ideas on how the variables in a before-battle situation should be expressed. I would doubt that you could harmonise another man's psychological terms of reference and a specific military episode so effectively without knowing your Thucydides so well that you had unconsciously begun to think along his lines. Bornemann, I may say, has recently shown Procopius achieving much the same result.[11]

Agathias does differ from Thucydides in the way he describes personalities and motivations — how could he not? And because his is a less subtle and original mind, the moments where his analysis diverges betray his cruder and more simplistic approach. Hence his description of Narses' appearance: used to luxurious living at Court (and being a eunuch as well), Narses had dieted himself to spare — and thus soldierly — proportions: but being short he remained an unimposing figure, so much so that the Alamans referred to him as a palace midget, 'skin and bones', an effete and effeminate nothing (1.16, 1.8). This is more like the *Secret History* of Procopius than Thucydides.

Agathias' overworked concept of 'due measure' reveals a similar inadequacy. Fulcar, for example, is energetic 'beyond due measure' (1.14.3), the Romans are confident 'beyond due measure' (5.17.3), Narses is energetic 'but' (of course) 'in due measure' (1.8.2), and so on. This '$\mu\acute{\epsilon}\tau\rho\sigma\nu$' (or, $\acute{\epsilon}\nu$ $\delta\acute{\epsilon}\sigma\nu\tau\iota$) explains nothing and is a device for evading further analysis.

Finally, though it is not spelled out clearly, it sometimes seems in Agathias as if irrationality comes, in the last resort, from outside. His (very frequent) use of the word $\tau\grave{o}$ $\pi\alpha\rho\acute{\alpha}\lambda\sigma\gamma\sigma\nu$ is not identical with Thucydides', for whom it means flatly $\pi\alpha\rho\grave{\alpha}\cdot\lambda\acute{o}\gamma\sigma\nu$, contrary to expectation. In Agathias, I suspect, the meaning is nearer to 'misguided', as in the phrase (1.73) $\tau\grave{o}$ $\pi\alpha\rho\acute{\alpha}\lambda\sigma\gamma\sigma\nu$ $\kappa\alpha\grave{\iota}$ $\check{\epsilon}\mu\pi\lambda\eta\kappa\tau\sigma\nu$ $\tau\tilde{\eta}\varsigma$ $\delta\acute{o}\xi\eta\varsigma$: 'the misguided and demented element in their calculation'. There is also the pair $\dot{\alpha}\lambda\acute{\alpha}\zeta\omega\nu$ $\kappa\alpha\grave{\iota}$ $\dot{\alpha}\tau\acute{\alpha}\sigma\theta\alpha\lambda\sigma\varsigma$, 'boastful and presumptuous' (of Xerxes, and of lesser figures like Ragnar the Goth, 2.14) to suggest that miscalculation has its moral dimension. So too, the Sicilian Expedition of 416, says Agathias, was the result not merely of $\check{\alpha}\nu\sigma\iota\alpha$, folly, but also of $\dot{\alpha}\delta\iota\kappa\acute{\iota}\alpha$, wickedness (2.10.2–6). There is thus an intrusion of the moral and metaphysical into the Thucydidean analysis of action. We need not immediately say that such an analysis is not there, but rather that it is not so well done.

III: The utility of history

Both Averil Cameron and Evans have in fact already argued that Agathias 'went some way towards writing a Christian history in a completely classical framework'.[12] He did this, they suggest, by reducing the role played by $\tau\acute{v}\chi\eta$ and by raising the Herodotean $\mathring{v}\beta\rho\iota\varsigma\cdot\nu\acute{\epsilon}\mu\epsilon\sigma\iota\varsigma$ motif to the status of a moral law. Both these points might be queried. In paragraph 5 of the *proem.*, the possible sources for calamity are said to lie either in mistaken $\gamma\nu\acute{\omega}\mu\eta$ or adverse $\tau\acute{v}\chi\eta$ (a very Thucydidean opposition). It is not evident that Agathias' conception of the workings of $\mathring{v}\beta\rho\iota\varsigma$ and $\nu\acute{\epsilon}\mu\epsilon\sigma\iota\varsigma$ are different — or specifically more moral — than Herodotus. The sacrilege of the Alamans is the same as that of Xerxes at Delphi or in Athens. Finally the $\mathring{v}\beta\rho\iota\varsigma\cdot\nu\acute{\epsilon}\mu\epsilon\sigma\iota\varsigma$ theme, even given a moral connotation, is not obviously susceptible of a more than superficial Christianisation.

I would like to argue that the concept which Agathias used to combine the classical genre of historiography with his own Christian beliefs was that of the utility of history.[13] Thucydides had said that he would avoid romancing ($\tau\grave{o}$ $\mu\grave{\eta}$ $\mu\upsilon\theta\tilde{\omega}\delta\epsilon\varsigma$) but would, he hoped, be of enduring usefulness ($\dot{\omega}\phi\acute{\epsilon}\lambda\iota\mu\alpha$) to his readers (1.22.4). And de Romilly has elucidated in more than one place the extreme subtlety of the balance struck in Thucydides between the general, the particular, and the possibility of forecasting the future on the basis of the past. It is then in a blend of intellectual satisfaction and a cautious but reasoned extrapolation towards the future that (for Thucydides) the utility of his subject is to be found. Agathias has this passage in mind in 1.7.6–7, I think. After excursuses on the Franks and Alamans, he makes a token apology for including this material, particularly for such personal pronouncements as are included. 'My intention is', he continues, 'to set out all the known facts and then to praise the good, while condemning the bad *and exhibiting the unprofitability [ἀξύμφορον] of the same'*. Without this, history cannot be helpful or useful for men's lives (χρήσιμοι, βιωφελέσταται) but is reduced to old wives' tales (μυθολογήματα). I find the verbal echoes of Thucydides' ὠφέλιμος and μυθῶδες suggestive here.

How then, did the by then widely accepted belief in the utility of history aid Agathias? On the one hand, it prevented his history from becoming merely a series of cautionary tales, of Christian *exempla* set down without trace of professional argument. He could answer the ancient question of the παιδεία ('how shall a man live well, εὖ πράττει?) by showing that Christians in some sense prosper and non Christians in some sense come to grief.[14] In Agathias' narrative the latter go mad, consume their own flesh, fall dramatically ill, are flayed alive, etc. On the other hand, he could also avoid the aridity of some kind of Christian theodicy by making use of all the colour and variety that history (as opposed to φιλοσοφία) allows. This I take to be the meaning of *proem.* 5–6, the contrast between history and theory. Thus time and again we find the moral pointed in such phrases as 'wicked *and unprofitable*' (3.10.12), 'seemly *and profitable*' (3.11.4), 'unjust *and, what is more, unprofitable*' (3.12.7) and so on. The most striking instance is 2.1.9. Having described the looting and sacking of churches by the Alamans up and down Italy, he looks ahead to the dreadful fate which lies in store for them. 'For wickedness and sacrilege are always to be avoided *and are unprofitable*, especially in time of war and hostilities' (φεύκτα καὶ ἀσύμφορα). Thus, the *Histories* take on a universal as well as a particular reference and there is room for the forethought and good judgment (προμηθεία and εὐβουλία) mentioned earlier.

Unfortunately, Agathias is not wholly successful in the execution of this plan. In the case of the marauding Alamans small incidents (a surprise encounter with the Huns of the Roman army, the unfortunate consequences of gorging themselves with unripe grapes) have to be inflated into disasters and, even less plausibly, interpreted as foretastes of the major calamities which lie ahead (a typhoid epidemic, the rout at Casilinum, 2.1–10). Even more striking is Agathias' obvious embarrassment at the fact that in Book 3 Martin, the man most responsible for the murder of Gubazes, is not executed like his fellow-conspirators but left in command of the army till the end of this phase of the war in the East (4.21.1–4, a nice piece of special pleading).

It is not so easy after all to demonstrate the coincidence of virtue and prosperity, wickedness and misfortune. Rather the significant point for us, if I am right, is that when Agathias tried to Christianise the writing of history in the classical manner, he made use of a theme taken not from Antiquity's notion of what went on in history but directly and centrally from *the idea of history* itself. Could he have done this (any more than interrelating speech and action, or concentrating so exclusively on psychological thought processes) if he had not had a thorough knowledge of Thucydides and a clear understanding of what a true mimesis of Thucydides would involve?

Notes

1. J. de Romilly, *Histoire et raison chez Thucydide* (Paris 1956) was as much of a land-mark as *Thucydide et l'impérialisme athénienne* (Paris 1947). Among more recent studies, those of P. Huart, *Le vocabulaire de l'analyse psychologique dans l'oeuvre de Thucydide* (Paris 1968) and V. J. Hunter, *Thucydides, the Artful Reporter* (Toronto 1973) reflect the impact of her approach most clearly.

2. Averil Cameron, 'Herodotus and Thucydides in Agathias', *Byzantinische Zeitschrift* 57 (1964), 33–52 (rp. in *Continuity and Change in Sixth Century Byzantium* (London 1981)) and *Agathias* (Oxford 1970) gives a detailed statement of this position.

3. J. A. S. Evans, 'The Attitude of the Secular Historians of the Age of Justinian towards the Classical Past', *Traditio* 32 (1976), 353–8. H. Hunger, *Die hochsprachliche profane Literatur der Byzantiner*, I (Berlin 1978), 308 is less definite.

4. Hunter, *op. cit.*, chap. 10.

5. *ibid.*, chap. 2.

6. *ibid.*, chap. 3, Κρείττων Λόγος.

7. For a useful outline of the background and a map see B. Rubin, *Das Zeitalter Justinians* (Berlin 1960), 360ff., map 8.

8. Hunter, *op. cit.*, 178.

9. Cf. Averil Cameron, 'Herodotus and Thucydides' (n.2 above), 51: 'where it is not just a matter of vocabulary, it is a search for *flosculi*'.

10. Cf. P. Huart, Γνώμη *chez Thucydide et ses contemporains* (Paris 1973).

11. F. Bornemann, 'Motivi Tucididei in Procopio', *Atene e Roma* 22 (1974), 138–50, esp. 150: 'Procopio non sia un puro stilista, o peggio ancora, un centonatore che deriva le tessere del suo mosaico da questa o quella lettura'.

12. Averil Cameron, 'The "Scepticism" of Procopius', *Historia* 15 (1966), 479 (rp. in *Continuity and Change* [n.2 above]); Evans, *op. cit.*.

13. J. de Romilly, 'L'utilité de l'histoire selon Thucydide', *Entretiens sur l'antiquité classique* 4 (Geneva 1958), 41–66.

14. Agathias' one direct allusion (3.12.8) to the New Testament is to Matthew 16:26 'What does it *profit* a man . . .' (τὶ γὰρ ὠφεληθήσεται ἄνθρωπος . . .).

Latin Panegyric in the Tetrarchic and Constantinian Period

C.E.V. Nixon

'His laudationibus historia rerum nostrarum est facta mendosior'.
(Cicero, *Brutus* 16.62)

'In summa meae res gestae tantae sunt, quantae sunt scilicet, quoiquoimodi sunt : tantae autem videbuntur, quantas tu eas videri voles'.
(Lucius Verus Imperator to M. Cornelius Fronto, ed. Haines II, 196)

It was long before Spätantike that Panegyric first infected History, and thereafter the two genres were seldom if ever completely distinct. As critical an historian as Ammianus Marcellinus appears to have had no compunction about using panegyrical techniques, or indeed an actual panegyric, in describing Julian and his exploits.[1] The place of panegyric in a book on historiography needs no elaborate justification.

Despite the title of the original conference it is not my brief (and indeed it would be otiose) to demonstrate either that my genre is 'old' or that its late antique manifestations are replete with traditional elements. Therefore I shall not mention (brace yourselves for an elaborate *praeteritio*!) *laudationes funebres*, nor the progress from praise of the dead to praise of the living (*Pro Lege Manilia, Pro Marcello*, which influenced late Latin panegyric), nor the fact that, while critics such as Lucian (*How to Write History* esp. 7, 13, 30f. and 61) identified and dramatised the problem illustrated in Lucius Verus' letter to Fronto, cited above, they did little to solve it.

But perhaps I should stress the enormous number of panegyrics that were delivered in the early Roman Empire, not just to princes and potentates but to *privati* such as one's literary patron (for example the pseudo-Tibullan *Panegyricus Messallae*). The accident of survival and a certain prejudice against the post-classical age has sometimes led to an association of panegyric with the late antique period which is quite misleading. For example it is clear that the *Gratiarum Actio* became panegyrical at a very early stage. In the Republic, a speech of thanks would be delivered to the *senatus populusque Romanus* for one's consulship. Ovid describes the change: the incumbent now thanks the gods — and Caesar (*Pont.* 4.4.35–9; there is the procession to the Capitol and the speech to the Senate, 'ubi . . . egeris et meritas superis cum Caesare grates'). Had we all the *gratiarum actiones* of all the *novus homo* consuls of the Augustan era we might not sneer so much at Pliny the Younger.

Pliny's speech of thanks to Trajan heads the co-called 'Gallic corpus' which is my main subject here, but the fact that the next earliest speech is dated to *c*.289 of course does not imply a long gap in the genre. Fronto, for one, was active in the Antonine period (panegyric on Antoninus' victory in Britain, *Pan.* IV/VIII.14.2;[2] cf. Fronto, ed. Haines, I, 130, §1; 134, §4), as was Eumenius' grandfather, at the height of the disturbances in the mid-third century, until the sack of Autun in the late 260s closed the Maenian schools (*Pan.* V/IX 17.3).

How, then, do we account for the composition of the Gallic corpus which, in addition to the speech of Pliny's, is made up of nine speeches dating from *c.*289 to 321, plus speeches of A.D. 362 and 389? The contents of the corpus are said to reflect pride in the revival of the Gallic schools of late Antiquity, and, as we shall see, there is much to suggest a literary motive for the collection.

To return to the theme of the original conference for just a little longer, the occasions on which the late Latin panegyrics were delivered – the foundation day of a city (*Pan.* II/X, VII/VI); the birthday of a ruler (*Pan.* III/XI);[3] the anniversary of an accession (*Pan.* IV/VIII, VIII/V); Constantine's Quinquennalia, 25 July, 311 (*Pan.* X/IV);[4] the arrival of an important official (*Pan.* V/IX); an imperial marriage (*Pan.* VI/VII); the return of the Emperor from a successful campaign (*Pan.* IX/XII, XII/II); and the receipt of a consulship (*Pan.* XI/III) – these occasions were traditional ones for such speeches, as the handbooks of rhetoric make clear. By and large, our panegyrics are traditional, too, in structure, theme and style. The more skilful speakers adapt the handbook rules to suit their requirements (as Mesk, amongst others, has shown[5]) but the conventional basic structure is usually preserved intact.

In style, the panegyrics are remarkably 'classical', indeed Ciceronian, for their time and place. The goals for which the panegyrists strove are clear, even if they did not always attain them; one speaker complains of the unfair advantages enjoyed by the 'real' Romans (in all likelihood he was from Trier):

> 'neque enim ignoro quanto inferiora nostra sint ingenia Romanis, siquidem latine et diserte loqui illis ingeneratum est, nobis elaboratum et, si quid forte [!] commode dicimus, ex illo fonte et capite facundiae imitatio nostra derivat.'
>
> (*Pan.* IX/XII 1.2)

> ('Nor am I ignorant how greatly inferior my talent is in comparison with the Romans, since indeed it is inborn among them to speak in Latin and eloquently, while for us it is a product of much labour, and, if perchance we should speak with any elegance at all, our simulation of fluency derives from that very font and source.')

Klotz and others have traced, not always convincingly, the borrowings of the panegyrists from previous writers.[6] Cicero is prominent in their tables, but there is considerable variation between speakers. The reminiscences of Eumenius, for instance, are only of Cicero's *Oratorica*; Mamertinus (the elder) is more learned, drawing (allegedly) on the *Philosophica*, and on much more. Some panegyrists seem to copy the phrases of others, the significance of which I shall comment upon in a moment. There are Vergilian quotations and tags, and occasionally what looks like a piece of personal research or autopsy. For example, in speaking of the cult of Hercules at Rome, Mamertinus remarks that 'it is no fable stemming from poetic licence, nor mere belief based on the assertion of by-gone eras, but a manifest and confirmed fact, as the great altar of Hercules attests even today – *sicut hodieque testatur Herculis ara maxima* – together with the Pinarian family, guardian of the cult of Hercules,' that Hercules was received as a guest within the *Pallantea moenia* . . . (*Pan.* II/X, 1.3). But this is borrowed knowledge – note Servius Auctus, *ad Aen.* VIII 271: 'ingens enim est ara Herculis *sicut videmus hodieque*'. Elsewhere Mamertinus locates the rostra in the Circus Maximus (*Pan.* III/XI 19.5)! Evidently he picked up the phrase via a chain of earlier Vergilian commentators – Julius Hyginus, Suetonius, Aemilius Asper *et al.* who repeat each other just as modern scholars do, and who are repeated in turn by Donatus, Servius and the later commentators.[7]

I do not wish to speak at length of the content of the panegyrics, which again is traditional and predictable: praise of rulers for time-honoured virtues, martial and moral — for *pietas* and *felicitas* (*Pan.* III/XI), for *clementia* or *severitas*, as the occasion demands. Our skilful orators are for the most part unruffled by delicate political matters or abrupt imperial tergiversations; they respond with the gamut of familiar techniques — rationalisation, explication, exculpation, gloss, silence or what have you: their conventions see them through.

A moment ago I said the panegyrics are, or purport to be, occasional. Scholars have sometimes suggested that they are 'school products, that the speeches we have were not actually delivered'.[8] Yet there is a wealth of evidence to confirm that speeches were given on such occasions — for example the Letters of Fronto (Haines, I, 130 §1; 134, §4); indeed there is a reference to a panegyric of his on Antoninus' victory in Britain in one of our panegyrics (*Pan.* IV/VIII 14.2). The panegyrists refer to the speeches of others celebrating imperial exploits (*Pan.* III/XI 5.1; IX/XII 1.1) and introduce circumstantial details about the occasions on which they themselves spoke — the presence of the Emperor (for example *Pan.* IV/VIII 1.1, 1.4), and on one occasion his absence (*Pan.* X/IV 3.1), the nature of the audience (*Pan.* VIII/V 2.1; see below, p.93–4) and so on. I think there is no real reason to suspect their authenticity in this respect; that would be to postulate a very elaborate charade, as we shall see.

I even doubt whether they were polished up or amplified after delivery, which was what Pliny did with his panegyric (*Letters* 3.18, 1–2; cf. 3.13, 7.17.5ff., 1.20). Our panegyrics, unlike Pliny's, are short — with one exception (*Pan.* XII/II, to Theodosius, A.D. 389); they would seem not to have been elaborated. Why believe that they had rough edges when delivered before such an august audience, and that they needed subsequent revision? Let us assume, then, and it is important to my case, that our corpus is a collection of speeches actually delivered, substantially in their present form. With a couple of exceptions they will have been delivered at the imperial court at Trier, as internal references make clear.

I have now set the stage for the main topic of my paper, namely the relationship of panegyric and panegyrist to the imperial Court. The period of the Tetrarchy and the early years of Constantine is a shadowy one. In the absence of a detailed narrative history the Gallic panegyrics, along with Lactantius' *De Mortibus Persecutorum*, loom larger than such sources normally would. It is of some importance, then, to try and establish the status of the panegyrics and the relationship of their authors to the imperial government. How dependent upon the Court are the panegyrists, and what is the function of their speeches?

A sensitive student of the panegyrists, M. René Pichon, whose *Les derniers écrivains profanes* (Paris 1906) is still one of the best treatments of the subject, has suggested that the late Latin panegyrics were purely ceremonial without political aim, unlike earlier panegyrics.[9] On the other hand Johannes Straub bases an argument on their quasi-official character and political significance: '. . . und das verdient angesichts des unbestreitbar offiziösen Charakters eines solchen publizistischen Werkes Beachtung . . .'.[10] A more recent writer, none more aware of the ceremonial importance of the genre, Sabine MacCormack, avers that 'these panegyrics were all used as a medium to announce imperial programmes and policies',[11] and frequently refers to them as an instrument of propaganda.[12] None of these statements in my opinion, does justice to the significance of the corpus. Without denying the immediacy of the political message of some of our panegyrics, I should like to emphasise that they have a public and political life which transcends this, that they are not merely occasional, nor merely ephemeral pieces of propaganda (when, indeed, they are that at all). They have a 'hidden audience' of which more later on. I shall also explore as far as possible the individual circumstances of the panegyrists, and their careers, in order to determine the sense in which the label 'official' or 'offiziös' may be attached to their products.

To generalise about the corpus is perhaps admirable in principle, but it is to do less than justice to the very real differences between individual panegyrics. Let us look more closely at specific panegyrics. If we were to take *Pan.* VII/VI of A.D. 310 as typical we might well subscribe to MacCormack's view. It is hard to believe that a panegyrist would dare to publicise a previously all but unknown and surely fictitious genealogy for a reigning Emperor (Constantine) without some kind of encouragement from the Court, nor that he would deal with such a delicate matter as the downfall of Maximian without first 'clearing' his version with it. Indeed, rather than to postulate such boldness and imagination from an independent speaker it would seem more reasonable to conclude that he had been primed by the Court. On the other hand it is equally hard to believe that the imperial government would be much concerned with the details of a speech, delivered in Rome in 321 in the absence of the Emperor (*Pan.* X/IV), which largely consisted of a narrative of Constantine's invasion of Italy in 312, or with the details of the way in which Constantine was thanked for relieving the city of Autun of some of its tax burden (*Pan.* IV/VIII). But much depends on one's preconceptions, as a perusal of scholarly debate reveals.

In order to test the proposition that panegyric was a medium selected by the imperial government to *announce* imperial programmes and policies one might proceed by looking at individual panegyrists and attempting to determine their relationship with the Court, the circumstances of the delivery of their speeches, and, if possible, the procedure of selection of speakers for official occasions. It has to be conceded that this is a difficult project. Most of our speakers are anonymous, and while some divulge information about themselves, others are pertinaciously reticent. In the period under scrutiny, the Tetrarchic and Constantinian period, we have eight speakers and nine panegyrics. Let us tabulate and review them in chronological order:

1. Mamertinus (*Pan.* II/X, 289; *Pan.* III/XI, 291); refers in III/XI 1.2 to an *honor* received from Maximian which far exceeds his expectations; the incipit of III/XI reads 'eiusdem magistri'; Mamertinus has spoken before Maximian previously (III/XI 1.2, 5.1) and confidently expects to again, five years hence (III/XI 1.3); he is probably from Trier (II/X 12.6 and Galletier, Vol. 1, 6–7).

2. Anon. (*Pan.* IV/VIII, 297). The speaker has come out of retirement (1.1; 1.4); he once taught youths (1.2); a considerable time ago he was introduced to the Court of Maximian by Constantius and delivered a speech on Maximian's exploits 'qui me in lucem primus eduxit' (1.5); that is, it led to a Court post, apparently as some kind of secretary (1.4 and Galletier, Vol. I, 71–2); he participated in an expedition of Maximian against the Alemanni (2.1); in this speech he conveys the congratulations of Autun to Constantius for his anniversary and victory in Britain (21.2).

3. Eumenius (*Pan.* V/IX, 298): grandson of an Athenian who taught rhetoric at Rome and then at Autun (17.2–3); a teacher of rhetoric himself (1.1, 2.2–5), but who had not spoken *in foro* before (1.1, 3.1); now speaks there at Autun, in the presence of the governor of Lugdunensis; formerly *magister memoriae* of Constantius (11.2; cf. 6.2); recently appointed by him director (*praeceptor moderatorque*) of the Maenian schools (5.3, 14 and *passim*).

4. Anon. (*Pan.* VI/VII, 307): no personal information discoverable; aware of the panegyrics of Mamertinus (cf. Galletier, Vol II, 10).

5. Anon. (*Pan.* VII/VI, 310): 'mediae aetatis' (1.1), he has had considerable experience employed in 'diversis otii et palatii officiis' (23.1); he commends his children to the Emperor Constantine, and especially his eldest son, 'summa fisci patrocinia tractantem'; he has numerous protégés 'quos provexi ad tutelam fori, ad officia palatii'; he is now engaged by 'privatorum studiorum ignobiles curae' but hopes for another Court post (23.3); he is from Autun (22, esp. 22.7).

6. Anon. (*Pan.* VIII/V, 311): a rhetorician from the Schools ('iam non privati studii litter-arum . . . orator', 1.2); a local senator (1, 3; 9.4) from Autun (4.2) who volunteered to convey the city's thanks to Constantine for tax cuts (1.1–3).

7. Anon. (*Pan.* IX/XII, 313): A Gaul (1.2), and a rhetor, one 'qui semper res a numine tuo gestas praedicare solitus essem' (1.1), but in the Schools or at Court? He doesn't mention any imperial post.

8. Nazarius (*Pan.* X/IV, 321): speaking in Rome (1–3.1, with 38.6); a distinguished professor of rhetoric in the School of Bordeaux (Ausonius, *Prof. Burdigal.* XIV); his daughter a Christian? (Prosper Aquit., *Chron. Min.* I, 452; cf. Jerome, *Chron.* s.a.336).

So of the seven speakers for whom some biographical information is recoverable, four (numbers 1, 2, 3 and 5) have been in imperial service. But with the probable exception of Mamertinus and only in the case of his second speech, none of them was *currently* engaged in such service at the time of delivery of his panegyric.[13] Number 2 (*Pan.* IV/VIII, 297) speaks of *otium*; he was called out of retirement to convey the felicitations of Autun to Constantius. Eumenius (no.3) has moved from his post as *magister memoriae* to a new appointment as director of the Schools of Autun. The Panegyrist of 310 (no.5), while angling for a job at Court, is currently engaged in private studies (*Pan.* VII/VI 23.3). Clearly they are not imperial 'Press Secretaries', indeed they are not part of the imperial administration at all, and so their speeches are not *formally* official pronouncements on imperial policies or events of the day.

In fact many of the speakers seem to be (nos. 3, 5, 6, 8 and perhaps 7), or to have been (no.2), professors of rhetoric (or law, in the case of no.5?) at Autun, Trier (?) and Bordeaux. But they are speaking at Court in formal surroundings on important ceremonial occasions. How did they get there, seeing that they were not already employed at Court? How independent were they? One might still be able to argue that 'these panegyrics were all used as a medium to announce imperial programmes and policies' despite the observations I have made. I shall return in a moment to these questions, noting only — at this point — that there is very little direct evidence on the subject of selection and briefing of speakers.[14]

I wish to turn now to a test case, which I regard as a salutary warning to exponents of the 'propaganda' argument in its extreme form, and which incidentally also raises other relevant questions. In 321 Nazarius spoke in Rome on the occasion of the Quinquennalia of the Caesars Crispus and Constantine II, but in the absence of Constantine himself. His speech, in essence, centres on the expedition of 312 against Maxentius (*Pan.* X/IV 6–35), after brief praise of the young Caesars. Subsequent events are dismissed in a few lines (38.4 on recent legislation, Constantine's 'moral revival'). This is disappointing for us, for Nazarius adds comparatively little to the panegyric of 313; we have a 'lost decade'. Especially if your expectation is 'propaganda' or an 'official line', Nazarius seems obviously 'out-of-date'.

What is the explanation? Was there really nothing of interest to say about recent events? Or is it the absence of the Emperor that is crucial – the Emperor was not there to brief him? But surely someone at Court could have? Or did Constantine or his ministers choose not to have the events of 312–321 aired? A show-down with Licinius was obviously looming. In 320 Constantine had held a (sixth) consulship with Constantine Junior, out of turn, and in 321 when Crispus and Constantine II (again) were consuls, Licinius refused to permit the publication of their names in the East. On the other hand, one might argue the reverse case – now was the time for propaganda! As I remarked earlier, it would seem to depend on one's preconceptions.

But something may be learned from our example if we put it beside its 'parallel', the Panegyric of 313. The latter panegyric was delivered in the imperial presence, and in its narrative of the invasion of Italy seems altogether 'up-to-date'. The juxtaposition might seem to illustrate graphically the difference between being 'briefed' and not being 'briefed'. But it is delusive, for the panegyric of 313 is *not* 'up-to-date' at all. The panegyrist himself refers to the speeches of *disertissimi* which the Emperor has already heard, both at Rome *and in Trier*, 'in urbe sacra et hic rursus' (1.1), but cannot refrain from adding his feeble (and non-Roman) voice 'inter tantos sonitus disertorum'. In other words, panegyrics on the defeat of Maxentius were already 'old hat'. Even at Trier, their news value or impact as political messages must have been slight. This is a clear warning. It is hazardous to assume that any speech that happens to be preserved in our corpus is the first on its subject, and therefore announcing for the first time an imperial programme or policy. Imperial programmes and policies may have been announced 'publicly' in this fashion, but we cannot *assume* that there is any such announcement in our collection. I do not know, nor does Seston,[15] the date, occasion or manner of announcement of Diocletian and Maximian's relationship to Iuppiter and Hercules, but I wager it was not first announced by Mamertinus in Trier on April 21st, 289 (*Pan.* II/X).

A better candidate for really 'hot' news items is Panegyric VII/VI of 310, with its avowedly novel Constantinian genealogy ('quod plerique adhuc fortasse nesciunt', 2.1), its undeniably local 'Vision of Apollo' (21.3ff.), and an account of the downfall of Maximian for which the orator awaits the approval of Constantine himself ('de nutu', 14.2) before proceeding. But even here the apparent novelty may be misleading, and the 'boldness' arises not because the panegyrist has been briefed, but because he is an experienced old professional (see 'biography' above) and 'knows the ropes'.

Let me revert to Nazarius. Surely the key to our mystery is the venue – Rome – and the audience, which is bound to have included senators. Constantine, despite his appointment of aristocrats to important imperial posts[16] had scarcely given unequivocal support and comfort to the pagan aristocracy of Rome: the best political mileage for the panegyrist was obviously to concentrate on the liberation of the Sacred City from the Unspeakable Tyrant, no matter how dated or hackneyed the theme. I cannot *prove* that Nazarius was not briefed for the occasion, but I assume that a rhetor who rose to become a leading professor in the Schools of Bordeaux was capable of making a professional judgement of this kind without the assistance of the Court.

Our Nazarius case has raised another question. What was the audience of our panegyrists? We know less than we would like, but for speeches delivered at the Court of Trier we may assume the Emperor, courtiers, senior officials and palace bureaucrats . . . and frequently a greater public throng. The Panegyrist of 311 specifically tells us (*Pan.* VIII/V 2.1) that the

Emperor is present, his whole 'amicorum . . . comitatus, et omnis imperii apparatus' (all the imperial *apparatchiks*), 'and a whole host of men from practically every city [in Gaul], either on public missions or with private petitions'. The occasion was the Quinquennalia of July 25th, 311. (The speaker had passed up an earlier opportunity to address the Emperor in the vestibule of the palace on the ground that the audience was inappropriately small.) Nazarius (1.1) speaks more vaguely of a throng (coetus), again for a Quinquennalia.

Oswyn Murray, in an interesting review of Johannes Straub's *Vom Herrscherideal in der Spätantike*, tilts against the line that the panegyrics have a 'publicising function': talk of propaganda is inappropriate when it is a question of appealing to the converted; evidence for an 'immediate' (a cunningly chosen adjective!) impact on a wider public is scanty.[17] But this may not be enough to unseat his adversary. The fact that the audience on these occasions was not confined to the Court itself is significant; it offers the possibility of a wider dissemination of ideas and viewpoints, and rapidly, too, with the return of visitors to their respective *civitates*. But I do not wish to seem to disagree with Murray; rather, I would direct our attention elsewhere, to a 'hidden audience', but more of this in a moment.

I wish now to revert to the question of how independent the panegyrists were of Emperor and Court. Can something be learned from the tone of the panegyrics? The corpus shows a complete range. On the one hand we have the confident Panegyrist of 310 who has been around the Court for a long time (*Pan.* VII/VI 23.1), who can even contemplate extemporising in the presence of the Emperor (were it not unbefitting to his age and the audience; for as he says, somewhat sententiously, 'he who extemporises before an Emperor of the Roman people has no feeling for the greatness of the Empire'), who can also put in a recommendation for his five sons and boast of his pupils in imperial service and private professions and, in closing, angle for a post as Court orator. On the other hand, there are those who confess to nervousness at speaking at Court. The Panegyrist of 311, the local senator who thanks the Emperor for tax remissions, vividly evokes a subject's feelings of awe in the presence of the *sacratissimus imperator*:

> 'It is no small business to ask the Emperor of the whole world for a favour for oneself, to put on a bold front before the aspect of such great majesty, to compose one's features, to shore up one's spirits, to think of the words, to utter them confidently, to know when to stop, to wait for a reply.'
>
> (*Pan.* VIII/V 9.3)

But he delivers a fine speech which rather belies his pose, and this reminds us that our speakers are professionals; all (or nearly all) are or have been professors of rhetoric. Some, as we have seen above, have been called to Court from the Schools; others, such as Eumenius, moved in the reverse direction. But whatever the nature of their experience at Court or in the imperial administration one might expect them to be thoroughly conversant with 'the rules of the game' and to have a professional pride in their ability to compose an appropriate oration for any occasion. In other words, given the biographical data available, the apparent lack of novelty of the material — the absence of political 'news' (with the notable exception of the Panegyric of 310) — and the unlikelihood of its uniqueness, one need not conclude that the imperial input in the panegyrics was very great at all.[18]

That, however, does not mean that the panegyrics were never 'instruments of propaganda'. But they were seldom instruments of propaganda in the crudest and most direct sense of the phrase. Rather, they usually reflected imperial wishes in a more subtle way. For the Schools themselves were under imperial patronage. Upon the death of a distinguished *praeceptor* of the Maenian Schools in Autun, Constantius appointed as its new head, at a very handsome salary, Eumenius, 'cuius eloquentiam et gravitatem morum ex actus nostri habemus administratione compertam' (*Pan.* V/IX 14.1) ('whose eloquence and seriousness of character we have ascertained from your administration of our affairs'). Let me emphasise that the initiative was taken by the Emperor; Eumenius was ordered to exchange his secretarial post at Court for one at Autun: 'qui [Constantius] honorem litterarum hac quoque dignatione cumulavit ut me filio potius meo ad pristina mea studia aditum molientum ipsum iusserit disciplinas artis oratoriae retractare . . .' etc. ('he added to the prestige of letters as well as by this distinction, that when I myself was striving for an entry to my former studies, this time for my son, he ordered me to undertake anew the discipline of the art of rhetoric . . .'). This solicitude for the education of the youth of Gaul – 'Merentur et Galli nostri ut eorum liberis, quorum vita in Augustodunensium oppido ingenuis artibus eruditu' (14.1) ('Our Gauls, too, deserve that we should desire to make provision for the talents of their children, who are instructed in the liberal arts in the town of Autun . . .') – was, of course, not entirely disinterested . . . 'et ipsi adulescentes, qui hilaro consensu meum Constanti Caesaris ex Italia revertentis suscepere comitatum, ut eorum indoli consulere cupiamus' (14.1) ('. . . and those youths, too, who cheerfully joined my retinue when I, Constantius Caesar, returned from Italy').

This imperial patronage of the Schools is scarcely surprising, for the Schools were the nursery or training ground for the imperial civil service, a recruiting ground for future officials and administrators. Another passage from Eumenius illustrates this very well. In the context of his appointment as *praeceptor moderatorque* Eumenius says (*Pan.* V/IX 5.4) that the Emperors 'litterarum . . . habuere dilectum, neque aliter quam si equestri turmae uel cohorti praetoriae consulendum foret, quem potissimum praeficerent sui arbitrii esse duxerunt, ne hi quos ad spem omnium tribunalium aut interdum ad stipendia cognitionum sacrarum aut fortasse ad ipsa palatii magisteria provehi oporteret, veluti repentino nubilo in mediis adulescentiae fluctibus deprehensi, incerta dicendi signa sequerentur' ('held . . . a levy of letters, and just as if they were providing for the command of a cavalry squadron or a praetorian cohort, they held it to be a matter for themselves to decide whom to put in charge in preference to all others, lest those who by rights had hopes of promotion to all the tribunals or on some occasions to service in the sacred (i.e. imperial) law-courts, or perhaps even to the palace secretariats themselves, as if caught in a sudden cloud amidst the billows of youth, should pursue wavering standards of rhetoric' [or 'untrustworthy guides to eloquence'].) The Schools must have been especially important in Gaul where the recent location of the Court at Trier will have created a great demand for educated men.[19] We have seen above how many imperial officials the Panegyrist of 310 claimed to have trained. We should ask what the educational goals of the Schools were, and what was the nature of the training. I spoke before of a 'hidden audience' of the panegyrics. That audience was the youth of Gaul. Let me clarify my point by reminding you of the disparate nature of the Gallic corpus of panegyrics. It is a collection of panegyrics ranging in date (Pliny's excluded) from A.D. 289 to 389, united by no common political or historical theme. Indeed, it must be stressed that the speeches are patently untampered with, politically or religiously speaking. For example, there is no process of 'Constantinification', no attempt to revise the portrait of Maximian: he appears in various guises, now as brother and assistant of Diocletian (*Pan.* of

289 and 291), now as promoter and patron of Constantine and Senior Augustus (*Pan.* of 307), and finally as traitorous villain (*Pan.* of 310). One might contrast Eusebius' *Ecclesiastical History* with its series of revisions. Or take the panegyrics of 313 and 321. In the former, Constantine is portrayed as the bold (indeed even brash) invader of Italy and aggressor against Maxentius, heedless alike of advice and entrails (*Pan.* IX/XII 2.4). Nazarius, speaking in 321, portrays Maxentius as the aggressor, presumably in line with, if not compelled by, the current official view of the matter. Again, there is no attempt to suppress, or tone down, Constantine's Vision of Apollo, when that may have been regarded as inappropriate in many circles.

The collection of such a corpus of occasional speeches, some of very ephemeral and parochial interest, is at first glance surprising, and the motive for the compilation has naturally been seen as a literary one — these are examples of the best products of the Gallic Schools of rhetoric. I have no quarrel with this conclusion, but wish to draw attention to the very survival of these politically ephemeral pieces. The implication is that they were read and used as models in the Schools. Indeed, several of the panegyrists betray an awareness of the work of their predecessors, and borrow their phrases. Thus the panegyric of Eumenius (*Pan.* V/IX, 298) and that of 297 (*Pan.* IV/VIII) have parallels. This is not surprising, for their authors were contemporaries teaching at Autun.[20] More revealing is the fact that the Panegyrist of 307 (*Pan.* VI/VII) borrows or adapts the phrase of Mamertinus' speeches delivered more than fifteen years before.[21] The Panegyrist of 297 (*Pan.* IV/VIII) had already done the same, [22] and the Panegyrist of 310 from Autun was perhaps to do so too.[23] The latter seems to draw upon the Panegyric of 297 for information about Constantius' campaigns between 293 and 296.[24] He certainly utilises Eumenius' panegyric, especially at *Pan.* VII/VI 22,[25] and, at times slavishly, the Panegyric of 307.[26] Finally the Panegyrist of 313 borrows several striking phrases from Mamertinus and the Panegyrist of 310.[27]

The inference is clear. Although this was not the primary intention of their authors, the influence of these panegyrics extended far beyond their immediate audience at the imperial Court. It spread from Trier to Autun, into the Schools, and thence into the generations to come. Eumenius has some remarks, instructive in this context, to make on the educational goals of the Schools which Constantius was so eager to restore. In stressing the importance of restoring the School buildings themselves he points to their situation, 'in the very path of our most invincible princes as they arrive here' (*Pan.* V/IX 9.2), 'as if between the very eyes of the city, between the Temple of Apollo and the Capitolium' (9.3). 'Assuredly, your Excellency [*vir perfectissime*; he addresses the governor of Lugdunensis], it is of importance to the fame which our great princes earn for their most frequent victories and triumphs *that the minds which are being carefully cultivated to sing their virtues* are honed not within private walls but in the public eye, and under the gaze of the city itself.'[28] The Schools of Gaul were in the service of the State. Not only did they provide the imperial government in Gaul with educated recruits, they inculcated the upper-class youth of Gaul with the right attitudes. The panegyrics had their part to play in this process. They were influential not only as rhetorical exemplars, but inevitably, in helping to form the political attitudes of the élite of Gallic youth who would go into public service, in affecting their sense of history, indeed in moulding their very historical knowledge. Brian Warmington has stressed the purely local and immediate nature of the 'propaganda' in the panegyrics.[29] The point is well worth making, but we must not neglect the wider and more enduring influence of these speeches, or underestimate their impact on the youth in the Schools of Gaul.

The late Latin panegyrics are both manifestations of the political and intellectual control of the educated classes by the central government, and an important tool in the process of that political and intellectual control — that is in the education of youth.[30]

Notes

This is, essentially, the conference paper as delivered. I have at some points expanded or clarified the text in response to criticism, but on the whole I have not attempted to alter the tone or style of the original version.

1. Cf. S. MacCormack, 'Latin Prose Panegyrics', in T. A. Dorey (ed.), *Empire and Aftermath* (London 1975), 153, n.70 and the works there cited. .

2. I give first the number in Galletier's edition, then that in the edition of Mynors.

3. For the occasion, see C. E. V. Nixon, 'The "Epiphany" of the Tetrarchs? An Examination of Mamertinus' Panegyric of 291', *Transactions of the American Philological Association* 111 (1981), 157–66.

4. Not 312, as Galletier would have it; cf. C. E. V. Nixon, 'The Occasion and Date of Panegyric VIII (V), and the Celebration of Constantine's Quinquennalia', *Antichthon* 14 (1980), 157–69.

5. J. Mesk, 'Zur Technik der lateinischen Panegyriker', *Rheinisches Museum* 67 (1912), 569–90.

6. A. Klotz, 'Studien zu den Panegyrici Latini', *Rheinisches Museum* 66 (1911), 513–72.

7. Further on (II/X 13.5) Mamertinus pointedly tells the story of Hercules' acquisition of the cognomen Victor; it was given to him by a merchant who defeated pirates with Hercules' help. 'Adeo, sacratissime imperator, multis iam saeculis inter officia est numinis tui superare piratas'. Well might Carausius quail! The same story turns up in Macrobius, *Sat.* II 6.11, who cites the Julio-Claudian jurist Masurius Sabinus. Macrobius then cites (Aemilius) Asper the Vergilian commentator. The world of Macrobius and that of our panegyrist are similar: we are among Schoolmen.

8. For example, M. Durry, *Pline le Jeune: panégyrique de Trajan* (Paris 1938), 4, n.6.

9. *op. cit.*, 42–3.

10. J. Straub, 'Konstantins Verzicht auf den Gang zum Kapitol', *Historia* 4 (1955), 298.

11. *op. cit.*, 160.

12. *ibid.*, 154 and 159–66 (passim) and *Art and Ceremony in Late Antiquity* (Berkeley 1981), 5; cf. too, Galletier, *op. cit.*, II, 114.

13. They are not 'fonctionnaires de l'empire' (Pichon, 'La politique de Constantin d'après les Panegyrici Latini', *Journal des Savants*, 1906, 289) but former 'fonctionnaires'.

14. *Pan.* VII/VI 1.1 (A.D. 310) gives us some information about a specific instance:

> Facerem, sacratissime imperator, quod paulo ante mihi plerique suaserunt ut, quoniam maiestas tua hunc mediocritati meae diem in ista civitate celeberrimum ad dicendum dedisset, de eo ipso ducerem sermonis exordium, nisi me ab hoc duplex ratio revocaret, considerantem neque mediae aetatis hominem ostentare debere subitam dicendi

> facultatem [dicendi] neque ad aures tanti numinis quicquam nisi diu scriptum et saepe tractatum adferri oportere.

> ('I would do, O most hallowed Emperor, what a great number of people have been advising me just now (*paulo ante*) to do, namely, since your majesty has allotted to my modest talents a day so celebrated in this city for my speech [he speaks of the foundation-day of the city of Trier], derive the introduction to my discourse from that very circumstance, did a double reason not dissuade me from this procedure. I consider first that a man of mature age has no business making a display of his talent for extempore speaking, and secondly, that nothing should be brought to the ears of such a great divinity which has not been composed over a period of time and frequently revised.')

From this one may deduce that the Emperor himself, or his representative, put the speaker on the programme, and perhaps it was normal for speeches to be prepared carefully in advance. Both these deductions are reinforced by *Pan.* III/XI of 291; at 5.1 the speaker comments that he has celebrated the expeditions and victories of the Emperor 'whenever your divine estimation has accorded me the favour of your audience' (cum mihi auditionis tuae divina dignatio eam copiam tribuit), and in the exordium he reveals that he had prepared a panegyric for Maximian's Quinquennalia, but for some reason or other (presumably the unexpected absence of the Emperor) had been unable to deliver it — he now, in its stead, delivers a speech celebrating Maximian's birthday.

But can we also deduce from the passage of *Pan.* VII/VI cited above that the speaker had no idea when, i.e. on what occasion, he was going to speak? Surely not. In this case it looks to me as if the panegyrist was not told exactly what day he was 'on' until his arrival at Court. The festival in question lasted several days (2.1 and esp. 3.7: 'these days on which the origin of [Hercules'] immortality is celebrated'), and the reference in 1.1 would then be to his luck in being chosen to orate on the very foundation day of Trier, as distinct from the day before or after.

15. See the article mentioned in note 3 above, for a critique of his views.

16. See M. T. W. Arnheim, *The Senatorial Aristocracy in the Later Roman Empire* (Oxford 1972), Ch. III; not undermined, in my opinion, by D. M. Novak, 'Constantine and the Senate: an early phase of the Christianisation of the Roman aristocracy', *Ancient Society* 10 (1979), 271–310.

17. *Classical Review* 80 (1966), 104.

18. Let me offer a further illustration, from *Pan.* III/XI of A.D. 291. As we have seen above, its author Mamertinus probably occupied an official post at the time. Here, if anywhere, we might expect obvious signs of imperial input. Now the centre-piece of the panegyrics is a description of the crossing of the Alps by the Emperors Diocletian and Maximian, and their meeting at Milan (Ch. 8–12). The orator discourses amusingly on the confusion arising when privileged subjects were confronted by the unaccustomed obligation to pay *adoratio* to two rulers of like status. But the meeting is described entirely from the viewpoint of the spectator; there is no hint that Mamertinus was apprised of their counsels. If there were an announcement of an imperial programme policy, it certainly does not appear here. This is scarcely surprising. We can be sure that the main topic of conversation at the meeting was what to do about the rebel Carausius after the failure of Maximian's expedition of 289 against him (cf. *Pan.* II/X 12 with the silence of *Pan.* III/XI about its fate and the revealing snippet in *Pan.* IV/VIII 12.2). It were best for Mamertinus to avoid the subject for the time being! In sum, deductions about imperial policy can be formed here from the panegyrics, but not as a result of any imperial announcements.

19.   This is not to discount pre-Tetrarchic Gaul as a centre of education. After all, Eumenius' grandfather, who was born in Athens and who had settled in Rome, left there and migrated to Autun, drawn by 'amor doctrinae', in the days before the Imperium Galliarum. But Gaul's pre-eminence can be exaggerated; for example, Haarhoff, *Schools of Gaul*, 141, suggests without any trace of humour that perhaps the reason the Emperors resided in Gaul in the fourth century was that, needing to mould public opinion, they selected the home of rhetoricians! Rather, Gallic pre-eminence was the consequence of imperial residence.

20.   See Table p.91 above (Numbers 2 and 3).

21.   Cf. Galletier, *op. cit.*, II, 10–11.

22.   Klotz, *op. cit.*, 548–9; this speaker was (probably) from Autun, while Mamertinus was probably from Trier.

23.   Klotz, *op. cit.*, 556–7 (alleged *Anklänge* not compelling).

24.   See Galletier, *op. cit.*, II, 48.

25.   Quondam fraterno populi Romano nomine gloriatam (22.4): cf. *Pan.* V/IX 4.1: olim fraterno populi Romano nomine gloriata; loca publica et templa (22.4): cf. *Pan.* V/IX 4.2: non templis moda ac locis publicis; restitues (22.3): cf. *Pan.* V/IX 4.1: restitutionis; liberalitate (22.4): liberalitatis (4.1); sedemque iustitiae (22.5): cf. *Pan.* V/IX 1.2: sedes ista iustitiae; and cf. Klotz, *op. cit.*, 557.

26.   Galletier, *ibid.*; Klotz, *op. cit.*, 557–9.

27.   Klotz, *op. cit.*, 564–5.

28.   For an example of the method, *ibid.*, ch.20.1–3: a geography lesson, complete with maps; the spirit of the lesson is in keeping with those of yesteryear, when our maps were painted red: 'Let the youth, moreover, see and gaze at every day in those porticos all lands and every sea and whatever cities, nations and tribes our most invincible princes are restoring in their piety, conquering by their valour, or holding fast by terror'. (20.2)

29.   'Aspects of Constantinian Propaganda in the Panegyrici Latini', *Transactions of the American Philological Association* 104 (1974), 371–84.

30.   Johannes Straub, writing in Germany in 1939 of the importance of the panegyrics in the 'politische Meinungsbildung der Jugend', *Vom Herrscherideal in der Spätantike*, (rp. Stuttgart 1964), 148, comes closer to the mark than many.

The Roman Antiquarian Tradition in Late Antiquity

G. Maslakov

Aeneas, capiturque locis et singula laetus
exquiritque auditque virum monumenta priorum.

Aeneid 8.311–12.

A paper on the Roman antiquarian tradition in a collection devoted to late antique historiography requires justification for two very good reasons. First, it may not be at all self-
evident that the antiquarian tradition of scholarship belongs to the sphere of historiography.
Second, its influence in late Antiquity is not so much on the writing of history as on particular conceptions of what a study of Roman customs and institutions entails. One may
observe the influence of the tradition on Ausonius, Servius, St Augustine and Macrobius, yet
to do so is merely to sketch in a chapter in the history of certain key ideas about the development of the Roman State and civilisation and not to illuminate historiography proper.

It is clear that the antiquarians did not write history in the formal sense in which it was
understood at Rome.[1] However, this technicality need not prevent us from appreciating the
extent to which their research and speculation produced coherent and influential accounts
of Roman history. Both Cicero and St Augustine give us a telling illustration of the true
historical character of antiquarian writing. Cicero's detailed praise of Varro in the *Academica*
is subsequently repeated in *De Civitate Dei*:

> 'Tum ego, "Sunt", inquam, "ista, Varro; nam nos in nostra urbe peregrinantis
> errantisque tamquam hospites tui libri quasi domum reduxerent, ut possemus
> aliquando qui et ubi essemus agnoscere. Tu aetatem patriae, tu discriptiones temp-
> orum, tu sacrorum iura, tu sacerdotum, tu domesticam, tu bellicam disciplinam, tu
> sedem regionum, locorum, tu omnium divinarum humanarumque rerum nomina,
> genera, officia causas aperuisti".'[2]

For orators of the Ciceronian period the notion of the *mos maiorum* may have been a
convenient rhetorical abstraction, but antiquarians of the late Republic and early Empire
(for example, Varro, Atticus, Nepos, Verrius Flaccus) gave substance and detail to the
evolution of the distinctive Roman community, exploring in their work the legal, social,
cultural and religious institutions of antiquity.[3]

The influence of these writers on the intellectual life of the fourth century and beyond has
not as yet been adequately evaluated. For those who had access to these massive collections,
their speculations and reflections on historical change formed an important part of historical
knowledge. While classical historiography degenerated into epitomes, to be supplemented by
extensive chonographies, men such as Varro were keenly read and imitated.[4] It is not
surprising therefore that when St Augustine comes to develop his rigorous critique of traditional Roman beliefs and values he chooses Varro's work as a target. However, as will be
demonstrated shortly, St Augustine does not challenge the antiquarians solely because they

are intellectually fashionable, he tackles Varro because Varro's conception of the role of religion in Roman history had particular relevance for him.[5]

All this is by way of a general justification for including the antiquarians in the context of historiography. More specifically, it may be helpful to isolate three distinct historical strands as they emerge from Varro, Nepos and the Elder Pliny, the latter being one of our best sources for the third strand below:

i. Concern for the *totality* of historical development of the *res publica* (as observed in Cicero's praise of Varro's intellectual scope at the beginning of the *Academica*) and within that *totality* for the place of religious history, its organic connection with the growth of the Roman community.

ii. Interest in the establishment of customs and in the introduction of the use of particular materials and objects (for example, who first used the plough, established cities and introduced writing).

iii. Related but not identical concern for the excesses of civilisation demonstrated through moral reflection on the extension of the use in Rome of such materials as marble, gold, silver in the context of charting the growth of excess in public and private building — pyramids, labyrinths, elaborate theatres.

This focus on the material history of Rome is much more than a simple domestication of the Hellenistic tradition of cataloguing invention, explicitly acknowledged by the Elder Pliny as one of his sources in his *Natural History*. Taking an overview of the product of antiquarian studies and the serious aims of their authors, it may be urged that here we have an important contribution to the history of Roman civilisation. In any history of Roman historiography these concerns should be noted and their achievement justly assessed.

This need becomes more clear as we detect the survival and influence of the antiquarian tradition in the fourth century. The last two aspects noted above have a resonance in the work of Ausonius. His *Mosella* proceeds by integrating its allusions to the *Aeneid* with those to Varro's *Hebdomades* and Pliny's *Natural History*. Ausonius' poetry illustrates the phenomenon that is to be seen in greater depth and detail in Servius and in Macrobius' *Saturnalia*. Antiquarians form an indispensable historical background to the study of poetry, particularly that of the Augustan age.[6]

Ausonius and Macrobius assume that a true understanding of the Roman literary heritage can be achieved by absorbing and interpreting the conclusions of scholars like Varro and Verrius. Acceptance of this proposition raises a wider question. No historiography exists in a vacuum. This is particularly true of the fourth century. The period was marked by a fundamental divergence between traditional and Christian historiography.[7] In discussing St Augustine's views on history, R. A. Markus sums up the essence of the parting of the ways:

'Notwithstanding his realisation of a need for a new Christian historiography, his own attitudes to history were very like those of most fourth-century Christians. It is unlikely that he read Ammianus Marcellinus. History of this kind held little interest for him, and in so far as the pagan opposition with which he set himself to deal in the *City of God* had historical roots, they lay elsewhere. The sort of history

Ammianus wrote had not even the distinction in his eyes of standing in need of refutation.'[8]

Equally, the interests of traditionalist intellectuals lay not in the writing of history on Tacitean and Sallustian models but in the reconstruction and study of the ancient historical heritage. In a very important way historiography ceases to be the vital method of dealing with the past. Arrangement, preservation and reflection on a tradition inherited from the late Republic and early Empire takes over.[9] Christians and their opponents cease to write history as traditionally understood. Ammianus is an exception that proves the rule. The implications for students of historiography of this situation are considerable, but the most relevant one for purposes of this discussion involves a reappraisal of the setting in which late antique historiography survives. Therefore, though the survival of certain key texts like Varro's *Hebdomades* and *Antiquitates* and Pliny's *Natural History* is not in itself mirrored in history written on their model, the study of Antiquity which these works made possible and the historical conceptions transmitted by means of that, have a direct bearing on the history of historiography in late Antiquity.

It is now widely accepted that the *Antiquitates* play a crucial part in St Augustine's scheme of arguments against his intellectual adversaries in *De Civitate Dei.*[10] I hope to show in the following analysis how Varro's works help St Augustine to sharpen his attack and in a positive way to formulate his ideas on the kind of historical study proper to a Christian. These ideas are worth investigating even though St Augustine avoided writing history as such and his protégé Orosius failed to appreciate their import.

It is clear from the *De Civitate Dei* (and clearer of course from Macrobius' *Saturnalia*) that antiquarian material was not only a source of information about ancient civic institutions and customs but also an important source of information and reassurance about the antiquity and nature of traditional religion. It demonstrated how the Roman community developed its laws and institutions and how inextricably these were bound up with the worship of the ancient gods.

If Varro's books did have the kind of impact on Cicero and his contemporaries that is attested in the *Academica* (compare praise of Atticus' *Liber Annalis* in *Brutus* 3–4), it may be conjectured that the impact on fourth-century intellectuals was equally profound. This was where they could discover systematic accounts of religious and cultural history, permeated by a serious moral purpose of reviving their relevance to current concerns.[11] To those who felt that the existing cults and rituals were in themselves an insufficient defence against the challenge of the Christian religion, antiquarian studies provided a useful reinforcement of traditional practices. However, as the whole thrust of St Augustine's polemic demonstrates, the use to which this antiquarian material might be put by embattled traditionalists was inadequate to perform the job at hand. The contemporary problems were not just the old Roman mixture of political unrest, moral decline and external threats (fully illustrated in the Livian tradition). With those things the Romans could always deal. The radically new ingredient at this time was an ideology requiring a revision of religious history.

St Augustine makes much of this and he frequently uses Varro's learning to underline the point. First, he selects those statements of Varro's which demonstrate that in remote Antiquity divinity was bestowed on men for service rendered to their respective cities. For Varro this seems to have been an important theme in *De gente populi Romani*, as well as in his discussion in the *Antiquitates* of the human origins of gods and religious ceremonies. As St

Augustine (*Civ. Dei* 6.3) reminds his readers, for Varro *res humanae* (25 books) preceded and conditioned *res divinae* (16 books).

St Augustine's arguments in *De Civitate Dei* tackle head on the assumption that study of Varronian material can silence those who are critical of ancestral religion. In the early books St Augustine selects for special attention the assertions of Varro:

i. that it may be politically expedient for leaders to encourage belief among the people that these leaders trace their descent from the gods; and

ii. that it is proper to encourage mistaken notions about the gods and that there are many truths that it is expedient for people not to know.[12]

In so far as Varro advocated a type of falsehood as a socially desirable thing, St Augustine is able to make effective criticism of his systematic theology. Subsequent illustration by a wealth of mythical examples of instances where men were deified for services to their cities (particularly in Book 18) is part of the same argument. St Augustine does not challenge Varro as an authority. He draws out of Varronian speculations those themes and concepts that seem to undercut the veracity and hence for him the validity of Roman religion. In St Augustine's view it is this implicit and explicit justification of deception as a socially profitable goal in religious matters that undermines the arguments of those who seek to assert the relevance to contemporary challenges of these inherited and time-honoured rites.

Condoning of deception is an open invitation to daemonic powers to involve themselves more fully in the deception of the worshippers. Varro's acceptance of deception and the criticism of it in *De Civitate Dei* fits in well with St Augustine's repeated exposure in the first ten books of the nature and activity of these daemonic forces.[13]

By illustrating that the ancient Romans were fully conscious of the artificiality of their religion, St Augustine appears to direct his message at those of his adversaries who are genuinely concerned to find a religious solution to the current turmoil. You will not find religion in Varro, he tells them. This is the very essence of his polemic and it indicates that the *De Civitate Dei* is a genuine plea to a hostile intelligentsia to think again, to review their favourite source for the nature and development of the *res publica*. In harmony with this aim, at the end of the first book St Augustine explicitly leaves the way open for those who are presently outside the church. Amongst her current enemies are those who are predestined to be its future citizens.

These future citizens of the City of God need to be shown the devastating falsehood at the heart of the religious practices that they meticulously reconstruct and explain from Varro's history of the Roman community. In St Augustine's view one must use Varro to defeat Varro. This may explain why it is Varro and not the contemporary manifestations of paganism (the mystery-cults, the Oriental religions, Mithraism) that provides the focus for attack.[14] Varro's studies symbolised a history that needed to be confronted in order to be properly transcended. No alternative historiography was called for or envisaged; intellectual cut and thrust of debate was deemed to be sufficient. This was partly because St Augustine did not himself wish to write an alternative history of the *res publica* from its mythical origins, and also because he was not fighting a living historiographical phenomenon. His adversaries were the lovingly preserved vestiges of ancient scholarly glory.

Notes

1.   The role of invention in Roman historiography is gradually getting adequate recognition; see in particular T. P. Wiseman, *Clio's Cosmetics* (Leicester 1979), 27–53. If one were to describe most of the history that was written in Rome as fiction largely inspired by current rhetorical and political preoccupations, one may look with greater tolerance at the directions and achievements of the antiquarians. It may even be argued that a Varro belongs to true historical writing more than a Livy or Dionysius. However, there is no need to push the point to that extent. It should be sufficient to urge that historiography, as conventionally conceived, and antiquarian studies belong to historiography broadly defined. For an appreciation of the antiquarian contribution to the study of Roman history, see A. Momigliano, 'An Interim Report on the Origins of Rome', *Journal of Roman Studies* 53 (1963), 96–8 in particular. It was recognised in Antiquity that Varro contributed more to historical knowledge than to eloquence (Quintilian, *Inst. Orat.* X, 1.95), surely a point in his favour. How Varro's eagerness to convey information affected his style is shown in detail by E. Laughton, 'Observations on the Style of Varro', *Classical Quarterly* 10 (1960), 1–28.

2.   Cicero, *acad. post.* 9; B. Cardauns, *M. Terentius Varro: Antiquitates Rerum Divinarum* (Wiesbaden 1972) I, 12–3 (*Testimonia* 1); C. O. Brink, 'Horace and Varro', *Entretiens sur l'ant. class.* (Geneva 1962), 182; N. Horsfall, review of Cardauns, *Classical Review* 29 (1979), 46–8.

3.   In order to appreciate the value of these antiquarian studies as history, see the discussion of the nature of historical investigation in J. H. Plumb, *The Death of the Past* (Harmondsworth 1973), 84–5. Particularly helpful is Plumb's conception of the scope of historical enquiry. This visualises historians as giving attention to the manifold aspects of human existence – language, religion, economics, politics; in short, it sees them as ideally aiming to investigate the totality of man's social and cultural setting. This notion of 'total' history owes a great deal to the *Annales* school of French historiography (see M. Aymard, 'The *Annales* and French Historiography', *Journal of Economic History* (1972), 491–511). Without wishing to take the comparison too far, it is illuminating to observe a degree of similarity in the broad directions of Roman antiquarians such as Varro and modern historians like Marc Bloch (see comments on Bloch's method by F. R. H. Du Boulay in *Land and Work in Medieval Europe* (London 1966), vii–xii). A number of recent studies have added significantly to our understanding of Roman antiquarian research: A. Momigliano, 'Ancient History and the Antiquarian', *Studies in Historiography* (London 1966), 4–5; E. Rawson, 'Cicero the Historian and Cicero the Antiquarian', *Journal of Roman Studies* 62 (1972), 33–45; G. V. Sumner, *The Orators in Cicero's 'Brutus': Prosopography and Chronology* (Toronto 1973), especially pp.161–75 devoted to Cicero's and Atticus' scholarship; T. P. Wiseman, *op. cit.*, index s.v. Cicero, Atticus, Nepos and Varro.

4.   Symmachus' father knew and imitated Varro's *Hebdomades* (Symmachus, *Epistulae* 1.2.8); see also N. Horsfall's studies cited in n.6 below.

5.   Both Servius and the Scholia Danielis have numerous references to a wide range of Varro's works; see Robert B. Lloyd, 'Republican Authors in Servius and the Scholia Danielis', *Harvard Studies in Classical Philology* 65 (1961), 291–341. If, as Lloyd argues, both Servius and the Scholia Danielis derive from the extensive commentary by Aelius Donatus, then one may suppose that that work set the standard in making Varro the authority on Roman religion, customs and legendary history. Even a commentary designed for school use (*ibid.*, 325–6) of the type prepared by Servius had to

incorporate references to Varro's opinions. Whether these references can be taken as evidence of direct familiarity with Varro's works by Servius and Macrobius is open to debate; see N. Marinone, *I Saturnali* (Turin 1967), 41–51. But even if much of Varro was known at second-hand only, the large number of extracts and references to his work should be taken as sufficient grounds for accepting that many of Varro's ideas and theories were known by the educated community. After all, Varro wrote so much and on so many topics that if only one tenth of his total output was excerpted and read this should amount to substantial survival. St Augustine doubted that anyone found time to read it all (*Civ. Dei* 6.2). For historiographical developments in the fourth century, see A. Momigliano, 'Pagan and Christian Historiography in the Fourth Century A.D.', *The Conflict between Paganism and Christianity in the Fourth Century* (Oxford 1963), 79–99; note especially p.99 on St Augustine's choice of Varro as his intellectual adversary. This last point is also picked up and discussed by R. A. Markus, 'Paganism, Christianity and the Latin Classics', *Latin Literature of the Fourth Century*, ed. J. W. Binns (London 1974), 8. On Varro and St Augustine in general, see H. Hagendahl, *Augustine and the Latin Classics* (Oslo 1967), Vol. II, 589–630.

6.   Lines 48–54 of the *Mosella* may be taken as an example of Ausonius' allusive method. Here Ausonius indicates his preference for walking on the firm sands of the river shores rather than spending his time in marble encrusted atria of luxury houses. This moral censure of human extravagance in matters of costly buildings draws directly on the third strand of the antiquarian tradition noted above. Cutting of marble slabs for veneer was invented in Caria, according to Pliny (*Nat. Hist.* 36.47; see also 51, explaining the role of *sand* in this process). The first Roman to use marble veneer to cover whole walls of his house on the Caelian hill was Mamurra, an eques from Formiae who was Caesar's *praefectus fabrum* in Gaul. This was originally noted by Nepos and recorded again by Pliny (*ibid.*, 48). Ausonius singles out Phrygian marble as a symbol of private ostentation. Pliny records (*ibid.*, 102) that the Basilica Aemilia had columns of Phrygian marble, so Ausonius may be deliberately highlighting the point that what was once a mark of public splendour is now extended to individual indulgence. Ausonius' preference for sand may also be read as a criticism of pavements (*pavimenta*). These, as Pliny records (*ibid.*, 184), had their origins in Greece and were called in Italy 'foreign' (*barbarica*). The fashion for mosaics came in under Sulla and spread from pavements to vaulted ceilings (*ibid.*, 189), but the latter by another leap of human ingenuity were later made of glass. Sand, of course, is the constituent of glass (Pliny gives the story describing its fortuitous origins in Phoenicia, *ibid.*, 190). These are all foreign inventions and imports, transforming by degrees the simple dwellings of old Italy. Having directed us to Pliny and his catalogue, ranging from marble to glass, Ausonius follows his description of sand (that fails to retain the imprint of his passing) with an image of the river's transparency. This is nature's *glass*, revealing the deep mysteries in a proper and natural way.

   If lines 48–54 of the *Mosella* are read as an implicit reference to the antiquarian tradition, then it would come as no surprise to the reader to have an excellent mention of Varro's *Hebdomades* (known also as *Imagines*) in lines 305–310. The poet's theme is the magnificence of the architecture to be seen on the banks of the river: such structures would not be scorned by Daedalus himself. Perhaps these wonders were built by the seven architects celebrated in the tenth volume of Varro's *Hebdomades*, the poet muses. *Hebdomades* was a magnificent illustrated book, more extensive than Atticus' *Imagines* by which it may have been inspired; see *Nat. Hist.* 35.11–2 and Gellius' *Noct. Att.* 3.10–1. Pliny's *in omnes terras misit* attests wide circulation for the *Hebdomades*. Further, on this work, see F. Della Corte, *Varrone* (Florence 1970),

192–5; K. Weitzmann, *Ancient Book Illumination* (Cambridge, Mass. 1959), 116–7; N. Horsfall's review of R. Daut, *Imago: Untersuchungen zum Bilderbegriff der Römer* (1975) in *Classical Review* 28 (1978), 161 and 'Virgil, Varro's *Imagines* and the Forum of Augustus', *Ancient Society: Resources for Teachers* 10 (1980), 20–3.

7.   A. Momigliano, *op. cit.* (n.5 above), 88–9.

8.   R. A. Markus, *Saeculum: History and Society in the Theology of St Augustine* (Cambridge 1970), 5.

9.   In this respect the outlook and aspirations of the presumed compiler and the author of the *Origo gentis Romanae* is of relevance: A. Momigliano, 'Some Observations on the *Origo gentis Romanae*', *Journal of Roman Studies* 48 (1958), 56–73. Momigliano's sketch of both scholars as types brings into relief the kind of interests that make up the new intellectual environment assumed in the present discussion.

10.   See the essays by Momigliano and Markus cited in n.5 above.

11.   Even though Varro placed his discussion of human affairs before systematically investigating matters pertaining to the gods, his interest in preserving Rome's religious tradition was fundamental to the whole enterprise. This is clear from the crucial programmatic statement preserved in *Civ. Dei* 6.2, where Varro compares his task with that of Aeneas and Metellus who rescued the *sacra Vestalia*. Varro's self-image was that of another Aeneas, performing a vital and arduous task in preserving (by unifying and explaining) the religious institutions of the State. The whole of the *Antiquitates* provided a moral *exemplum* for Varro's contemporaries. In so far as it revived civic and religious traditions it furnished patterns of conduct and precedent to set against prevailing ignorance and neglect. To the oratorical abuse of history it gave a counterpoint of systematic investigation. It is not surprising that Cicero, torn between the demands of scholarship and politics, found in Varro's studies security and reassurance.

12.   In the first book of *res divinae* (fr.20 Cardauns = *Civ. Dei* 3.4) Varro argued that it is expedient in a *civitas* for brave men to believe, though it be a fiction (*etiamsi falsum sit*), that they are descended from the gods. Fragment 21 (Cardauns = *Civ. Dei* 4.31) takes the matter further in suggesting that some truths are best kept hidden from the people.

13.   See his discussion of Varro's treatment of Numa's hydromancy (in *de cultu deorum*) in *Civ. Dei* 7.34 and 35.

14.   P. Brown, *Augustine of Hippo* (London 1967), 305.

The Exegete as Historian:
Hilary of Poitiers' Commentary on Matthew

Philip Rousseau

First I should explain how this paper fits into the wider context of my present research. From one particular point of view, I am anxious to know how the empire of the late third century turned into the empire of the early fifth. I am concentrating for the moment on the West, and on the way in which articulate citizens related their understanding of Providence to their understanding of individual responsibility and freedom. It would seem that a familiar preoccupation about the divine protection of the State persisted, even in its terminology. At the same time the guarantees of that protection, attaching to participation by individuals in the current religious and political system, came to depend more and more on the enforcement of interior attitudes, opinions and loyalty not least.

Part of the explanation for this 'inward shift' may reside in the current understanding of history, particularly in Christians' understanding of what they regard as 'their' history. But where is that understanding reflected? Eusebius, at the beginning of our period, has no true heirs in the West: that is to say, 'ecclesiastical history. in the stricter sense seems a predominantly eastern development.[1] (Chronicles are another matter![2]) Jerome and Rufinus introduce into what might seem extensions of Eusebius' work a new note that I would label briefly ascetic and biographical.[3]

Jerome and Rufinus conjoined recall the Origenist Controversy, which I believe is essential to our understanding of changes of emphasis in the minds of western Christians during this period. The Origenist Controversy involved, among other things, a debate about the uses to which Christians might put the methods of the classical culture. It also helped to express mistrust of one type of cosmology, as well as a growing historical interest in the text of the Bible.[4]

It is this last thread that I wish to pick up here. Reflection on the biblical text may have been the method whereby Christians of the later fourth century developed a new 'sense of the past'. It seemed useful, therefore, to conduct a few experiments among exegetes known to Jerome and to his immediate successors. Hilary is a good place to begin. He is mentioned by Jerome, in suggestive passages.[5] He displays moral preoccupations that might support other links in my wider argument.[6] Above all, he was responsible for a text, the *Commentary on Matthew*, which marked in many ways a new beginning in western exegesis, relatively untouched however by the thought of Origen and by the pressures of the Arian Controversy.[7]

It becomes clear very quickly that the whole *Commentary* is based on one simple confrontation, that which occurs between the Jews and the true believers, between the Law and the Gospel. A woman touches the fringe of Jesus' garment, her haemorrhage stops, and 'quod Israeli parabatur, plebs gentium occupavit'.[8] Jesus leaves the temple and the city and goes out to Bethany: 'infidelem videlicet Synagogam deserens, in Ecclesia gentium demoratur' (xxi.5).

Two striking images make the point clear. Scandal, and the preferable millstone, bring to Hilary's mind a patient, plodding donkey, blindfold, working the mill. The donkey stands for the lucky *gentes*, lucky in their ignorance (blindfold). The Jews, through the Law, ought to have known better, but instead are scandalised.[9] And so the camel, which — as we shall see — brings John the Baptist to mind (skins), is an obedient beast, and passes along the narrow way, through the eye of the needle, into the kingdom. The Jews, however, get stuck, and are forced to offload the 'opulentia divitis, id est, gloriantis in lege' (xix.11).

Now the first point I want to make is already hidden in these examples. Hilary is not simply making a contrast, but describing a transition, from Law to Gospel: a real event, or series of events. Series, because once the note of transition is struck, his analysis quickly goes beyond the binary. There are vivid touches that tip us forward in time. The Magi are on a journey; and so for them there is no going back — to Judaea! (i.5). Jesus says to the High Priest, 'tu dixisti'; but to Pilate, 'tu dicis'. The Jewish High Priest, *passé*, has had his moment; whereas Pilate, the Gentile, brings us to a new present (xxxii.7).

Even there the contrast may be too sharp. Hilary was anxious not only to describe how prophecy reached across from antiquity into, as he says, 'our times' but also to dwell seriously on the extent to which the Law really did speak, in its own day, of nativity, passion and resurrection (iv.14). The kingdom is like leaven in the meal because a unity results: 'quod lex constituit, prophetae nuntiaverunt, id ipsum evangeliorum profectibus expleatur' (xiii.5). So an organic quality attaches to the transition. The Gospel really grows out of the Law — 'Christi ortus et adventus ex lege est'; but of course the Law failed to recognise its own future (xii.13).

It is this sense of growth that gives John the Baptist his special importance for Hilary. John preaches in a Judaea that is a desert, symbolic of infidelity and absence of the Spirit; but he offers a chance of repentance, and a kingdom: we of course, believers, have wandered (like locusts), but now we find new nourishment (wild honey) (ii.2). John is in a very special way the point at which the transition most importantly takes place. He fulfils the Law; and that is why the Law tries to kill, in him, the Gospel (xi.2). One can almost feel the shift in Hilary's text, after Herod's party: 'finitis igitur legis temporibus, et cum Joanne consepultis, discipuli eius res ita gestas Domino nuntiant, ad Evangelia scilicet ex lege venientes' (xiv.8).

The process is more detailed than that; but first it is worth mentioning a feature mixed in with these categories of Law and Gospel, namely a varied readiness on the part of Hilary to deal in periods. For example, the paralytic is forgiven, raised up, carries his bed, and returns home. So the preaching of the Gospel sets us free from sin and guilt, so too we share in Christ's resurrection, though we labour first, as we journey back to that state of paradise lost by Adam (viii.7).[10] In another example, Christ visits the favoured disciples in Gethsemane three times. On the first occasion he rebukes them, because he is anxious about their probable doubt and dispersal after his resurrection. On the second occasion he remains silent: the Holy Spirit is now the one to speak. On the third occasion he tells them to take their rest; a rest that will follow from his second coming (xxxi.11). There are two points to hold in mind here, for later reference: the inner quality of the middle period, the silence; and the long gap, so to speak, between Pentecost and Parousia.

More specifically linking Law and Gospel, the labourers in the vineyard report at conveniently different hours. The first is the hour of Noah, the third of Abraham, the sixth of Moses, the ninth of David and the prophets. Only with the eleventh hour do we come to the incarnation — and everything after it! By calculating five hundred years to the hour, Hilary is able to clock up the required six thousand — though he carefully avoids predicting the end in another century and a half! (xx.6).[11]

My favourite example is when Christ walks on the water. The apostles in the boat are in the church (and more on that in a moment), and Christ comes in the fourth watch — the hour of the Parousia. The other watches refer to the periods of the Law, the prophets and the incarnation; and again, note that long (and stormy) gap (xiv.5).

Hilary is most interesting when discussing in greater detail the link between Jews and believers. It was not a question of Jews disappearing and of believers coming to the surface: the general historiographical 'plot' demanded that potential believers should always be in the wings, waiting to take up the opportunity of Jewish infidelity. So we find that there was a Gentile faith before the coming of Christ, which is represented for example by the Queen of the South, while followers of the Law were faithless and condemned to wander among the nations (xii.22). Very attractive is the confusion in a later passage: '*sunt* enim atque *erant* duo populi, circumcisionis et gentium' (xiv.7). Such a *longue durée* was needed to accommodate the passing of the torch from one group to another. I will anticipate one of my final comments by saying that we should always be alert to antecedents of the *City of God*. These 'duo populi' are interesting, although no recent author (as far as I am aware) has counted Hilary among the *prolegomena* to Augustine in this respect.

And yet Hilary avoids loading the historical dice. It was fully intended by God that the Jews should find salvation. Not only did many of them do so, but they reflected the variety of response possible in the face of the incarnation. Some were unable to wean themselves from the Law, but they admired the teaching and achievements of Jesus. Others explored more fully the *libertas* promised by the Gospel, but allowed themselves to be led into heresy. Total acceptance, therefore, and total rejection were joined by hesitancy and confusion (x.9). Jewry was the city, the *civitas*, which was divided against itself (by allowing itself to harbour Jewish persecution of the new believers): that alone made its fall intelligible (xii.14).

It is worth emphasising, therefore, how varied a view of the Jews Hilary displayed. The parable of the talents illustrates the point. The man who had one talent, and who buried it, was the fruitless and persistent rejecter of Jesus. Those who had two were the *gentes*: their faith and their works brought them their increase and reward. But those who had five were those who really made something of the Pentateuch, and doubled their endowment by faith in the Gospel (xxvii.7f.).

Thus we have straightforward images of uncomplicated conversion. Crowds run from the city (now Jewish) to the desert (now Christian), following Jesus in the boat (again, the church): 'de Synagoga videlicet ad Ecclesiam concedit' (xiv.19). But others are more hesitant, and no less praiseworthy in the end: they may resist Christ, but will fall under the spell of the apostles (xxi.13). And this slow and partial change of heart only makes sense against a long background of optimism on God's part, and of goodwill. It was from Jewry, after all, that sprang the disciples of John the Baptist (xx.11). Jesus himself embodied the ancient decision, formulated by Isaiah, that the smouldering flax would not be extinguished: during the 'time of penance' (between incarnation and Parousia) it might flare up in redeeming faith (xii.10). The Pharisees in particular were made part of this enduring plan: they were called to the same task as the apostles themselves (xii.7, repeated at xx.11). It is all a measure of how precisely historical Hilary was: for Jesus was first a Jew. 'Sed suis Dominus atque in sua venerat, primitias ergo fidei ab his quibus erat ortus exspectans, caeteris deinceps Apostolorum praedicatione salvandis' (xv.4). It was this fact that made a rejection most piquant: 'quia ab his perimebatur, quos primum genitos filios retinere voluisset' (i.7).

The apostles represented a very specific moment in the growth of the Gospel from the Law: 'apostoli quidem iam ex lege crediderant, quae eos in fidem evangelicam nutriverat' (xx.9); and again, 'credentes primi ex Israel apostoli, et inter legem et evangelia grossorum modo inhaerentes' (xxi.9).[12] So they had a very special role vis-à-vis the Jews. In the parable of the great banquet, 'qui autem admonentur ut veniant, invitati antea populus Israel est: in gloriam enim aeternitatis per legem est advocatus. Servi missi, qui invitatos vocarent, apostoli sunt: eorum enim est proprium, commonefacere eos quos invitaverant prophetae' (xxii.4). Only after that does their vocation carry over into what we might call the 'resurrection period': 'resurrectionis testimonium proprium est apostolorum' (xvi.8).

So the apostles represented as it were the poised holding of the historical breath, between John the Baptist and the *praedicatio*, the full flowering of the Gospel. In the feeding of the five thousand, they have to make do with five loaves, representing the Law, and two fishes, representing the prophets and John himself; and these five thousand foreshadow the first believers mentioned in *Acts*, who are clearly Jews (xiv.10f. See also xvii.13). Then, and only then, comes the feeding of the four thousand, who represent the four corners of the earth, the *gentes*; and they feast on seven loaves, representing the gifts of the Spirit (xv.7f.)[13]

A fuller chronology, so to speak, should by now have begun to emerge. In addition to a panorama, variously divided, stretching from Adam to the final judgment, we have different stages, more carefully described: the Law, the exile, the predisposition to salvation among both Jews and Gentiles, the various Jewish successes and failures in response, the circle of John, the apostles, the church of the *Acts*, and the first addresses beyond the Jewish people.

At this point it is worth looking at how the church is described; in particular at the emphasis on a segregated and beleaguered community. It is true that there are references, like those mentioned, in which the church is described as the 'magni regis . . . civitas'; but it is one formed by Christ's taking flesh, and we are simply taken up into what one might describe as an 'incarnation polity' (iv.12,24).[14] Similarly, when describing the church as a lamp, shining out to others, the light is Christ, and the church is simply the place where the light shines (iv.13).

There is one rather interesting text where Hilary records the great sheet let down before Peter in a trance: it reminds us that the church is to be buried (in a winding sheet) with Christ; but the recollection underlines also the variety to be found within the church (another slightly Augustinian premonition) (xxxiii.8).[15]

But on the whole a more rigorist note is struck, evoking a minority. The church is the place where the 'salty' ones are: others are cast out, out of the *ecclesia* (iv.10). The church is the boat where the chosen ones go with Christ, to be buffeted into the bargain by enemies and evil spirits (vii.9). The church is the tree in whose branches we take refuge, with the apostles, from the demons abroad in the world (xiii.4). When the disciples are sent out two by two to offer peace to deserving houses, those houses *are* the church — the implication being that believers will be scattered and exceptional (x.7).

It should be pointed out that believers appear also to be segregated from civil society and the Empire. The ideal is to have nothing left to 'render to Caesar': the church has its own *principes* — its bishops! (xxiii.2; xvii.1)[16]

Complementing these somewhat harsh impressions are the exegetical opportunities that Hilary deliberately missed or twisted. References to marriage, which inevitably recall Paul's interpretation in *Ephesians*, are hurried over (xix.2; xxii.3; xxvii.4). To love one's neighbour is to be Christ loving the Father, an image simply of Trinitarian intimacy (xxiii.7). When two or three are gathered together in Christ's name, he is in their midst, but in a special sense that destroys the social allusion: 'ipse enim pax atque charitas, sedem atque habitationem in bonis et pacificis voluntatibus collocabit' (xviii.9).

So when we come to the 'church' stage of Hilary's 'history', the momentum appears to slow down somewhat. There is certainly no impression of the inevitable growth of a triumphant Christian society. We cannot say that the momentum stops completely, because both the faithless and the heretics are excluded from a history precisely. They have, quite literally, a different future. They are condemned to an eternity of bodily burning, whereas believers 'put on incorruption' (v.12). In other words, unbelievers will not share in the life of the resurrection (ix.8). Hilary is particularly sharp with heretics: they are the possessed swine, who then plunge to share the death of unbelievers (viii.4). No compromise is possible: you are either a good tree, bearing good fruit, or a bad tree, bearing bad. Heretics try to accept this, and reject that; but 'neutrum facientes, nec inter gentes sub venia ignorationis habitantes, nec in veritatis cognitione versantes' (xii.18. See also 19).

Nevertheless the stillness of the present age is undeniable. It is the *spatium poenitentiae*. Images of the end make this clear. We await the bridegroom, who delays: 'mora sponsi, poenitentiae tempus est' (xxvii.4). A man gives out talents before making his journey: the reckoning will come; but 'peregrinationis tempus poenitentiae spatium est' (xxvii.6). And the wait is a long one, as in the comment on the fig tree: 'dato enim poenitentiae spatio, eo videlicet tempore quod inter passionem et reditum claritatis est medium'. Even the Jews must wait — for it is the Synagogue that the returning Christ finds fruitless and deserving of judgment (xxi.6).

It is only when he comes to deal with the passion that Hilary makes a very necessary attempt to bridge the gap between the incarnation and the *claritatis adventus*. 'Wherever the body is, there the eagles will be gathered together.' Eagles fly, and therefore stand for those who become at the end spiritual and holy; but it is around the passion that this final *conventus* will take place: 'et digne illic claritatis adventus exspectabitur, ubi nobis gloriam aeternitatis passione corporeae humilitatis operatus est' (xxv.8). The point is repeated in a later phrase: 'ut sacramentum crucis admixtum esse gloriae aeternitatis agnoscerent' (xxviii.2). The *gentes* share in the sacrifice of Christ: his chalice passes to men, and they are buried with him (xxx.1; xxxi.7; xxxiii.8).[17]

Men participate, therefore, as well as wait; *poenitentia* has that sense too: the momentum is restored, but it becomes more clearly moral and personal. Here is the clue, I think, to what history means for Hilary. However, before we examine further this penultimate transition from the primitive post-Jewish community to the moral combat of relatively isolated individuals, I would like to avoid any suggestion of sleight of hand at an important point in the argument, and am perfectly willing to stare long and hard at some potentially embarrassing passages.

The apostles, for example, are intent upon building up a society in the image of Christ, fulfilling the lost promise that Adam was made in the image of God. Men thus become heavenly (*coelestes*), and reign with Christ, the *regnum* here being a 'consortium veritatis' (x.4; cf. xii.18). It is all somewhat static and interior. Even more striking is a passage worth quoting in full:

Merito praedicationem suam reti comparavit, quae in saeculum *veniens*, sine saeculi damno habitantes intra saeculum congregavit, modo retis, quod mare *penetrans* ita agitur *de profundo*, ut per omne elementi illius corpus *evadens*, clausos intra ambitum suum extrahat, nosque ex saeculo in lumen veri solis *educat* (xiii.9).

There is much more cosmology here than history, although there may be a certain momentum in those words which are italicised.[18] So at the last trump, the emphasis is again on a change from the corruptible to the spiritual, a change of status rather than an event (xxvi.1).[19] The very composition of man predisposes the interpreter to that scenario: man is above all a mind, like a light, infused into the body.[20] At the marriage feast attended by the wise and foolish virgins, the lamps are the lamps of the mind, and the marriage is one of corruption with incorruption. But then of course there is a touch of history here: the bride-groom comes! (xxvii.4) Similarly with the hen gathering her chicks about her: eggs are earthly, representing the body; but chicks have wings, and represent the promise of a spiritual life. Jesus, likening himself to the hen, has this task, therefore, of carrying us from one state to the other. However, the historical allusion is once again there: 'O Jerusalem, Jerusalem, killing the prophets . . . how often would I have gathered . . . you will not see me again, until you say, "Blessed is he who comes in the name of the Lord" ' (xxiv.11).

So we have to admit to a certain degree of confusion. When Hilary has brought us beyond the *Acts* to the plateau of expectation in the history of the church, we rightly ask where he will lead us next. But I do not think that he is then content merely to suggest some pro-gramme of cosmic 'ascent', in the Origenist style.[21] The *spatium poenitentiae* demands a moral response, yes, and by individuals; but this is not an alternative, adjunct, or postlude to history, but represents the same momentum being maintained at a new level — 'fidei haered-itas', as opposed to 'successio carnis' (ii.3). The historical *praedicatio*, no less than the human mind, is 'hominum corporibus infusa' (x.23); and morality has, after all, its own inner history: Adam, Christ, and we ourselves are all tempted by the same devil (iii.1; see also 5).

So it is not just that Hilary emphasises the importance of the inner life. He asserts, of course, that 'damnum corporis otiosum est, relicto voluntatis instinctu' (iv.21); that prayer is conducted within, a matter of *conscientia* more than *verba* (v.1); that when Matthew is called from his house, he is called from the body, so that Christ may enter his *mens*, to illuminate it and feed it upon the Gospel (ix.2). But, as we saw in some of those 'embarras-sing' passages above, this inner movement is constantly linked with, and is indeed a diverted impulse from, the historical images which we have detected. John the Baptist comes from the desert of Judaea, part of Hilary's history; but he stands also as a model of tough life and inner perfection: 'zonae autem praecinctio, efficax in omne opus bonum est apparatus: ut ad omne ministerium Christi *voluntate* simus accincti' (ii.2).[22] John' s disciples go to Christ, again a piece of the history; but Christ present there among his non-fasting apostles is a Christ in their mind (ix.3; cf. xviii.9), and after John's death, Christ will go in his boat (the church) to the desert, that is.'in vacua divinae cognitionis *pectora* transiturus' (xiv.9). In the case mentioned above, that of peace offered to worthy houses, as a representation of the church (an allusion that follows a step-by-step 'historical' description of the Jews, pagans and heretics that true believers are likely to meet) the peace itself is interior in quality, as witnessed by the phrases 'viscera miserationis', and 'intra propriam eorum conscientiam' (x.9). With reference more specifically to the end of things, we find the same conjunction:

'erit enim Dominus in claritatis suae adventu gentes possidens: earumque *mentibus* tamquam vector insidens'; but then the historical dimension: 'toto comitatus sui agmine praedicabitur, patriarcharum, prophetarum, atque apostolorum' (xxi.2). In the case of Peter's sheet, there are the more historical allusions to both the variety of peoples within the church and to its burial with Christ; but then the burial is said to be in a 'new tomb', 'scilicet in *pectus* duritiae gentilis quodam doctrinae opere excisum Christus infertur' (xxxiii.8).

Now I really think that Hilary is trying here to tie the individual into the historical process. To some extent (though I am well aware that one should not play with words) this reflects the very nature of allegory, as used by Hilary to extend the history within restricted events: 'in his quae gesta narrantur, subesse interioris intelligentiae ratio reperiatur' (xiv.3; see also xii.12). For his interpretation is always very much the interpretation of *gesta*, of the historical phenomenon. He never allows the *interior intelligentia* to take off, as it were, but to provoke clearer understanding within the boundaries of the event. 'Res evangelica, ut diximus, inter praesentis et futuri effectum, mediam utrique rei et congruam rationem temperavit: ut his, quae efficiebantur, futuri species adhaereret' (xix.3).[23] That other surface, the *futuri species*, overlaying history, is perceptible only to the inner eye; and only the moral subject can bring its *effectum* into play. Christ in the flesh is like the treasure in the field, and lucky is the man who finds it. The news of the find is given: the Gospel is preached, as a fact of history. But the 'utendi et possidendi . . . potestas' depends on your finding the price: you have to work for it (xiii.7). All are called; but it is the will that distinguishes man from man (xxii.6).

There is no need for laboured conclusions. Neither the occasion nor the research would justify them. Even the relationship of the *Commentary* to Hilary's other works and his career in general has yet to be explored. This is no more than an experiment and a beginning. I was simply anxious to discover whether texts of this sort could be used in such a way, to uncover an historical attitude. That much does seem clear: there is a history in the *Commentary on Matthew*. Even more important, Hilary does not bring his church to a level of triumphant achievement in the Christian Empire (which may or may not have been the 'Eusebian view'), but onto a plateau of doubt, danger, obscurity and individual moral challenge. How many other exegetes of the period were making the same point? The task ahead is clear enough.

That much, I confess, I hoped to find; but there are bonuses: the extent to which Hilary makes his later history an inner drama; the clear division between church and world; the frequent reflection (springing from a contrast with the Jews) on the relative importance of grace and of works. These are elements of the *praeparatio Augustiniana* at which I have already hinted.

There are also considerations attaching to *genre*. Hilary's ability to escape from the influence of Origen is obviously important, in the light of what was to happen in the 390s. Conversely Jerome's respect for his works is given reinforced significance. Hilary's alternative pedigree reaches back to Cyprian and Tertullian, and reminds us that an independent view of the church and its development had long been available to the Latin-speaking world.[24] Above all, we may revise our suppositions as to where Christian writers might betray their view of history. Here we have it embedded in a work closely allied to the homily, and therefore to traditions of public declamation and moral reform: history, so to speak, brought back to the marketplace.

Notes

1. It would be presumptuous to present here a bibliography on Eusebius. I particularly regret not having been able to consult, in the preparation of this paper, the current work by T. D. Barnes and R. M. Grant. I remain impressed by R. A. Markus, 'Church History and the Early Church Historians', *Studies in Church History* 11 (1975), 1–17. We have still to be grateful to A. Momigliano, 'Pagan and Christian Historiography in the Fourth Century' in A. Momigliano (ed.), *The Conflict between Paganism and Christianity in the Fourth Century* (Oxford 1963), 79–99. I am disappointed by the enclosed perspective of G. F. Chesnut, *The First Christian Histories* (Paris 1977), though it has the merit of suggesting implicitly that Eusebius' 'philosophy of history' is to be found most forcefully expressed in the *Praeparatio Evangelica*.

2. I had no prior access to Brian Croke's paper, published here (below 116–31), on the chronicle tradition. Some of his remarks may compel adjustment to my argument. I value in particular his subsequent inquiry as to where Sulpicius may stand in my scheme of things. On the other hand he reinforces my suspicion that it cannot be in *historiae* alone that we seek for philosophical, ideological, even political reflections on the past.

3. Jerome was tempted to the historian's task, before turning to hagiography or the *De viris illustribus*; and that conjunction should warn us historiographers to attend as much to Gennadius or the Cassiodorus of the *Institutiones* as we do, say, to Orosius or Gregory of Tours. As for Rufinus, his additions to his version of Eusebius have much to say about the recent importance of the ascetic in both church and state.

4. These reflections I attempted to substantiate in 'Jerome, his Failures and their Importance' in G. Harper and J. Veitch (eds), *The Heritage of Christian Thought* (Wellington 1979), 35–58.

5. Famous passages are discussed by J. Doignon, *Hilaire de Poitiers avant l'exil* (Paris 1971), 163, 169f. *Epp.* 57.6, 61.2, 82.7 and 84.7 are particularly important, because at those points Jerome links Hilary with his own exegetical methods. *Ep.* 58.9f. criticises Hilary for not addressing the *simplices*. For some earlier references and their context, see P. Rousseau, *Ascetics, Authority and the Church* (Oxford 1978), 102.

6. My suspicions here flow from points already made in Rousseau, *op. cit.* (n.5 above), 83f., 148f. I find them corroborated more than he would allow in the comments on Fortunatianus and Cyprian by Doignon (*op. cit.*, 208f., esp. 215).

7. Points emphasised by Doignon, on whose book (n.5 above) my dependence will be obvious. He dates the *Commentary* between 353 and early 355.

8. Hilary, *Comm. in Matthaeum* ix.6. All future references are to this work. In the preparation of this paper I was dependent on the text printed in *PL* 9.917–1078.

9. xviii.2, xii.20 fills out the theory.

10. Compare the return of the lost sheep to the company of ninety-nine angels (xviii.6).

11. The six thousand years occur also in Hilary's treatment of the Transfiguration 'after six days' (xvii.2).

12. 'Grossorum modo' I find obscure, being unable to follow Hilary's disquisition on the cultivation of figs.

13. Doignon, *op. cit.*, 189 emphasises how much 'history' is present here.

14. More social, perhaps, is the phrase 'deo civitas fidelium plebs est' (viii.4).

15. The reference is to *Acts* 10:9f.

16. xxiii.2; xxvii.1. Criticism of the clergy is very muted in the *Commentary*; but Hilary makes it clear that that is the *milieu* where the greatest purges are likely to be necessary (xxi.4, xxvii.2).

17. Note how it is just at this most human moment (in Gethsemane: 'Let this cup pass from me') that Jesus becomes, for Hilary, most divine (xxxi.4).

18. One might have italicised 'praedicatio' also, as marking a stage in Hilary's history.

19. There is an interesting link made between *praedicatio* and the angel's *tuba*, in the phrase 'publicae libertatis hortatu'.

20. v.4 is a very clear example.

21. The contrast is made very firmly by Doignon, *op. cit.*, 179. For more general doubts about dependence on Origen, even via Victorinus of Pettau: Doignon, *op. cit.*, 204.

22. And note the phrase in ii.3 'mores atque vita'.

23. The care represented by that word 'adhaereret' is rightly emphasised by Doignon, *op. cit.*, 179, not least as a contrast to Origen.

24. For the importance of these two authors, see Doignon, *op. cit.*, 183f., 210f. R. M. Grant has pointed out precisely how little Eusebius knew of them in 'The Uses of History in the Church before Nicaea', *Studia Patristica* 11 (Berlin 1972), 166–78.

The Origins of the Christian World Chronicle

Brian Croke

It has become traditional to dismiss the annalistic chronicles of late Antiquity as feeble and inferior products symptomatic of the decadence of a period of literary and cultural decline.[1] While there may be a trace of truth in that judgment, it is essentially an unhelpful and deficient explanation for the origins and early development of the Chronicle as a stylised historiographical genre in the period from the third to the sixth centuries. A more constructive approach can be based on the realisation that the Christianisation of the Roman world made new demands on the presentation and interpretation of the past, and that the Chronicle represents a response to such demands.[2]

This new genre had an historiographical purpose different from that of narrative history writing, so that it was now possible for particular individuals to write both simple annalistic chronicles and larger scale histories. In other words, the new style was not a substitute for the old but each had a life independent of the other. Eusebius, Jerome, Prosper, Cassiodorus, Isidore and Bede, for example, all compiled comprehensive chronicles in the course of a vast literary output that included narrative histories, a fact which by itself should arrest any tendency to impugn the intelligence and literary culture of an author when only his Chronicle survives.

Eusebius of Caesarea (*c.* 260–340) was, as he himself claimed and as was acknowledged by later writers, the first to establish the format and style of the Christian world chronicle.[3] His *Chronicle*, first published in the 280s and updated *c.* 326 was translated into Latin by Jerome (*c.* 345–419) and continued to 378.[4] Subsequent writers in the West continued Jerome and each other in order to keep the record continuous and contemporary, so that the chroniclers, like the church historians, constituted a kind of 'diachronic syndicate'.[5] Likewise, in the East, Eusebius' *Chronicle* formed the fountainhead of a long tradition of chronographic writing at Constantinople,[6] and its Armenian and Syriac translations greatly shaped the development of chronicle writing in these languages.[7] At the other end of the known world, in Ireland, Jerome's translation provided the backbone of the earlier Irish annals.[8]

While Eusebius' claim to originality is secure, little attention has been paid to the background and literary antecedents of his historiographical invention. It has been correctly observed that the chronicle, as a genre, owes a great deal to the tradition of anti-pagan polemic as it developed in the second and third centuries, particularly in Antioch and Alexandria.[9] At the same time attention has been drawn to the fact that, in terms of layout and content, the chronicle had forerunners in both Roman consular *fasti*[10] and Hellenistic and later Greek chronographical writing.[11] Yet, precisely what these various elements contributed to the Eusebian invention of the Christian world chronicle, and how they fitted together, have not been properly investigated and explained. Quite recently Momigliano has remarked, without offering any guidance himself, that 'the jump from the creation of scientific chronology in the third century B.C. (Eratosthenes) to the Christian canons [Eusebius] is a wide one'.[12] This paper aims to make an initial attempt to cover that wide jump; in particular it seeks to explain more fully than hitherto exactly how Eusebius came to compile his chronicle and what marked it off from previous chronographic works.

All literate societies, not least our own, have demonstrated a need to keep continuous records of various kinds, both private and public. We are all familiar with those impressive polished boards displayed in the vestibule of many a club and school which list the office-holders or award-winners and have space for many still to come. Keeping such a record has always been the natural inclination of such societies and communities and it has had the effect not only of promoting solidarity but also of reinforcing a group's identity and sense of tradition. From classical times, there survive lists of public officials from annual consuls[13] to the magistrates of individual regions of Rome itself;[14] lists of officials of the household of the Roman empress[15] and so on. Some of the most lasting and influential of such lists were those relating to particular temples or cults (for example, the priestesses of Hera at Argos[16] and the Arval brotherhood at Rome[17]) as well as the winners of athletic events like the *stadionikai* at Olympia and those of musical and dramatic contests.[18]

There was a great variety of such local records throughout the ancient world and these lists of kings, civic officials and competition winners provided, by their potential synthesis, the framework for a more elaborate and comprehensive chronological record of the past, in addition to being the framework of local histories. Indeed, Dionysius of Halicarnassus (*de Thuc.* 5) noted that Greek historiography originated in the local histories of individual cities. Since the chronicles and annals of late Roman and early Medieval/Byzantine times possess a format and character similar to some of these local records such as the *Fasti Ostienses*,[19] the question arises of the relationship and degree of continuity between them as well as the role of these Classical lists in shaping the nature and scope of the highly influential *Chronicle* of Eusebius.

As far as we know the Hittites did not conserve data for chronological purposes: at least no eponymous lists survive; so the honour of having the first king lists belongs to the Sumerians.[20] Their cultural successors, the Assyrians and Babylonians, not only kept lists of kings but other annalistic records based on astronomical diaries and with notices confined to imperial campaigns and victories. In addition, the Assyrians compiled detailed narratives of campaigns, in which the king played an essential role, and used lists of annual officials they called *limu*.[21] These latter records correspond to lists of Roman consuls or Athenian archons. Likewise, the Egyptians had lists of kings and records of imperial campaigns, sometimes with other events attached,[22] while the Israelites were meticulous in recording their genealogies and also possessed, on the model of the Assyrian king lists, chronicles of the royal-diary type.[23]

In the fifth century B.C. Herodotus (*Hist.* 2.77.1) found that the Egyptians were 'the most diligent of all men in preserving the memory of the past'. With respect to keeping detailed historical records the Greeks had a lesson to learn; while centuries later Josephus (*contra Apionem* 1.2) was able to disparage the accuracy of Greek history on the grounds that they were still less accustomed to keeping proper records like those of the Jews and Babylonians.

By the time of Herodotus, however, the Greeks were in fact beginning to grapple with problems of chronology and dating. Hecataeus had been trying to establish some sort of time scale for the heroic age, at the time when the earliest archon list was being set up in the Athenian *agora*,[24] and when the first list of Olympic victors was drawn up by Hippias of Elis.[25] So too, individual cities had their local origins and history reconstructed and kept up-to-date as an annalistic record. These *horographiai*, as they were known, were especially common in Ionian cities but had their counterparts elsewhere.[26] In fact the most celebrated of all local histories was that of Athens and was the basis of the successive 'Atthido-graphers'.[27]

It was in the late fifth century B.C. with the availability of public lists that more elaborate accounts of the past could be attempted, now that some degree of synchronism among these diverse and scattered local records was possible. So far as we can tell, Hellanicus of Lesbos made extensive use of these lists in his work,[28] although it was not until the time of Timaeus in the third century that the potential for a more comprehensive history with a common numerical rather than eponymous dating — that is by Olympiads — was fully exploited.[29] Throughout the fourth century B.C. local histories continued to be written while there was a proliferation of lists of local office-holders, priests and victors.[30] Yet the absence of any common chronological yardstick prevented the development of the widespread synchronisms essential for comparing and narrating the simultaneous history of several states. So it was left to the Hellenistic era — alert to the unity of the Greek world and its past — and to the city of Alexandria in particular to fill this gap. One of the most significant aspects of the new society of Ptolemaic Alexandria, and this point deserves emphasis, was the presence there of a large Jewish community alongside both the descendants of the ancient Egyptians and the more recent Greeks. Sooner or later the problem was bound to arise concerning the respective antiquity of the Greeks, Jews and Egyptians, and the careful attention to records by the latter two provided the potential for settling the question.[31]

In the early third century B.C. the Egyptian priest, Manethon, compiled a list of Egyptian dynasties which he compared with the chronology of the Hebrews and other oriental nations, and five hundred years later Eusebius relied on this for his account of the Egyptian dynasties.[32] Thereafter Jewish scholars at Alexandria refined and expanded their calculations.[33] Demetrius wrote lengthy genealogies in an attempt to establish the precise chronology of the Genesis narrative,[34] while a writer called pseudo-Eupolemus (*c.* 200) first tried to identify the Noachite generations with their Babylonian and Hellenic equivalents.[35] By the second century the Greeks had become (for the Jews) the main target of chronological polemic. The issue at stake now — and the implications for the history of philosophy and culture were profound — was how the chronology of Greek history meshed with that of the Hebrews. Did Moses steal ideas from Plato or vice-versa? Perhaps the most successful attempt at this kind of research was that of a Palestinian, Eupolemus, writing about 158. His calculations demonstrated that Moses had given the alphabet to the Phoenicians who had in turn passed it on to the Greeks.[36]

Consequently, by the first century A.D. in the time of Josephus the comparative chronology of Greek and Hebrew history had long been well established although in the volatile society of Alexandria the issue continued to burn. What had been happening, though, in the three centuries during which this chronological analysis was slowly maturing was that the style and methods of calculation had become increasingly detailed and elaborate. It had produced a full-scale synchronism of Hebrew history with that of the Egyptians and Babylonians and, to an increasing extent, the Greeks too. The necessary research had doubtless been made easier and been largely concentrated at Alexandria because of the unique library built up there.[37]

It was the availability of so many works that gave rise to the creation of a new universal chronology of Greek history. The most celebrated of these works of Hellenistic chronography was that of Eratosthenes (*c.* 275–194 B.C.) who composed, while librarian at Alexandria, a schematic unified history of the Greek world from Troy to the time of Alexander.[38] It has failed to survive. The other important chronological work of this period was the *Chronika* of Apollodorus which was dedicated to the king of Pergamum. Although Apollodorus' work was based on Eratosthenes he had done most of his research at Alexandria.[39] Both Eratosthenes and Apollodorus seem to have set out their books on an Olympiad scale. In these new chronicles there was a certain completeness and comprehensiveness characteristic of the Hellenistic view, and they provided useful handbooks for reckoning and research. In addition they contained much important historical information. From the preface to Apollodorus' *Chronika*, preserved in a later work, we can see precisely what sort of material such a chronicle could be expected to contain: destruction of cities, migration of races, games, alliances, treaties, deeds of kings, lives of famous men and so on.[40]

The need for disseminating this type of presentation of the past more widely is reflected in the so-called *Parian Marble* in which the writer prefaces his work by explaining that he has compiled his annalistic account from all sorts of writings and histories. It covers the period from Kekrops (1581 B.C.) to 264/3 B.C., dating first by kings, then by archons.[41] Like Apollodorus' *Chronika*, the *Parian Marble* bears many resemblances to the chronicle of Eusebius and its continuators. It contains great battles and victories, political events, establishments of games and festivals, literary figures (for example Homer, Hesiod, Sappho, Aeschylus) plus natural phenomena like comets, eclipses and earthquakes.[42]

A strictly annalistic record like the *Parian Marble* easily lent itself to interpolation, at least in normal manuscript form; that is to say, it was easy to insert under particular years extra events culled from other sources and these would become less detectable than normal glosses. This is certainly the case with the numerous chronicles of late Antiquity. However, by chiselling up his record the author of the Parian chronicle averted this sort of contamination just as did those who composed the numerous *fasti* at Rome and elsewhere during the reigns of Augustus and Tiberius.[43] The increased sophistication of chronographical composition represented by the *Parian Marble* and influenced by the work of Eratosthenes and his contemporaries, gave rise to other works in which various king lists and/or history in a universal framework in the Alexandrian tradition is reflected in various Olympiad chronicles. Some of these exist in only a single scrap of papyrus, for example the Oxyrhynchos chronicle in which Roman events are sandwiched into what is essentially a record of Greek history.[44]

One of the most successful of these chronicles, it appears, was that of Phlegon writing in Tralles in the time of Hadrian. His work, which apparently summarised the period 776 B.C. to *c.* A.D. 140, was being consulted in the sixth century at Alexandria and by Photius at Constantinople in the ninth.[45] Once again the influence of the chronographical tradition we saw in Apollodorus and the Parian chronicle is evident. In a fragment quoted by Photius which covers the years 72/69 B.C. we read of the siege of Asimos by the Roman general

Lucullus (cos. 74), an earthquake and the birth of Vergil.[46] It was just such an Olympiad Chronicle which formed the framework for Eusebius' notices of events in both Greek and Roman history.[47]

Meanwhile, at Rome the same Hellenistic differentiation of style and content in chronographical works was maintained. On the one hand, records of local office-holders, particularly consuls and *triumphatores*, were kept up-to-date, and in the time of Augustus and his successors there were various attempts to put these records onto stone, while there arose other local chronicles (on the model of the *Parian Marble*) which are misleadingly called *fasti*.[48] Besides these, the Romans had developed a strong tradition of what they labelled *annales* based originally on the *tabulae* of the priests and becoming elaborated much like the work of the Atthidographers.[49]

Nonetheless, the Romans did not completely ignore the achievements of Alexandria in defining the scope of universal chronography. There was a sudden outburst of activity at the time Cicero was engaged in his antiquarian researches in the 50s and 40s. Copies of Apollodorus' *Chronika* were available at Rome: Atticus, for example, possessed one.[50] In fact it was at precisely this time that Nepos compiled his *Chronica* which was largely a translation of Apollodorus.[51] Atticus too composed an annalistic record of events in Rome itself,[52] while Varro is attributed with a *liber annalis* about which nothing else is known.[53] This efflorescence of chronographical writing seems to have petered out as abruptly as it started. The works of the local historians of Rome – the 'annalists', who arranged their histories according to the sequence of years – survived, however, and the tradition continued in an abbreviated form in the historical works of Velleius Paterculus, Florus and the later (fourth-century) epitomators.[54]

When Eusebius came to write his *Chronicle* in the late third century he had this rich tradition of classical chronographical writing to draw upon, so he made full use of Apollodorus, Eratosthenes and the later writers who collected and synchronised lists of kings and officials – Castor of Rhodes, Alexander Polyhistor, and the anonymous Olympiad chronicler in particular. As we shall see, Eusebius' highly intricate format and ambitious scope presupposes a total view of the unity and span of history. It takes for granted, although it begins with Abraham, a fixed starting point in the human story and that the history of all known kingdoms and countries can be fitted into a single calculated sweep. This authentic universal history had only become possible of course with Christianity although the Romanisation of the whole Mediterranean had considerably expanded the Hellenistic concept of universal history,[55] and historians like Diodorus were able to combine this perspective with a Stoic view of Providence in history.[56]

It is manifest from the very sources Eusebius uses in his chronicle that he was most indebted to the Alexandrian tradition of chronographical writing. Another, again particularly Alexandrian, preoccupation which is evident in the very purpose of the chronicle is the role of chronographical argument in the arsenal of Christian polemic. Indeed, this is probably the most important element in explaining the nature and purpose of Eusebius' chronicle, just as it significantly shaped the equally new genre of ecclesiastical history.[57]

As noted above, the Jewish communities of the great Hellenistic cities, especially Antioch and Alexandria, had become embroiled in an interminable debate over the relative antiquity of Moses and Plato.[58] Josephus, for example, in his treatise against the views of Apion gave a clear statement of the issue and dismissed it swiftly since the documents of the Greeks were unreliable, compared with those of the Jews who maintained accurate genealogical records. He went on to prove his point by basing his case on Manethon and the Babylonian priest, Berosus.[59]

Forced to defend and explain itself against the formidable attacks of scholars like Celsus and Porphyry, Christianity, particularly at Alexandria, soon began to make its own the tested arguments of Josephus. Moreover, these arguments became central to the issue and as they developed they acquired greater sophistication and conviction so that ultimately Eusebius could say in a definitive and comprehensive work of apologetics, the *Praeparatio Evangelica* (written *c.* 313/4):

> Now it would be well to examine their chronology, I mean the dates at which Moses and the prophets after him flourished: since this would be one of the most conclusive evidences for the argument before us, that before dealing with the learned men among the people we should first decide about their antiquity.[60]

Eusebius had long seen the self-evident fact that had not always been fully appreciated, that is, the way forward on this question was to tighten up the chronological proof. The *Praeparatio Evangelica* represented the culmination of a century of chronological argument and research centred in the tradition of the so-called catechetical school at Alexandria. Before moving to this, however, it is necessary to emphasise the importance of chronology in the Christian view of man, his past and destiny.

In their formative early stages the Christian communities were concerned with a not too distant Second Coming (*parousia*) but slowly came to accept that God's time was not man's and that the *parousia* might be generations away. Attention then focussed on Psalm 90:2: 'A thousand years to you are like one day', and the idea gained currency that the world's life span would be 6,000 years on the analogy of Creation (Gen. 1). So in order to calculate the Second Coming one had to establish when the world began, the date of the Incarnation and where the present age stood in this scheme.[61] A parallel and increasing concern of early Christian chronography was calculation of the date of Easter but that is something that remains outside the scope of the mainstream of chronographical development.

The other major clue to the Christian teleology was embodied in the prophecy of the four kingdoms in the Book of Daniel. The Christians came to identify the fourth kingdom not with the Seleucids but with Rome. This necessitated the development of a chronology which effectively interpreted the 'seventy weeks of years' in Daniel 9:24 and was able to accommodate Christ's nativity.[62] Tertullian (*c.* 160–225), for example, employed a careful computation of the Hellenistic monarchs and the lengths of their reigns in his explanation (*adv. Jud.* 8); while Eusebius later set out the various attempts, particularly that of Julius Africanus, at explaining the chronology of Daniel from a Christian viewpoint.[63] When Augustine came to consider the question he refrained from working over the detailed computations once more but acknowledged that this had been satisfactorily unravelled by several of his scholarly predecessors (*de civ. Dei* 18.3.4). The chronological explanation had now been settled.

The development of the Christian interpretation of history herefore had as its cornerstone the necessity for an accurate chronology of the whole of human history. In the course of time these computational explanations became progressively more sophisticated and elaborate. At the same time anti-Christian critics like Porphyry needed to counter-attack with equally sophisticated alternative explanations of the chronology of world history. Porphyry's demolition of the Christian version of Daniel in the twelfth book of his *Against the Christians* became a classic,[64] while it is not unlikely that Eunapius' denigration of chronicles was aimed at a primarily Christian obsession.[65] This preoccupation with chronology was reinforced by the increasing need for the Christians to show that their religion was not a discordant novelty but did in fact possess a respectable antiquity. This was done by explaining the continuity with the Hebrew nation, in the context of the idea that all religions and nations ultimately spring from a common fount[66] — which returns us to the issue at hand.

The Christian apologists took over the firmly established arguments for the priority of Hebrew history over that of the Greeks,[67] and eventually absorbed the Old Testament as the precursor of God's plan. Justin (*fl.* 150–60) first made the point that Moses' account of the creation had been used by Plato, thus asserting the priority of the Jewish scriptures (*Apol.* 1.44, 51, 54, 59). This idea was passed on to his pupil Tatian (*ad Graecos* 1.1, 31–41) who described Moses as the first historian (the later Byzantine view) and in order to demonstrate the fact that Moses predated Homer drew on the genealogies of the Chaldaeans, Phoenicians and Egyptians, making use of Eratosthenes and Apollodorus. His work reaches its finale with various calculations using Olympiad dating and lists of kings (*ad Graecos* 41). Tatian was probably writing at Antioch.[68]

A contemporary of Tatian and bishop of Antioch, Theophilus, concluded his work to Autolycus (*c.* 180) with several chapters of detailed chronology. He aims, so he says, 'to give you a more accurate demonstration, God helping me, of the historical periods, that you may see that our doctrine is not modern nor fabulous, but more ancient and pure than all the poets who have written in uncertainty' (*ad Autol.* 3.16). Theophilus then proceeds to provide detailed genealogies and synchronistic arguments based on the Pentateuch, Manethon, Josephus and Menander the Ephesian (*ad Autol.* 3.23–7). Yet he shows no clear understanding of the totality of universal history.

Meanwhile in the West, at least in the influential Latin circles of Carthage, Tertullian had become aware of the significance of Moses' predating the Trojan War. Although leaving the detailed computations for the future because of the length involved (*non tam difficile est nobis exponere quam enorme, nec arduum, sed interim longum*), he realised that a comprehensive table of synchronisms which would demonstrate the priority of Hebrew history could be compiled from the proper sources: Manethon, Berosus, Menander the Ephesian, Thallos and others (*Apol.* 19.1–8). More elaborate exposition of the argument developing in both East and West is found in the *Miscellanies* of Clement of Alexandria who may well have been a pupil of Tatian.[69] In a lengthy discussion, drawing on a host of ancient authorities and in the perspective of Hellenistic chronography (using Eratosthenes and Apollodorus), Clement provides what amounts to a chronology of history from Moses to the present day.[70] He demonstrates a new thoroughness and comprehensive view in this chronological polemic. Clement's successor in the school at Alexandria, Origen, also wrote a *Miscellanies* which may have been consciously constructed as a continuation of Clement. It certainly included a discussion of the chronology of Daniel.[71] Elsewhere, in his answer to the anti-Christian critique of Celsus, Origen adopted these arguments of the apologists quoting the authority of Josephus and Tatian (*contra Celsum* 1.16, 4.11).

This leads to an important point, for it is in the person of Origen and the school of Alexandria that the pioneers of Christian chronography — Julius Africanus, Hippolytus and Eusebius — thread together, and it is in the nature of the arguments of which Origen was master and in the tradition of Alexandrian Christianity in which he originally taught that the usefulness and necessity of chronography became clear and established.

Julius Africanus had been attracted to Alexandria by the spell of Origen and there wrote in *c.* 221 five books under the title *de temporibus* (chronographiai).[72] He apparently set out to take the argument of Clement a step further by synchronising the whole of sacred history, or at least the whole of the Old Testament with secular (Greek and Oriental) history. As he explains in his preface:

> By seizing upon one action in Hebrew history contemporary with an action narrated by the Greeks and adhering to it, while either deducting or adding and indicating what Greek or Persian or any one else synchronised with the Hebrew action, I shall perhaps succeed in my aim.[73]

In other words, what Africanus wrote was not an annalistic chronicle like that of Eusebius but provided lists of synchronisms and genealogies, making full use of the chronographical sources familiar at Alexandria: Alexander Polyhistor, Manethon, Castor of Rhodes and so on in order to link sacred and profane history.[74]

The first to take advantage of his work was one of Africanus' coevals at Rome, another Greek who knew Origen and was much imbued with Alexandrian theology, Hippolytus, who wrote a *Chronika* in *c.* 234/5.[75] It is not unlikely that Africanus' work provided the impetus for Hippolytus' venture. Hippolytus did not compose an annalistic chronicle of world history either but a record of history from Adam to his own day, relying on the Old Testament generational reckoning, interspersed with lists of mountains and rivers and concluding with a catalogue of Roman emperors and the length of their reigns. Hippolytus intended to make it easier for the not so learned to appreciate the context of biblical history.[76]

When Origen was obliged to transfer his school to the no less cosmopolitan city of Caesarea, this chronological activity at Alexandria came to an abrupt halt. It was at Caesarea, however, that Eusebius came to know and admire the work of Origen; he even completed a defence of Origen begun by his own mentor Pamphilus and he wrote on Origen at some length in the *Church History*.[77]

It was clearly the tradition of Alexandrian Christian chronography preserved in the school at Caesarea that attracted Eusebius to this kind of work, provided him with the necessary materials and suggested the next stage in its development.

In the tenth book of his massive *Praeparatio Evangelica* Eusebius, as noted above, defined the main challenge to Christian chronography and set out his chronological method, quoting all the traditional authorities — Tatian, Clement and Africanus. Furthermore, he claimed originality for working out a method of counting backwards and forwards from key dates. All ultimately revolves around the date of Moses. Eusebius noted that others had attempted to establish the date of Moses and then went on to explain his own approach to the question. He begins by taking two epochal events: the beginning of Christ's public life in the fifteenth

year of Tiberius (Luke 3:1) and the rebuilding of the temple in Jerusalem in the second year
of Darius (Ezra 4:24). The interval between these dates is 548 years from the first year of
the 65th Olympiad (520/19 B.C.) to the fourth year of the 201st Olympiad (A.D. 28/9).
From here Eusebius was able to reckon backwards: from the second year of Darius to the
1st Olympiad (776 B.C.) is 256 years so this period in Jewish history takes one back to the
350th year of Uzziah in the era of the prophet Isaiah. Since Greek historians and chronographers counted a period of 408 years from the fall of Troy to the first Olympiad, then
continuing to reckon backwards in Jewish history brings us to the third year of Labdon.
Moses lies another 328 years further back than that and is contemporary with the Greek
giant Kekrops. This means quite simply that Moses was earlier than all the gods and heroes
of Greek mythology. Finally there are still another 505 years back to Abraham, the same
interval from Kekrops to king Ninus of Assyria.

Establishing the date of Moses was the key problem in the whole apologetic tradition.[78]
The scholarly predecessors cited by Eusebius had reached a variety of conclusions, the most
widely accepted being a date of 700–600 years before the Trojan War, usually by making
him a contemporary of Ogyges of Athens.

Eusebius therefore provided a novel calculation but one that facilitated synchronisation
of Hebrew and pagan history. This research had already been accomplished by the late third
century when the results were incorporated into the structure and span of his *Chronicle*.

Eusebius' *Chronicle* was divided into two parts.[79] In the first (*chronographia*) he set out
what amounted to the raw material for the second part, the chronological tables. This raw
material consisted of extracts of lists of rulers and officials compiled from the standard
chronographical sources: Apollodorus, Castor of Rhodes and others. In addition to copying
out the relevant sections of his sources Eusebius provided occasional comment on them plus
a standard chronological summary for each kingdom. This first book is preserved only in an
Armenian version and even then the last portion recording the consuls and emperors of
Rome is missing.

The chronicle proper, or *canons*, which is best preserved in the Latin translation of
Jerome, began with Abraham and recorded each year from then to the year A.D. 277/8.
This was the most revolutionary feature of Eusebius' work. Whereas Hellenistic and Roman
chronographers had compiled a continuous annalistic record of certain portions of the past,
and whereas previous Christian writers had attempted to synchronise sections of Greek and
Hebrew history, Eusebius surpassed all these efforts by providing a thorough synchronisation
of all known nations from the beginning of recorded time right up to the present. To achieve
this he hit upon a novel but extremely intricate format in which the years of individual
rulers were recorded vertically with different kingdoms juxtaposed in parallel columns. The
overriding framework of the chronicle, however, was the year of Abraham with every tenth
year marked in the extreme left-hand column. The other universal numerical dating system,
that by Olympiads, was employed from 776 B.C.

Since the chronicle began with Abraham it started out with three columns (Hebrews,
Assyrians, Egyptians). As the work progressed new columns had to be added when the time
arose — Persians, Greeks (various), Romans; while others dropped away when they became
effectively extinguished by conquest. As Eusebius approached his own day the format had
become far simpler. All that was required now, besides the years of Abraham and Olympiads,
was a column for Roman emperors and Persian kings. Throughout the chronicle in the
middle of the page, or, when two pages were necessary, at the adjacent edges of each page,

were recorded particular events or persons under a particular year. On the left-hand side were notices of biblical history (prophets, etc.) and on the right-hand side notices of pagan history (battles, literary figures, etc.). What Eusebius achieved by this mammoth work was the incorporation of the whole of human history, Christian and pagan, into a single grid. This enabled anyone interested to see at a single glance the relationship between various kingdoms and the relative antiquity of individuals and events, just as he tells us he intended: 'to offer the effortless discovery' of what particular time of Greek or barbarian history corresponded with which of the Hebrew prophets, priests and kings, and so he concludes: 'we will locate everything in its place with the utmost brevity' (*Praef.*).

Such a work was an invaluable reference tool to increasing numbers of Christian scholars and apologists. It illustrated with absolute clarity the prior antiquity of the Hebrew-Christian nation and provided an indispensable handbook for the historical chronology and exegesis of the Old Testament. For example, in his famous *Commentary on Daniel* Jerome was primarily concerned to refute Porphyry's chronological reconstruction by showing that the 'seventy weeks of years' (Dan. 9:24) embraced the time of Christ. So, in the course of explaining the chronology of the Hellenistic kings and the computations required he had only to turn to Eusebius' *Chronicle* —which he duly did, and he made thorough use of it.[80] Indeed, Eusebius had made use of his own chronicle in the *Ecclesiastical History* in order to clarify the date of the Incarnation (1.4.12, cf. 1.1.2), and it played an important ancillary role in the chronological argument presented in the *Praeparatio Evangelica* (10.9.1).

In the decisive years of the later fourth century many well-educated Romans such as Ambrose, Augustine and Paulinus of Nola turned to Christ. When they came to Christianity fully imbued with the consummate literary taste and style acquired from their classical education they were confronted with a view of the past that was foreign to the classical view in its scope and purpose. They were able to locate this in Jerome's recent translation of Eusebius' *Chronicle*, judiciously augmented for a Latin audience and continued to his own day (378).

Consequently, we find Paulinus of Nola writing to Alypius, a protégé of Augustine, in 395· to tell him that he has made arrangements to send him a copy of Jerome's *Chronicle* (*Ep.* 3.3). Paulinus does not have his own copy but he was able to obtain one from a certain Domnio at Rome, as Alypius had suggested to him. A few years later (*c.* 403) Paulinus was asked by Sulpicius Severus, a Gallic nobleman who was engaged in a summary of Biblical and Christian history, for advice ' on those points not of national but of universal history on which you are ignorant' (*Ep.* 28.5). Paulinus confesses that he had never himself become involved in collecting and collating historical data. In fact, so he says, even in the days when he was immersed in Latin literature he used to give the historians a wide berth.

It is apparent, nonetheless, that Paulinus was familiar with the problems of Christian chronology and he knew how to make use of Eusebius/Jerome. He was clearly able to provide some information for Severus whose project involved him 'in analysing and comparing the accounts of past ages in the interest of our faith' (*Ep.* 28.5). Again we note the pragmatic apologetic purpose of Christian chronography. Finally, Paulinus tells us that the particular queries he was unable to handle himself he passed on to a known expert, Rufinus of Aquileia, with the frank advice that 'if he cannot account for the vagaries in the reckoning of years and reigns which rightly trouble you as gaps in history' then no-one else can.

Through Paulinus we catch a glimpse of the involvement of the newly Christianised aristocracy in studying and explaining the Christian account of world history and its chronology. It was from Ambrose at Milan that Augustine first learnt the utility of history (*de doct. crist.* 43, cf.*Retract.* 2.24), and his close knowledge of the Eusebian chronology proved an important instrument in both his own understanding and explanation of human history, especially in the *de civitate Dei*, and the exegesis of scripture.[81] It enabled him to argue, for instance, that Plato could not have heard Jeremiah on his visit to Egypt.[82] He also quotes the chronicle for the date of Abraham (*de civ. Dei* 16.16), the duration of the Assyrian empire (4.6) and for many other points, always assuming and sometimes positively asserting the accuracy of the Eusebian chronology (12.11, 18.2–8, 13, 25, 27, 31, 37, 47).

Finally, it is in Augustine's programme for the education of all children that we find the clearest statement of the role and importance of Christian history and chronology:

> Anything, then, that we learn from history about the chronology of past times assists us very much in understanding the scriptures, even if it be learnt without the pale of the church as a matter of childish instruction. For we frequently seek information about a variety of matters by use of the Olympiads and the names of consuls; and ignorance of the consulship in which Our Lord was born, and that in which he suffered has led some into the error of supposing that he was forty-six years of age when he suffered.
>
> (*de doct. crist.* 2.28).

At a single blow Eusebius had taken the tradition of Alexandrian chronological argument which had been becoming progressively more elaborate to its limit. This he achieved by combining two features of Alexandrian literary culture which he had absorbed at Caesarea: that of universal history exemplified by Eratosthenes and Apollodorus; and that of Judaeo-Christian/Greek polemic. To these he added a universal time scale he invented himself so that it was now possible for the whole of human history to be laid out end-to-end. Within this complex chronographical edifice, Eusebius inserted a variety of historical notices according to the practice of Hellenistic chronographical literature explained in Apollodorus' preface and illustrated by the *Parian Marble* and other Olympiad chroniclers — battles, treaties, lives of famous men, inventions, games, natural disasters and so on.

The *Chronicle* of Eusebius was a very intricate document and copying of its multicoloured contents must have been very difficult. What happened, since the work was so popular and useful, was that the format was modified and simplified. At the same time the local chronicles and other records that had always been maintained now won a new prominence. The *Chronicle* had made it possible to fit local history into the context of God's time. Jerome's translation is a good example of this. Not only did he update Eusebius to 378 but he built into it a larger number of notices relating to Roman history where Eusebius had been particularly thin. Jerome was continued with the same format and content by others such as Prosper in mid-fifth-century Gaul and Marcellinus in sixth-century Constantinople, who were themselves continued in turn. At the same time the local chronicles of places like Rome, Ravenna, Arles, Antioch and Constantinople were sometimes written up on the Eusebian model and attached to a manuscript of the *Chronicle*. This explains why so many of these anonymous local chronicles survived in some form. While writers in the West, or at least in Latin, were content to continue Jerome or one of his continuators, in the East the practice appears to have been quite different. These chroniclers chose to recopy or modify the totality of world history available in Eusebius' *Chronicle*, not just continue it. In fact the Byzantine chronographic tradition from the time of Panodorus and Annianus in the early fifth century began not with Abraham but with Adam.

It was, as we have seen, the demands of apologetic which provided the intial impulse for the production of Eusebius' *Chronicle*. By the late fourth/early fifth century that demand had diminished so that the interest was now not so much in the details or accuracy of Eusebius' reconstruction but its results. For the exegete and polemicist alike here was the full story of God's people on earth. For those still interested in establishing the correct date for Easter or those aiming to establish accurately the precise date for the origin of the world and for its duration – for all these Eusebius' *Chronicle* constituted a basic working document. From Ireland to the Orient the chronicle performed the same function and became the most popular mode of recording the past for a Christian public. The diversity in structure and style of content that soon arose only obscures the fact that the chroniclers of East and West could trace the canons of their art back to a single pragmatic document that grew out of the needs of early Christian apologists – the *Chronicle* of Eusebius of Caesarea.

Notes

1. For example, A. H. M. Jones, *The Decline of the Ancient World* (London 1966), 3: 'For the history of the west we are often reduced to bare annalists who give lists of the consuls with occasional notes of battles and church councils'; S. Dill, *Roman Society in the Last Century of the Western Empire* (London 1899), 441: '... jejune chronicles, arid in style, and often ludicrously capricious in their selection of events deemed worthy of narration, occasionally rousing the curiosity which they never satisfy'; F. Lot, *The End of the Ancient World and the Beginning of the Middle Ages* (New York 1961), 161: 'dry chronicles in which the facts of history are strung together'; implicit even in B. Croce, *History as the Story of Liberty* (London 1941), 18: 'when there is a sudden break or suspension in the process of civilised life, as there was in Europe in the early Middle Ages, then the writing of history almost ceases and relapses into barbarism together with the society to which it belongs'.

2. A. Momigliano, 'Pagan and Christian Historiography in the Fourth Century A.D.', in A. Momigliano (ed.), *The Conflict between Paganism and Christianity in the Fourth Century* (Oxford 1963), 83–5 (the clearest statement of the role of chronicles).

3. B. Croke, 'The Originality of Eusebius' Chronicle', *American Journal of Philology* 103 (1982), 195–200. For this and all the other complex problems presented by the versions and manuscripts of the chronicle: A. Mosshammer, *The Chronicle of Eusebius and Greek Chronographic Tradition* (Lewisburg–London 1979).

4. J. Karst, *Die Chronik des Eusebius* [*GCS* 20] (Leipzig 1911); R. Helm, *Die Chronik des Hieronymus* [*GCS* 47] (Berlin 1956). The most convenient edition, in that it incorporates the Greek excerpts and the Armenian version (in Latin translation) of the *Chronographia*, is A. Schoene, *Eusebii Chronicorum libri duo* (Frankfurt 1875, rp.

1967) vol. I. For the date of the chronicle: T. D. Barnes, *Constantine and Eusebius* (Cambridge, Mass. 1981), 111 (arguing for *c.* 280, which would make Eusebius 20 years of age at the time, an unlikely but not impossible fact) and R. M. Grant, *Eusebius as Church Historian* (Oxford 1980), 7–8 (arguing for a later date). Eusebius' role in the history of chronography is underestimated in J. W. Johnson, 'Chronological Writing: Its Concepts and Development', *History and Theory* 2 (1962), 124–45.

5.   R. A. Markus, 'Church History and the early Church Historians', *Studies in Church History* 11 (1975), 8.

6.   For the Byzantine chronographical tradition: H. Hunger, *Die hochsprachliche profane Literatur der Byzantiner* I (Munich 1978), 254–78 and the useful synthesis of C. Mango, *Byzantium: The Empire of New Rome* (London 1980), 189–200.

7.   Mosshammer, *op. cit.*, 29ff. and H. W. Thompson, *A History of Historical Writing* I (Gloucester, Mass. 1942, rp. 1967), 324–34.

8.   J. Morris, 'The Chronicle of Eusebius: Irish Fragments', *Bulletin of the Institute of Classical Studies* 19 (1972), 80–93 and K. Hughes, *Early Christian Ireland: Introduction to the Sources* (London 1972), 100.

9.   R. Helm, *Eusebius' Chronik und ihre Tabellenform* (Abh. Berl. phil.-hist. Kl. 1923, 4) (Berlin 1924), 1; S. Prete, *I Chronica di Sulpicio Severo* (Rome 1955), 105.

10.   R. L. Poole, *Chronicles and Annals. A Brief Outline of their Origin and Growth* (Oxford 1926), 9.

11.   A. Momigliano, 'Greek Historiography', *History and Theory* 17 (1978), 17 (= M. Finley (ed.), *The Legacy of the Greek World* (Oxford 1981), 175).

12.   *ibid.*, 17 (175).

13.   Degrassi, *Inscr. Ital.* XIII.1, 24–63 = *CIL* 1^2.1, 16–29.

14.   Degrassi, *Inscr. Ital.* XIII.1, 280–6.

15.   Degrassi, *Inscr. Ital.* XIII.1, 322–7, 332–3.

16.   Jacoby, *FGrH* 4, F74–84.

17.   Degrassi, *Inscr. Ital.* XIII.1, 296–9 = *CIL* 1^2.1, 70–1.

18.   For details: R. Laqueur, 'Lokalchronik', *RE* 13 (1926), 1087–8.

19.   Degrassi, *Inscr. Ital.* XIII.1, 182ff.

20.   H. Hoffner, 'Histories and Historians of the Ancient Near East. The Hittites', *Orientalia* 49 (1980), 330.

21.   A. K. Grayson, 'Histories and Historians of the Ancient Near East. Assyria and Babylonia', *Orientalia* 49 (1980), 150, 176.

22.   For example the Palermo stone (A. Gardiner, *Egypt of the Pharaohs* (Oxford 1961, rp. 1980), 62–4).

23.   J. van Seters, 'Histories and Historians of the Ancient Near East. The Israelites', *Orientalia* 50 (1981), 137–85, esp. 174–83.

24.   Jacoby, *FGrH* 323a, with Mosshammer, *op. cit.*, 8.

25.   Jacoby, *FGrH* 6, F2.

26.   Laqueur, *RE* 13 (1926), 1091ff.

27.   F. Jacoby, *Atthis. The Local Chroniclers of Ancient Athens* (Oxford 1949 rp. New York 1973).

28.   Jacoby, *FGrH* 4.

29. Polybius, *Hist.* 12.11.1. For the problem of reconciling various histories in this way: Diod. Sic. 1.4.

30. Diod. Sic. 1.26.5 with Laqueur, *RE* 13 (1926), 1091.

31. P. M. Fraser, *Ptolemaic Alexandria* (Oxford 1972), 495–519. The same historiographical impetus arose, with less thoroughgoing results, in Palestine (M. Hengel, *Judaism and Hellenism*, I (London 1974), 88–102).

32. Fragments in the Loeb Classical Library edition of W. G. Waddell, (Cambridge, Mass. 1950).

33. B. Wacholder, 'Biblical Chronology in the Hellenistic World Chronicles', *Harvard Theological Review* 61 (1968), 451; A. Momigliano, *Alien Wisdom. The Limits of Hellenisation* (Cambridge 1975), 92–4.

34. Jacoby, *FGrH* 273; 722, F1–7.

35. Jacoby, *FGrH* 724, F1–2.

36. Jacoby, *FGrH* 723, F1a–b.

37. Fraser, *op. cit.*, 320–35.

38. Jacoby, *FGrH* 241, with Fraser, *op. cit.*, 456–7.

39. Jacoby, *FGrH* 244, with Fraser, *op. cit.*, 457.

40. Jacoby, *FGrH* 244, T2.

41. Jacoby, *FGrH* 239 A.

42. For details: Laqueur, *RE* 14 (1928), 1885ff.

43. Documents in Degrassi, *Inscr. Ital.* XIII.1 with useful synthesis in V. Ehrenberg and A. H. M. Jones, *Documents Illustrating the Reigns of Augustus and Tiberius*[2] (Oxford 1955 rp. 1979), 32–55.

44. Jacoby, *FGrH* 255 = *P. Oxy.* 12 cf. *FGrH* 257a = *P. Oxy.* 2082 and the *Chronicum Romanum* (*FGrH* 252 = *IG* 14, 1297). The anonymous chronicle of *P. Oxy.* 1613 (*FGrH* 258) was possibly used by Eusebius (Jacoby, *FGrH* IIA. *Komm.*, 853).

45. Jacoby, *FGrH* 257.

46. Jacoby, *FGrH* 257, F12.

47. A controversial question for which see Mosshammer, *op. cit.*, 137 (identifying him with Cassius Longinus).

48. That is the name *fasti* embraces not only calendars but also what amount to annalistic chronicles.

49. On the vexed question of the *tabulae pontificum/annales maximi*: J. Crake, 'The Annals of the Pontifex Maximus', *Classical Philology* 35 (1940), 375–86; H. Peter, *Historicorum Romanorum Reliquiae* (Leipzig 1906–14) I, iiiff.; and the sensible remarks of W. Kierdorf, 'Catos *Origines* und die Anfänge der römischen Geschichtsschreibung', *Chiron* 10 (1980), 206ff.

50. Cicero, *ad Atticum* 12.2.3.2.

51. Fragments in Peter, *op. cit.*, II, 25–6 and for commentary: W. St. Clair, *Ancient Chronography and the Latin Chronographic Tradition from Cornelius Nepos to Sulpicius Severus* (Diss. Cornell 1972), 50–65 (considerably overrating the extent and significance of Nepos' work), and T. P. Wiseman, *Clio's Cosmetics* (Leicester 1979), 157–74. Nepos' *Chronicle* was still in demand in the fourth century, to judge from Ausonius, *Ep.* 14.

52. Its thoroughness was acknowledged by both Cicero (*Brutus* 15) and Nepos (*Atticus* 18). For fragments: Peter, *op. cit.*, II, 6–8 and exposition: St Clair, *op. cit.*, 70–7.

53. Peter, *op. cit.*, II, 24.

54. In this respect, therefore, the thesis of St Clair is fundamentally misconceived. With his emphasis on brevity Velleius Paterculus was the prototype of Florus, Festus, etc. (A. J. Woodman, 'Questions of Date, Genre and Style in Velleius: Some Literary Answers', *Classical Quarterly* n.s.25 (1975), 283ff.); while Sulpicius Severus was not the Christian counterpart of Nepos and Atticus but of Eutropius and Festus (Momigliano, *op. cit.* (n.2 above), 87).

55. A. B. Breebart, 'Weltgeschichte als Thema der antiker Geschichtsschreibung', *Acta Historica Neerlandica* 1 (1966), 20–1.

56. Diod. Sic. 1.5.

57. Markus, *op. cit.*, 6 and G. Downey, 'The Perspective of the Early Church Historians', *Greek, Roman and Byzantine Studies* 6 (1965), 63.

58. R. Mortley, 'The Past in Clement of Alexandria' in E. P. Sanders (ed.), *Jewish and Christian Self-Definition* (London 1980), 186–200. For the Christians as a nation: Momigliano, *op. cit.* (n.2 above), 90.

59. *contra Apionem* 1.4–8. On Berosus as chronographer: R. Drews, 'The Babylonian Chronicles and Berosus', *Iraq* 37 (1975), 39–55.

60. *PE* 10.2 with R. Goulet, 'Porphyre et la datation de Moïse', *Revue de l'histoire des religions* 184 (1977), 137–164.

61. In general: R. P. Milburn, *Early Christian Interpretations of History* (London 1954); R. Bainton, 'Ideas of History in Primitive Christianity' in *Early and Medieval Christianity* (Boston 1962); W. den Boer, 'Some Remarks on the Beginnings of Christian Historiography', *Studia Patristica* 4 (1959), 348–62 (rp. in *Syngrammata. Studies in Graeco-Roman History* (ed. H. Pleket *et al.*) (Leiden 1979), 23–37). L. Koep, 'Chronologie, Christliche', *Reallexicon für Antike und Christentum* 3 (1957), 50–9. Particularly useful still is A. Bauer, *Ursprung und Fortwirken der christlichen Weltchronik* (Graz 1910), cf. V. Grumel, 'Les premières ères mondiales', *Revue des Etudes Byzantines* 10 (1952), 93–108.

62. Bauer, *op. cit.*, 15–7 and commentaries on Daniel (especially that of Hippolytus, plus his *Heresies* and *Christ and Anti-Christ*).

63. *PE* 10.9; *Eclogae Propheticae* 3.45.

64. It will be observed that I overlook the Chronicle of Porphyry. The fact is that the fragments usually attributed to a Porphyrian chronicle (Jacoby, *FGrH* 260) come from his *Against the Christians*. Porphyry never did write a chronicle. For detailed justification of this view: B. Croke, 'Porphyry's Anti-Christian Chronology', *Journal of Theological Studies* n.s.34 (1983).

65. Frag. 1 (*FHG* IV, 12). Eunapius was basically taking issue with the *Chronika* of Dexippus, a comprehensive work in the classical chronographic tradition, but not an annalistic chronicle in the Eusebian sense.

66. Mortley, *op. cit.*, 190–4 and 'L'historiographie et les pères', in *Paganisme, Judaïsme, Christianisme: Mélanges M. Simon* (Paris 1978), 315–27.

67. Treated broadly in M. Friedländer, *Geschichte der jüdischen Apologetik als Vorgeschichte des Christentums* (Zurich 1903).

68. On Tatian: C. A. Crutwell, *A Literary History of Early Christianity* (London 1893, rp. New York 1971), 338 ff.

69. H. Chadwick, *Early Christian Thought and the Classical Tradition* (London 1966), 32.

70. *Stromata* 1.2ff. with Mortley, *op. cit.* (n.58 above), 194–200.

71. Chadwick, *op. cit.*, 72. Origen, *Strom.* IX and X used by Jerome, *In Dan.* I.iv.5a [*CCL* 75A, 811 = *PL* 25, 514].

72. For Africanus: H. Gelzer, *Sextus Julius Africanus und die byzantinische Chronographie* 2 vols, (Leipzig 1880, rp. in one vol. New York 1967).

73. M. J. Routh, *Reliquiae Sacrae* II^2 (Oxford 1846, rp. Hildesheim/New York 1974), fr. 22 (p. 26).

74. Mosshammer, *op. cit.*, 36–7, 146–57. It is often thought that Africanus wrote a world chronicle of the kind we find in that of Eusebius (P. Meinhold, *Geschichte der kirklichen Historiographie* I (Munich 1967), 82).

75. A. Bauer and R. Helm, *Hippolytus Werke IV. Die Chronik* (*GCS* 4) (Berlin 1955).

76. *Praef.* (*PL* 3.659–60 = *PG* 92.1041–3).

77. A relationship well explained in Barnes, *op. cit.*, 81–105.

78. Goulet, *op. cit.*, 137–64 and J. Sirinelli, *Les vues historiques d'Eusèbe de Césarée* (Dakar 1961), 497–515.

79. For what follows: Mosshammer, *op. cit.*, 21–166 and Barnes, *op. cit.*, 111–20.

80. *In Dan.* ix.24 (*CCL* 75A, 880 = *PL* 25, 549) and elsewhere.

81. *Quaest. in Heptateuchum* 1.2.25; 2.47, 70.

82. *de civ. Dei* 8.11 — made possible by 'a careful calculation of the dates which are to be found in the chronicles'.

The Logic of Retribution
in Eusebius of Caesarea

Garry W. Trompf

In May 312, Maximin Daia, according to the church historian Eusebius, promulgated an official rescript — a mixture of pagan ideology and imperial ordinance — responding to anti-Christian urban petitioners in the eastern provinces of the Roman Empire (*HE* 9.7, 1–15).[1] About three years had elapsed since the Roman world had been subjected, 'for the first, and indeed the last time', to the rule of six emperors at once.[2] Although included in this unprecedented 'sexvirate', however, by 312 Maximin was one of only four great power-contenders in a divided Empire.[3] As the nephew to Galerius, he was as dangerous to the church as his uncle had been; and he came to be considered a tyrant by the partisans of the pre-Christian Constantine,[4] who was the subsequent victor in the whole struggle.

The space given to Maximin's rescript in Eusebius' *Ecclesiastical History* is intriguing. The effort spent in translating such a long[5] un-Christian document was clearly not simply for the sake of thorough documentation (for which Eusebius is famous), nor was it just to underline the tyrannical deeds of Maximin, whose death marked the end of the 'enemies of godliness' in the first edition of Eusebius' work (*HE* 9.11.1).[6] Those factors are to be acknowledged, but there is more besides. To allow his readers to hear these last[7] pleas of paganism was of strategic importance in the overall structure of his history.

The rescript, which Eusebius copied from a tablet of Tyre, basically restates the perennial assumptions of Mediterranean paganism both official and parochial — namely that the honouring of the gods results in security and prosperity, while impiety brings suffering and shame.

> Zeus . . . presides over your far-famed city, he who protects your ancestral gods and women and children and hearth and home from all destruction . . . For who can be so senseless . . . as not to perceive that it is by the benevolent care of the gods that the earth does not refuse the seeds committed to it, nor render the hopes of the husbandman vain?
>
> (*HE* 9.12.8)

Unholy war will not erupt and neither hurricane nor earthquake strike where and when there is piety (εὐσέβεια), with sacrifice and veneration to propitiate the deities (9.12.8, 11, 14). Julian, Symmachus and Zosimus were to state it more palpably, perhaps, but the rescript points the bone at 'godless men' who have fallen into 'deadly error' and directs them to be expelled from the city to avoid 'pollution and impiety'. To obey was proclaimed a pious deed before the deathless gods, a deed which would provide witness, μαρτυρία, that the citizens and their descendants had received from Caesar's benevolence a worthy 'prize of the contest' for their conduct.[8] The rescript voices the prevailing and in this case official understanding of divine rewards and punishments. *Do ut des*, and woe betide those who do not have anything to offer.

It is precisely this popular logic, however, which Eusebius was trying to turn on its head. The Eusebian contention was that the unprecedented rending of the Roman world was the result of persecution against the Christians (*HE* 8.13; 14.11–12, 18). During the ten years of διωγμός (303–313), he maintained, the Empire fell into great confusion — unnavigable seas, the torturing of people attempting to travel between warring parts, and the constant fear of enemy attack (8.15.1–2). Not without a certain relish, therefore, Eusebius can describe how it was that (following the proclamation of the rescript, which he considers arrogant boasting (μεγαλαυχία) before the true God (9.7.16; 8.3, cf. 8.10.1)) famine, plague, a disease named 'anthrax', and an unfortunate war against the Armenians ravaged the (eastern) provinces (9.8.1–2).[9]

Eusebius' vivid sketch of this famine and pestilence (9.8.3–12) appears important for the unity of his history, because it recalls the shocking and detailed accounts of famine in Jerusalem during the Jewish War and the plague of Alexandria in the days of Dionysius the Great, both calamities being highlighted by Eusebius through long earlier quotations from his sources (3.6.1–28: 7.21.2–22.10).[10] The great suffering of the Jews, it is plainly stated, was God's punishment for their impiety (δυσσέβεια) towards the Christ (3.7.1, cf. 3.5.6–7), and (although parallels were rather unexploitable) Eusebius also implies that Alexandria's pestilence took its toll while the virtuous and peace-loving Gallienus was struggling to supplant his wicked opponents (7.23.12–23.3, cf. 21.1; 22.1). Thus the situations are not so different from Maximin's promulgation of the rescript.[11] In the more recent situation Maximin was the most evil antagonist of the beloved Constantine, whose victory and order of peace were just around the corner (313).[12] In Eusebius' mind, then, the dreadful calamities which follow the rescript both call the lie to false indigenous assumptions and foreshadow the toppling of its tyrannical author, who must soon submit to Providence's vindication of the Christians (9.10.3–15).

Before Constantine eventually achieved final supremacy over his three rivals, he had already sought to present himself as the legitimate defender of the 'Senate and *populus Romanus*' against tyranny. Both he and Licinius memorialised the victory over Maxentius in 312 with this intent (cf. 9.9.11, *VC* 1.38), although Licinius was subsequently to fall into the category of tyrant himself, Constantine having to quell his uprisings (10.9.2–6, cf. *VC* 2.11–18). Eusebius' striking emphasis on the toppling of the three tyrants in the last books of his *Historia Ecclesiastica*, then, clearly plays on the official Constantinian ideology (the mature form of which Eusebius himself may have had some part in fashioning).[13] We find an authorised general statement of Constantine's more developed approach to the logic of retribution in his *Letter to the Provincials* (of 323). It notes how those who in former times have striven to place 'the basis of human affairs' on 'justice and goodness' have succeeded in

> the accomplishments they undertook, obtaining all kinds of temporal blessing [lit. sweet fruit from such pleasing roots] as a reward, while those working in unjust insolence, and driven mindlessly to oppose the Almighty (τὸ κρεῖττον) or the human race . . . were punished.
>
> (*VC* 2.25, cf. 28).[14]

In essence the letter simply appropriates the traditional Graeco-Roman assumptions so eagerly exploited by Maximin but suggests that Christianity, not paganism, brings those results which tyrants cannot achieve. It has done part of Eusebius' job for him, in turning the previously official line upside down.[15]

The Eusebian approach to *retributio*, it naturally follows, shares some basic ingredients with the new imperial platform. With an attitude for which he has been more than once criticised, the historian has espoused the naive, and some would add shallow, optimism of the welcome moment.[16] Moreover, he has exerted himself in defence of the Constantinian order by accentuating the injustices of the defeated triad and thus the deservedness of their defeats and dismal ends. Even Licinius — whose persecutions, after all, were localised and mainly concentrated on the army;[17] who was probably innocent of the official charges of tyranny brought against him;[18] and whom Eusebius had at first acclaimed, along with Constantine, as a pious ruler loving virtue and God (*HE* 9.11.9) — is eventually portrayed as the worst of all tyrants. With Licinius evil seems to reach its highest pitch, so that he appears rather like the Platonic τύραννος (opposed to φύσις), taking madness to the utmost, subverting time-honoured laws, exacting wealth for himself, revaluing land, imposing banishment,[19] all before the best Roman governance of them all is established.[20] Furthermore, it is shown of Licinius' defection in particular that he himself had foolishly forgotten the new understanding of retributive principles and the punishments which would be visited on those great tyrants who persecuted the Christians and who 'made war on God Himself' (*VC* 1.59, *HE* 10.8.9.)[21]

If these elements of Eusebiana match and sustain the new 'court ideology', however, one must still remember that the historian bishop of Caesarea was interested in many more episodes than those which had so recently seen the Empire reunified and the Christians given succour (cf. *HE* 10.9.2, 6–9, *VC* 2.19–24). His *Ecclesiastical History*, after all, takes us back to the life of Christ, even reminding us of Eusebius' interests in matters anthropological as well as the events of Old Testament times (*HE* 1.2.23; 5.1–13.22, cf. 5.2.18–22; 4.5–14, *PE* 1–2).[22] Eusebius' stress on tyranny and its penalties, moreover, comes towards the end of his history.[23] Although he labours the point that five evil emperors from Diocletian onwards died horribly for their sins, [24] he evidently lacked the inside information about Court history which was available to his contemporary Lactantius, who recounted the recurrently hideous deaths of the imperial persecutors from as far back as Nero.[25] In any case, the structure of Eusebius' ecclesiastical history is such that as much space is given to the internal concerns of the church, that 'indestructible, invincible' and 'most populous of all nations' (*HE* 1.4.2, cf. 5, pref. 4; 8.10.4, 24) as to the affairs of those bent on exterminating this νέον ἔθνος.

I stand by the statement which I have made elsewhere that Eusebius 'was less interested in *recurrent* instances of retribution . . . than in the plan of salvation which made world Christianisation possible under Constantine'.[26] One must concede, on the other hand, that retributive logic holds a central place in his historiographical hermeneutic because he felt so bound to explain why the divine Providence was actually working in favour of Christianity rather than for its opponents. A prominent part of that explanation lay in documenting the unpleasant visitations falling upon God's enemies. In general Eusebius was in this connnection the inheritor of both Biblical and Graeco-Roman perspectives, since it is a common preoccupation of historians and sages from both traditions to demonstrate a moral order behind the eventualities of the past.[27] In particular, the first two books of the *Historia* show him to have taken his cue from Luke-Acts. If one of Luke's motivations in writing a sequel to his Gospel had been to show how the wicked were punished — Judas the betrayer falling headlong, Herod[28] riddled with worms, the Jews rejected, the High Priest's assassination and Jerusalem's destruction both predicted[29] — then Eusebius, for his part, dilates upon these verdicts of history with a good deal more detail and intricate argument, using them as lessons to foreshadow the retributions of his own day.

Herod the Great, for daring to act against the Christ (and those of the same age) received Divine Justice ($\dot{\eta} \theta \epsilon i a \delta i \kappa \eta$) in the form of a terrible wasting disease (shistasomiasis?) (1.8.3–15) there being no comparable (and thus exhaustive) account of a persecutor's last ailments until we come to the fate of Maximin (*HE* 9.10.13–5).[30] Pilate, whose fate is left quite unmentioned in the New Testament, is said to have killed himself in accordance with $\dot{\eta} \theta \epsilon i a \delta i \kappa \eta$ (1.2.7), while both Herods Antipas and Agrippa I, who are left without differentiation in Luke–Acts, suffer punishments, the latter's belly of worms being ascribed yet again to the Divine Justice because he murdered James (1.2.4.1; 9.4–10.10).[31] Unlike Luke, Eusebius could quote Josephus *in extenso* on the dreadful famine and civil strife which overtook Jerusalem during the Roman siege of A.D. 70 (3.5.4–8.11, cf. 2.26.1–2). Although there is a touch of regret that it was the pagans who pitilessly destroyed the Jewish *ethnos* (2.26.2, cf. 2.5.1–6.2), the Jews suffer disasters from Pilate's time onwards because of their crimes against the Saviour (2.6.3, cf. 1.1.2). Indeed, the true Jewish priesthood had ceased just before Christ's coming,[32] as had the (pre-Herodian) Jewish kingship, so that since Jesus himself fulfilled the best of Israel's institutional life, only destruction could await the corrupt leftovers (1.6.1–11,[33] cf. 2.6.8, 11.1–3, 20.1–21.3; 4.2.1–5, 6.1–4, 8.4). Ἡ $\theta \epsilon i a \delta i \kappa \eta$ visited this people primarily because of their violence against the Christ (2.6.8, 3.5.3.6–7, 3.7.1), yet they were also the first persecutors of the Christians (2.1.8, 3.3, 23.1–25.24; 3.5.2–3, cf. 4.8.4, 18.7) and events are written up as if pagan opposition grew out of these first (Jewish) calumnies (cf. 2.9.1–4, 22.4, 25.1–8, 3.22,[34] 32–33).

Eusebius' language of retribution is geared to anticipate the preconceptions of two audiences — those steeped in the Biblical tradition (especially ecclesiastics) and those familiar with the devices of Greek historiography (particularly intellectuals at the Imperial Court unfamiliar with Christian history). The Old Testament histories, as well as Luke–Acts, play constantly on the theme of Yahweh's punishment of evil and vindication of obedience.[35] Much in the Prophets and Psalms (and thus much of the poetry which is so basic for the episcopal rhetoric) voices the prospect of extreme penalty befalling God's enemies.[36] However, the glimmerings of a virtually hypostatised $\Delta i \kappa \eta$ in either Septuagintal or New Testament literature are few,[37] and this encourages suspicion that the Eusebian choice of language was governed more by Hellenistic convention. Commending the ways of justice, of course, is characteristic of extant Greek literature, and most interpreters of history 'were comforted when it was satisfied, whether by men, by the gods, or by the natural order of things'.[38] Better known Hellenistic historiographers, on the other hand, had made much of the less predictable *Tyche* as a moral arbiter, and what distinguishes Eusebius' approach is the conspicuous absence of any significant reference to her. Even the Jewish Josephus, let alone Polybius and the moralising Diodorus Siculus who succeeded him,[39] could explain the outcome of events by appealing to both retributive Justice and a 'tamed' Fortune (who effected change in accordance with the virtues or baseness of a case) as if they were the same elevated Principle.[40] The Divine Justice of Eusebius is clearly more self-consciously de-Hellenised in flavour. Although he is capable of less monotheistic-looking alternatives ($\dot{\eta} \dot{a}\xi i a \delta i \kappa \eta$, for instance),[41] the early preponderance of the phrase $\dot{\eta} \theta \epsilon i a \delta i \kappa \eta$ reflects the influence of the pseudo-epigraphical 4 Maccabees (first century A.D.) — a short work which Eusebius himself attributed to Josephus (*HE* 3.10.6) but which unlike the Josephan corpus carries this distinctive expression, and as many as seven times.[42] Thus the age-old theme of just deserts (important in the 'then known' ancient world from as far east as Persia to the Latins of the west)[43] was intelligently redeployed along lines acceptable under the new dispensation, that unique unfolding order within which Gentiles had become inheritors of Jewish salvation history.[44]

It is at this point, however, that we should outline some of the problems facing Eusebius as he tried to exegete the divine distribution of recompenses in the first three Christian centuries. Between the dreadful συμφοραί experienced by the Jews and Constantine's crushing of the tyrants (that is, between the opening and closing portions of the *Historia*), much space is given to descriptions of some of the most horrendous tortures ever devised by men (esp. 3.31–36; 4.15–17; 5 pref.–3; 6.39–44, cf. 8.4–13 *MP*). Eusebius realised only too well that the hideous atrocities inflicted on the hundreds of martyred Christians registered in the pagan mind as the very opposite to prosperity and temporal blessing.[45] Thus he did spend some time documenting how figures closely implicated in the use of evil torments received their just deserts — how those who falsely accused the virtuous Narcissus could not escape 'the great eye of Justice' (6.9.7–10.1), or how two of the persecutor-henchmen of Maximin were themselves tortured and put to death (9.11.3–6)[46] — but their suffering seems tame beside the agonies of the martyrs. Since the Christians seemed to have suffered more than the pagans, being mauled to death by wild beasts, or roasted upon the dreaded 'iron chair' or else having their naked bodies furrowed by metal combs,[47] how then did Eusebius untangle the problems of retributive logic and so play the role, as we would expect, of an apologist?[48]

One method, of course, was to celebrate the 'happy ending'. The panegyrical notes have already been sounded at the end of the *Historia* (10.9.6–9) before being fully voluble in the *Vita* and *Laus Constantini*, and Charles Cochrane has rightly suspected Eusebius of extravagant dreams, of looking to the age of Constantine as one of universal (and perhaps perpetual) peace and prosperity.[49] The *Pax Augusta* was significant enough, since 'the wars of antiquity were due to polytheism' and Christ's coming into the world coincided with a 'sovereign, profound peace' under Rome's universal Empire (*LC* 16.4).[50] Yet this prior dispensation was no more than an unsatisfactory foretaste when compared to the new order which Eusebius proclaimed like Constantine's new Vergil; and thus it is no wonder that scholars have noticed far less emphasis on 'traditional' eschatology and much more hope in a this-worldly yet divinely planned πολιτεία,[51] as well as the lineaments of a doctrine of progress.[52] According to this trajectory in Eusebian thought, the fact that human affairs have now arrived to a state of unprecedented security and happiness[53] helps to justify the circuitous, unpleasant route taken to get there.

Imbedded in Eusebian panegyric, of course, is the celebration of victory, and thus the suppression of those agencies which unjustly persecuted the Christians.[54] There is no question that the new ruler Constantine acts as God's just arm of punition when he prohibits pagan sacrifices, idolatry and polytheism, and demolishes various temples (*VC* 2.42–7, 3.54–8). The new order both removes the causes of persecution (we may note by initiating another, if much milder one) and thus vindicates the cause of the martyrs.

Constantine's punitive measures, however, were hardly commensurate with the scale and persistence of the atrocities committed against the persecuted. Expectedly, the happy ending was not enough and constituted only one part of the solution. Eusebius has to resort to some of the more obviously theological devices so as to mitigate the discrepancies. We see him struggling with the issues most clearly in the *Vita* (2.26), where he has Constantine persuaded that the martyr's suffering and piety should be rewarded with 'happiness and blessedness in the next life'. The persecutors, it is added, not only have met with the 'miseries of war, devastations and famine . . . equal to their injustices' (all of which we have already heard about in connection with the last part of the *Historia – HE* 9–10), but they have also to face present 'misfortune . . . and torment of mind', and the 'expectation of a future punishment . . . in hell' (27, cf. 53, *MP* 7.8).[55] Such generalisations are not an afterthought in one so interested in the temporal future as Eusebius is. His use of martyrological quotations in the *Historia* and his own comments on select martyrdoms show him ready to confirm that there is indeed an ultimate victory – a crowning and perfection – awaiting these sufferers (for example, 8.10.12, 11.2 cf. 3.36.9; 4.15.33, etc.). Since the martyrs refuse idolatry, therefore they refuse to be 'utterly destroyed' in hell, which is by implication the destination of pagan persecutors (8.10.10 cf. 5.1.26). Perhaps one might have expected of Eusebius, who shows such favour towards Origen (*HE* 6.1.1–19.19), some universalist hope of the 'restoration of all things' (*apokatastasis*) in which even the persecutors would eventually find God in another order – yet history (and I suspect history rather than cautious theology) seems to have constrained him otherwise.

Another method by which the problem of martyrdom was handled (and one by which Eusebius struggled to make sense of suffering in terms of pagan predispositions, not just of Christian theology)[56] was to portray the martyrs as innocents who died bravely, even magnificently. It is of course false to imagine that in traditional Mediterranean cultures every ugly death was considered deserving and the will of the gods. A virtuous and guiltless person could be murdered, such being a case of κακία and ἀσέβεια; and it is this status – the status of totally unjustified killing – which Eusebius attributed to the slaying of Christians. If pagan reflection had already conceded that murderers were not always duly brought to heel, or received recompense much later than seemed appropriate, loopholes of logic appeared to include the continuing notoriety of the evildoers following their deeds, or else the favourable memory of virtuous sufferers in posterity.[57] Eusebius himself was clearly not above having recourse to such logic and he was also obviously aware that Graeco-Roman (not just Biblical) paradigms of victorious death could be put to use.

Eusebius not only underlines the savage, mindless injustices done to the Christians (especially 4.16.8, 26.6; 5.1.6, 9, 57; 8.9; 9.6.2), a people whom he portrayed as opposed to violence and as fighting 'peaceful wars for the very peace of the soul' (especially 5, pref. 3, cf. especially 5.4.7; 8.4.2, 13.9; 10.9.6; *VC* 2.57); he also presents martyr deaths as victorious and, far from being repulsive, as majestic (especially 8.6.3, 14.17, cf. 3.36.9; 4.8.5, 4.15–7). Even Christian suicide is justified, and so, possibly with a view to popularised Stoicism, Eusebius tells us how holy women preferred to dispatch themselves rather than to lose their virtue to ravishers (8.12.3–4, 14.17; *VC* 1.34). He rightly perceived it as significant that Christian women were capable of bearing agonies with equanimity and of standing their ground with a virtue equal to men's (*HE* 8.14.14–5). All in all, martyr's deaths are endowed with profound meaning: the Saviour Himself is the One giving strength to the tortured faithful; miracles (the allegedly divine muzzling of wild beasts in the arena, for example) confirm the guiding hand of God even behind these tragedies; stones and the earth weep for being unable to endure such foul deeds; the Devil, albeit a cause of persecution, is jealous of the martyr's achievements; and the noble deaths, sometimes paralleled with that of Christ himself, stand in continuity with the stricken Lord, although He alone took on the penalties (τὰ προστιμήματα) for human wickedness.[58] According to the *Historia*, and pointedly so, all this is the true and astonishing μαρτυρία — and if Maximin later came to promulgate a false alternative in his notorious rescript, Maximin himself showed publicly how resigned he was to the resilience of those who 'fear no punishment', having conceded in his earlier provincial epistle of 310 what 'so long a passage of time' had 'proved', namely, that 'they can in no way be persuaded to abandon' their 'obstinate conduct' (9.1.5 cf.4).

Eusebius' affirmation of a moral order *within* history, even despite such protracted execrable suffering, once more reveals his capacity for developing lines laid down in Biblical and pre-Christian Greek historiographies into a fresh (but by no means unpersuasive) paradigm. The greatest Jewish histories before him admittedly had confirmed the hand of God as chastiser behind such terrible troubles besetting the Jews as the Babylonian captivity (the Deuteronomist [s]) and the Jewish War (Josephus).[59] The great classical and Hellenistic Greek historians also deplored the enslavement of whole nations by tyrannical powers,[60] although they never made a virtue out of the consistent calamities experienced by minority groups or small, uncouth cultures.[61] Eusebius' own context, of course, made it easier to render the enormities intelligible: vindication at last presented itself with Licinius and (above all) with Constantine, yet to justify the carnage *en route* was hardly easy. A cue had already been provided for the bishop, at least, in the Jewish Maccabaica — 1 Maccabees recounting how the Jews obtained (albeit military) victory after the persecutions of Antiochus Epiphanes; and 4 Maccabees, which was so influential on Eusebius' phraseology, being distinctive in pre-Christian literature for approaching a theology of martyrdom.[62] In any case, other Biblical writers (the Chronicler and Luke among them) had commended the persistence of faithful heroes in the face of oppression.[63] However, it was Eusebius himself who created the first full-scale history with praiseworthy and ultimately effective suffering as its central motif.

As already noted, justification for the martyrs was not carried off as if history alone contained all the answers. It is misguided to suppose that Eusebius set aside fundamental Christian beliefs about extra-mundane Judgment in favour of a this-worldly outlook. But unlike Augustine (who knew the apostate Julian to have followed Constantine, and who lived later under an Empire so shaky that it seemed foredoomed), Eusebius made much less of the supra-terrestrial resolution of historical anomalies because present eventualities spoke louder than theological speculation. The real sharpening of this issue is not to be found in his work. I have written more generally about the matter elsewhere:

> In times of bloody persecution, Christians could afford to question a moral order *within history*. After all, certain Biblical writers had been uneasy about it. (see Jer. 12:1; Ps. 73:3 on the prosperity of the wicked; cf. John 9:2–3, Job); and there were also some non-Christian moralists who were sensitive about relevant discrepancies bypassed by the popularisers. Divine vengeance seemed to be frequently delayed, for instance, and innocent victims often died before they could see retribution fall on those who afflicted them. Questioning souls were justifiably troubled. The dogmas that in the event of delayed punishment the evildoer would suffer either inward torture in life or notoriety in death, and that those who suffered undeservedly would be honoured in posterity, came to be seen as flimsy rationalisations. Naturally enough, the belief in *other-worldly* rewards and punishments received a greater airing in later Antiquity, increasingly so the more there was

intellectual interchange between pagan and Christian. It is fair to assert that Christian beliefs about heaven and hell provided more intellectually satisfying solutions to the problems of the moral order than those offered by pagans, who often added a blind fatalism to their face-saving explanations. That is an interesting sidelight to the history of Christianity's rise to ideological supremacy.[64]

Eusebius was not among those who seriously doubted the moral order within history, however, because he could borrow capital from *Pax Constantiniana*, indulging in a questionable optimism which later generations had to unlearn.

All is not so simple, however, and Eusebius' solutions were not in every respect one-sided in favour of the Christians. In his exegesis of the more recent events, we find more sober, qualifying (and one might add episcopal) observations at the beginning of Book 8 — to the effect that the Church's opponents cannot take all the blame for the trials of history. The principles of retribution are evidently not interpreted either correctly or convincingly if the Church's own weaknesses are left ignored. Eusebius, nevertheless, refused to include the unedifying details of ecclesiastical logomachy (8.2.3 cf. 7);[65] yet it is the pride, the sloth, the hypocrisy and the factionalism which occurred within the fold during the hiatus before Diocletian's edicts that the bishop identifies as a cause of persecution (8.1.7–8 cf. 6, 8.2.4–51).[66] There are no names to go by, yet church rulers (ἄρχοντες) are the chief targets of his criticisms, for their ambitions are incipiently tyrannical and the psalmist's contempt of princes can be quoted as much against them as against the pre-Constantinian tyrants (8.1.8,[67] 8.2.2 cf. 9.11.8). Thus persecution is the payment for Christian divisiveness.

In the same breath, however, Eusebius writes of ἡ θεία κρίσις against the Church, not as an ordering τιμωρία but as a judgment falling μετρίως according to the divine ἐπισκοπή (8.1.7 cf. 8.2.2).[68] This notion of the measured permissions of God (which has an obvious affinity with the theologies of divine patience important for Lactantius and (later) Orosius[69]) is anticipated by Eusebius' comments on the later years of Aurelian. Divine Justice visited this Emperor before he had the chance to organise a persecution; 'thus,' writes the historian, 'the rulers of this world never find it easy to proceed against the churches of Christ unless our champion's hand were to permit this, at the time he approves, as a divine and heavenly judgment to chasten and turn us' (... θεία καὶ οὐρανίῳ κρίσει παιδείας ἕνεκα καὶ ἐπιστροφῆς, 7.30.21). Here there is a different ingredient in the explanation of events: the heavenly succour only comes after the correcting God deems necessary for His people, sufficient παιδεία, it appears, to make the Church worthy of the blessed peace of Constantine (9.8.15, 10.4.33–4).[70]

Broadly speaking, then, Eusebius saw the Church as being refined rather than punished by persecution, although he was under no illusion that certain weaknesses within Christianity, especially evident before Diocletian, could affect the sternness of divine measures (cf. 10.4.57–9). It is worth remembering here Eusebius' apparent acceptance of a view maintained by his predeccessor Hegesippus, namely that corruption and error first took root in the Church after the last of those who heard 'the divine Wisdom with their own ears had passed away' (3.32.8, cf. 6–7; 4.22.4–6).[71] The defilement, of course, comes with heresy — a persistent problem for the Church during its first three centuries, a period which Eusebius was the first to document as a whole — from Simon Magus to Arius.[72] In fact, it is in connection with heresy that Eusebius first introduced the Devil — a figure highly important as an agency influencing events (and thus as a means of explaining them). Ὁ πονηρὸς δαίμων, as he is called, is certainly characterised as a motivator of persecution (4.7.1–2; 5.21.2; 6.39.4, 10.8.2; *VC* 1.49, 57, etc.). Yet he is more decidedly the one who undermines the Christian 'nation' as it is — causing error, working against the martyrs[73] — and only with this accounted for can we concur with Momigliano's statement that Eusebius' history is 'a history of the struggle against the devil'.[74] If the panegyric in the newly dedicated church of Tyre is any indication, Eusebius' greatest fear of the Evil One was that he would seduce the Church and thus lead the 'Deity to depart from her' as unfaithful (*HE* 10.4.57). Thus matters were not so clear-cut that Eusebius could indulge in an unbalanced and uncritical polemic.

The bishop was only too well aware, moreover, that large scale calamities — those which Maximin's rescript held to be forestalled by pious attention to the gods — overtook Christians along with the unbelievers. He may have reckoned the floods, conflagrations, famines, plagues and wars of the distant past as the chastisements ($\kappa o\lambda a\sigma\tau\acute\eta\rho\iota o\iota$) of God (1.2.20) — but there was clearly no exemption for Christians in the sufferings of Alexandria's great epidemic in 258–9.[75] Using Dionysius the Great as a source, however, Eusebius could contrast (as he does in other places) Christian care with pagan brutality. The Christians tended the sick:

> . . . in Christ, and so most gladly departed this life along with them; being infected with the disease from others, drawing upon themselves the sickness from their neighbours, and willingly taking over their pains;

while

> the conduct of the heathen was the exact opposite. Even those who were in the first stages of the disease were thrust away, and fled . . . They would cast them out in the roads half-dead, and treat the unburied corpses as vile refuse, in their attempts to avoid the . . . contagion.
>
> (*HE* 7.22.7, 10 cf. 7.21.8–9; 9.9.13–4)

The eventual outcome of events in the *Historia*, therefore, is not merely determined by power struggles both imperial or cosmic, nor only by the degree to which the Church can avoid error and contention, but also by the superior qualities of the Church's new social outlook. Eusebius' insistence is that no one person can undermine the whole collective undertaking (cf. 7.32.33–3), upheld as it is by $\mu e\gamma a\lambda o\psi v\chi\acute\iota a$ (10.4.26).[76]

As a whole, however, we may conclude that the *Historia Ecclesiastica* presents itself as a record of Providence, and that although Eusebius inherited the concept of a divine $\pi\rho\acute o\nu o\iota a$ from both Hellenistic and later Jewish predecessors, yet his understanding and usage of it has a comparative freshness. Providence is much more than an overarching factor which can be appealed to in order to endow events with philosophical significance; it is the efficacy of a personal God who is intimately concerned for the whole universe, and especially for his own people. Thus Providence does not merely underly the foreordained principles which give history its typical event-complexes, its patterns and situations. It is also the manifestation of a Will, of the 'God who acts' with freedom (as the Biblical perspective had it).[77] Under God's Providence one can find what is surprisingly unwelcome — the agonies of the martyrs for example — yet also the emergence of a quite new social order, of 'a nation never even heard of since time began, which now no longer lies hidden in some obscure corner of the earth, but extends wherever the sun does shine' (*HE* 10.4.19). The hyperbole is commensurate, after all, with both the marvel of church growth and an enormous sense of relief.

Notes

1. On the dating of the rescript's promulgation, and its inscription on pillars (late in 312), see esp. H. J. Lawlor, *Eusebiana; Essays on the Ecclesiastical History of Eusebius Bishop of Caesarea* (Oxford 1912), 223–4; Lawlor and J. E. L. Oulton (eds), *Eusebius Bishop of Caesarea; the Ecclesiastical History and the Martyrs of Palestine* (London 1954), vol. 2, 287–8, 296–7. Publicising the rescript was clearly not confined to Phoenicia (Eusebius witnessing the inscription in Latin at Tyre, *HE* 9.7.3); the ordinance was meant for most cities of the Roman East (7.1; cf. *Orientis Graeci Inscriptiones Selectae* (ed. W. Dittenberger) (Leipzig 1905), vol. 2, n.569, 252. Cf. also H. Castritius, *Studien zu Maximinus Daia (Frankfurter Althistorische Studien 2)* (Frankfurt 1969), 48–51, 68 [Eusebius, incidentally, referring to Maximin as Daza rather than Daia].

2. Edward Gibbon, *Decline and Fall of the Roman Empire* (London 1910 edn), vol. 1, 397, cf. 385–6, 396–9.

3. Lactantius, *De mortibus persecutorum*, 27–32; Eutropius, *Breviarium* 10; cf. Aurelius Victor, *Liber de Caesaribus*, 39–40; Zosimus, *Historia Nova*, 1.2.10; Socrates, *HE* 1.2.

4. For Eusebius on Galerius, *HE* 8.16–17; Frg. 4; and on tyranny, *infra*.

5. Although there are indications that Eusebius excised some portions of the statement (cf. 8.7.10: τούτοις μεθ᾽ ἕτερα ἐπιλέγει), the rescript is the only anti-Christian document quoted in *HE* at length.

6. In all probability *HE* Book 10 was added as an appendix some twelve years after completing the first nine books (note *HE* 10.1.2–3, cf. 8, pref.; Lawlor, *Eusebiana*, 261), thus in completing his first edition, Eusebius acclaims Licinius (along with Constantine) as benefactor rather than tyrant (9.11.9).

7. Eusebius, who died in 339, was in no position to foresee the attempt at a pagan revival under Julian (361–3).

8. *HE* 9.7.9 (cf. τῶν ἀθεμίτων . . . ἀνθρώπων); 12 (μιάσματος καὶ ἀσεβείας); 14 (τοῦ δὲ ὑμᾶς ἀξίων ἐπάθλων τετυχηκέναι . . .). Eusebius clearly makes something special out of μαρτυρία here; the Latin equivalent in the extant Lycian inscription (cf. n.1 *supra*) is [testabi]tur (*1*.5).

9. One rightly suspects exaggeration here, since the natural disasters, although said to affect both cities and especially rural areas (8.8.5), are not placed geographically. The richness of detail (8.8.6–12), however, suggests an eyewitness report. As for the Armenian war, there exists no other record to help measure its significance.

10. Points in common between the later calamity and the two earlier ones include shamelessness (3.6.5, 20; 9.8.7 cf. 7.22.10), the selling of possessions for mere food scraps (3.6.3; 9.8.6), the rotting of many corpses (3.6.15; 7.22.8, 10; 9.9–10 cf. the phrase ὥσπερ εἴδωλα . . ., 3.6.12; 9.8.8), lamentations (3.6.13; 7.22.2; 9.8.11), as well as references to cannibalism (3.6.21–8, 9.8.10) and death as equaliser (7.22.9–10; 9.9.11. Cf. also 7.22.7, 10; 9.9.13, 14).

11.   I.e. Gallienus established peace after the κακοτροπία of Decius and his successors (22.12), and eventually overthrew Fulvius Macrianus (23.2). Cf., for example, R. M. Grant, *Augustus to Constantine* (New York 1970), ch. 11.

12.   Did Dionysius the Great's panegyric for Gallienus (7.23.1–4) provide a model for Eusebius' own acclamations of Constantine? It is very tempting to conclude so, more especially because the correct fixing of Easter dates, such an important issue for Eusebius (4.26.3; 5.23–5; 7.32.14–9, *On the Paschal Festival*), was made possible by Gallienus (*HE* 7.24.4, cf. 20) and settled by Constantine (*VC* 3.13). Cf. N. Zernov, 'Eusebius and the Paschal Controversy at the End of the Second Century', *Church Quarterly Review* 116 (1933), 24–41.

13.   Apart from a few earlier allusions to tyranny in *HE* (cf. sources quoted in 3.6.22, 5.1.27), all references to it are in the last three Books (8.1.8, 13.15, 14.3–17; 9.1.1, 2.1, 4.1; 9.7.16, 8.2–9.11, 13, 10.1, 11.7; 10.2.1, 4.14.35, 8.2, 9.2.9, cf. *VC* 1.3, 23, 26–7, 35–8, 47, 49, 59; 2.1–4, 18–9; 3.12; 4.12, *MP* 4.1(L), 7.7(S), 8.5(L), 9.1(L)). On Eusebius' panegyrical writing as an attempt to create a 'Constantinian perspective', esp. H. A. Drake, *In Praise of Constantine (University of California Publications: Classical Studies 15)* (Los Angeles 1975), 4–8, 59–60, 75–9.

14.   Historical problems surround the official Constantinian statements in *VC*, since the original MSS do not usually allow one to see where the quotations begin and end, and whether interpolations have been made. For background, esp. A. Crivelucci, 'I documenti della V.C.', *Studi Storici* 7 (1898), 412–29, 453–9; P. Batiffol, 'Les documents de la Vita Constantini', *Bulletin d'ancienne littérature et d'archéologie chrétiennes* 4 (1914), 81–90; I. Daniele, *I documenti Constantiniani della V.C. di Eusebio di Cesarea (Analecta Gregoriana 13, Ser. Fac. Hist. Eccles., Sect B1)*(Rome 1938).

15.   The previous quotation squares with what one would expect of the imperial stance at that time. Fertility is associated with virtue (as with Maximin's rescript), yet the allusions to oppressive attitudes remind the reader of the defeat of the Tyrants. Since the language is not characteristically Eusebian, and this is certainly true of the terms used for God (25, 26) and of retribution befalling the oppressors (τῶν ἀμοιβαίων τυχόντας), we have no reason to suspect editorial modification.

16.   See esp. T. E. Mommsen, *Medieval and Renaissance Studies* (ed. E. F. Rice) (Ithaca 1959), 291; G. W. Trompf, *The Idea of Historical Recurrence in Western Thought* (Los Angeles 1979), 224–5.

17.   Socrates, *HE* 1.3 (. . . διωγμὸς τοπικός), cf. Sozomen, *HE* 1.7.

18.   Eutropius, *Brev.* 10.6; Zosimus, *Hist.*, 1.2.28; cf. (Eusebius–)Jerome, *Chronicorum* (ed. A. Schoene) (Frankfurt 1875), vol. 2, 191.

19.   *HE* 10.8.11–4, 9.2; Plato, *Rep.* 566A, 573C–574A, cf. Polybius, *Hist.* 6.9.8–9, 7.13.7.

20.   The precedent set by Dionysius the Great (as panegyrist for Gallienus, cf. *HE* 7.23.1–4) I believe to be important for Eusebius' estimate of his own role (see n.12). With his sense of both recurrence and progress, however (cf. Trompf, *op. cit.*, 208, 224–5), Eusebius clearly understands Constantine's opponents to have taken injustice to an extreme not reached by those of Gallienus, and thus the victory in favour of Christianity by Constantine and Licinius (according to the first edition of *HE*), or by Constantine alone (according to the second), was so much greater and worthy of eulogy.

21.   Cf. also *VC* 2.18. Adjustments were probably made to the first edition of *HE* 9, so that in the second Licinius' defection would not come as a surprise (9.9.1, 12).

22.   See also *DE* 4.8 (157c–158b); 9 (160b–d), *Chronicorum* I (Schoene, vol. 1, 7–171).

Cf. J. Sirinelli, *Les vues historiques d'Eusèbe de Césarée durant la période préniceéne (Université de Dakar Faculté des Lettres et Sciences Humaine, Sect. de Lang. et Litt. 10)* (Dakar 1961), pts. 1–2.

23. See n.13 above.

24. *HE* 8.13.10–11 (Diocletian); 8.16.3; *VC* 1.57–9 (Galerius = Maximian II); *HE* 9.9.1, *VC* 1.38 (Maxentius); *HE* 8.13.15, 14.7; 9.7.2, 10.4–6, 13; *MP* 9.1 (L), 13.10 (L) (Maximinus [II] Daia); Licinius, *HE* 10.9.5–6. Earlier cases 7.1.1, 10.8–9, 13.1.23.

25. *De mort. pers.* 2–49, cf. Eusebius' generalisation in *MP* 7.8 (L, S).

26. Trompf, *op. cit.*, 235, cf. esp. *HE* 10.9.2, *MP*, 3.7, *DE* 3.7 (136a–137a). Apart from recurrence motifs discussed in *ibid.*, 204–5, 209, 213n, 219n, 224–5, others include the defeat of Maxentius at the Tiber (Oct. 312) depicted as a reenactment of Pharaoh's chariots destroyed in the Red Sea (*HE*, 9.9.3–8, *VC*, 1.38), parallels drawn between Constantine and Moses (*VC*, 1.12.16.38–9, 2.11–2, 14, cf. those between Christ and Moses in *DE*, 3.2 (90c–94c), and the message that insolent tyrants inevitably fall (*MP*, 7.8, cf. *HE*, 9.7.16, 11.6; 10.4.28–32; *VC* 1.6–7, 48, 52, etc.). Cf. also, 6.29.1–3, and see n.53 *infra*.

27. Trompf, *op. cit.*, 93–106, 155–174, 231–3.

28. Not specified as Agrippa (I) (cf. Josephus, *Antiq.*, 19.38–50), Luke apparently representing the King's ailment as a punishment against Herodianism in general.

29. Acts 1:18 (cf. Matt. 27:3–5), 12:20–3; 23:3, cf. Luke, 19:43–4 (*om.* Mark, Matt.), 21:20 (cf. Mark 13:14, Matt. 24:15), Acts 7:42–3. Cf. Trompf, *op. cit.*, 170–4.

30. Thanks to Dr. R. R. Trompf for suggested diagnosis of Herod's disease (cf. Z. Farid and R. H. Watten, 'Schistosomiasis', *International Medicine (Australia Edition)*, n.s., II/2 (1981), A146–53. She is much less sure about Maximin's case (a thyroid complaint?).

31. I.e. James the apostle. Eusebius does not understand Luke's (probable) motive for declining to specify Agrippa I (see n.28 above, cf. *HE*, 2.10.10). Unlike Luke he sees Herod Antipas' crimes are already requited — by exile (4.1). He also sought to harmonise the Lukan and Josephan account of Agrippa's death by making the king see an angel (10.6, ≠ the avenging angel of Acts 12:23) rather than an owl (Josephus, *Antiq.*, 19.346). His information concerning Pilate's suicide is ascribed to pagan sources in *Chron.* (Schoene, vol. 2, 150a), cf. the alternative tradition that Nero had him summarily executed; Joannes Malalas, (Slavonic) *Chron.*, 10.8 (B257–8) (Spinka, 63).

32. *HE*, 1.6.6–9, cf. 3.8, *DE*, 4.10 (166d); 15 (176b–177d), 8.2 (396d–397a). Thus there was no reason for Eusebius to recount the assassination of Ananias, the last high priest (cf. Josephus, *Bell. Jud.*, 2.441).

33. Cf. (on the foreigners of the Herodian line), 3.10.12, *DE*, 3.2 (96a). And did Eusebius also believe that Christ was the proper fulfilment of the pharaonic line? (*HE*, 1.5.2, cf. *Chron.* [Schoene, vol. 1, 100], *DE*, 3.7 [140a], 9.2 [421d–422d]). In fact Cleopatra VII died *c.* 30 B.C. and not, as Eusebius supposed, at the time of the Nativity, even though the death of her son Ptolemy XV 'Caesarion' (by Julius Caesar?) cannot be dated with any accuracy (see esp. Plutarch, *Vit. Ant.*, 86, cf. 81–2).

34. Here Eusebius refers to Domitian as the δεύτερος to promote persecution against the Christians, yet although the historian provided the basis for later models of five or ten persecutions, he did not persist with such numbering (cf. Trompf, *op. cit.*, 219, n.183).

35. G. W. Trompf, 'Notions of Historical Recurrence in Classical Hebrew Historiography',

in J. A. Emerton (ed.), *Studies in the Historical Books of the Old Testament* (Leiden 1979), 219–29.

36. Esp. W. Eichrodt, *Theology of the Old Testament* (trans. J. A. Baker) (London 1961–7), vol. 1, 263–82 (the best O.T. equivalent being Yahweh's vindicative *mishpatim*, e.g. Ps. 103:6, 146:7). Cf. Eusebius, *HE*, 10.4.30–2, *Comm. in Pss.*, and on appropriate δίκη in patristic literature before him, e.g. Justin, *Apol.*, 1.17, Methodius, *Symp.*, 10.

37. Sap. 1:8; 11:20; 14:31, cf. LXX Deut. 32:41, 43, Luke 21:22 (*om.* Mark, Matt.) and (put on another's lips), Acts 28:4.

38. Trompf, *Recurrence*, 93, cf. 85–8, 94–7 for fuller discussion.

39. On Polybius, Diodorus and Plutarch, *ibid.*, 63–6, 192–6.

40. Josephus, e.g. *Antiq.*, 19.77, *Bell. Jud.*, 4.622, cf. *Antiq.*, 8.251 (on fortune), 8.229, 11.274, 18.116–7 (on justice), cf. *Bell. Jud.*, 5.355, 572, 6.314 (on fate). In fact Josephus makes far less of Fortune than Philo Judaeus, who affirmed both *tychē* and *dikē* to be expressions of God's lordship over history; cf. Trompf, *Recurrence*, 167–8.

41. *HE*, 4.6.3; 8.14.7; 9.11.6; 10.4.59, cf. 6.10; 9.6.1, 11.5 and on other expressions, e.g. 1.8.3; 2.1.12; 3.5.7, 6.1; 9.10.14, *MP*, 13.10 (L). On ἡ ἀξία δίκη in Josephus, see *Antiq.*, 8.289, 9.282, 13.107, *Bell. Jud.*, 4.185, cf. also Polybius, *Hist.*, 4.81.5; 15.20.5; 18.44.11 (ἡ ἁρμόζουσα δίκη), etc. Note *HE*, 6.9.7 (ὁ τῆς δίκης μέγας ὀφθαλμός), cf. Polybius, *Hist.*, 23.10.5. For background in classical Greek historiography, esp. Herodotus, *Hist.*, 8.77; 106.

42. 4 Macc., 4:13, 21; 8:22, 9:9, 32; 12:12; 18:22, cf. 9:15, 11:3, 2 Macc. 8:13. In the Syriac version of *HE* the phraseology varies, although note kīnā dālhā in 2.6.8; 3.5.6 (W. Wright and N. McLean edn.[Cambridge 1898], 73, 119).

43. E.g. (using historiographical works only), Herodotus, *Hist.*, 9.116 (Persia), Acts 28:4 (Malta), Diodorus Siculus, *Bibliot.*, 5.71.1–2 (both Greeks and Romans), etc.

44. See Sirinelli, *op. cit.*, pt. 2.

45. *HE*, esp. 4.15.26; 5.1.31, 60; 9.10.12, cf. 9.18. Christians, it must be remembered, were still only a minority in the Empire under Constantine.

46. I.e., Peucetius and Culcianus; cf. 9.5.2–6.1 (for another case). See n.41 above on the 'Eye of Justice'.

47. *HE*, 5.1.38, 52; *MP*, 8.8 (L); *HE*, 5.1.59, 8.7.1–6, 13.4; 9.6.1, cf. 8.6.2–3, 9.1, 12.6–8; 10.8.14, etc.

48. Cf. Sirinelli, *op. cit.*, pt. 4.

49. *Christianity and Classical Culture* (New York 1957), 185.

50. Cf. also *DE*, 3.7 (139d–140b), 7.2 (345a); Sirinelli, *op. cit.*, 390–7.

51. *Comm. in Isa.*, esp. 2.36 (49:19), 43 (54:12), cf. 1.73 (18:4), 2.36 (48:16; 49:17), 56 (65:19–20), etc. (*Die griechischen christlichen Schriftsteller, Eusebius 9* [Berlin 1975], 315, *ll.*18–22; p.342, *l.*36–p.343, *l.*1, cf. p.121, *l.*18; p.314, *ll.*15, 32–3; p.397, *ll.*19–25, etc.). Cf. L. G. Patterson, *God and History in Early Christian Thought (Studies in Patristic Thought)* (London 1967), 80–2. In Eusebius we find an incipient doctrine of the City of God.

52. A. Funkenstein, *Heilsplan und näturliche Entwicklung* (Munich 1965), cf. 1, pts. 2–4, yet cf. D. S. Wallace-Hadrill, *Eusebius of Caesarea* (London 1960), 169–84.

53. Although note *HE*, 10.9.7 (κατὰ τὸ παλαιὸν παρεῖχον ἀρχήν) for an element of recurrence; cf. Dionysius, *apud* Eusebius, *HE*, 7.24.2–3, and (for a similar yet later and

pagan attempt to relate the new developments to the best of the old order), Ammianus Marcellinus, 14.6.6.

54. Cf. esp. *VC*, 1.59, where the nature of Licinius' death atones for his persecution.

55. It is possible that Eusebius had paraphrased parts of a document here, and thus injected some of his own conceptions (possibly adding the reference to γῆ τῶν κολαστηρίων at the end of 2.27?), but most of the passages (with the terms τὸ κρεῖττον, and τὸ θεῖον for the God, cf. *HE*, 10.5.4, 5 for the latter) fit in with what one would expect of imperial pronouncements.

56. For background, J. Ferguson, *The Place of Suffering* (Cambridge and London 1972), chs. 2–3, 6.

57. E.g., Polybius, *Hist.*, 8.30.9 (cf. 1–8), 18.15.7, Cicero, *Pro Sestio*, 67.40, Plutarch, *De sera numinis vindicta*, esp. 548C–549D, Diodorus, *Bibliot.*, 16.61.1–4.

58. *HE*, 8.7.2, cf. 5.3.3 (Christ strengthens the martyrs), 8.7.2–6 (instances of muzzled beasts), *MP*, 9.12 (L, S) (nature sheds tears), *HE*, 4.7.1–2, 15.40, etc. (on Devil and persecution, cf. above), 10.4.12, cf. *DE*, 3.7 (137d) (Christ takes on our penalties).

59. Esp. 1 Kgs 12:25–31, 2 Kgs 17:21–3; 21:1–15, Josephus, *Antiq.*, 8.225–9, 9.282, 10.78–81, 103–4, 139, 142.

60. E.g., Herodotus, *Hist.*, 1.170–1, 9.89–107 (on Ionia under Persia), Thucydides, *Hist.*, esp. 5.84–113 (on the problems of Athenian imperialism), cf. Plato, *Leg.*, 3.695b–696a, Livy, 1.25.1.

61. E.g., Thucydides, *Hist.*, 1.78–84 (on Corcyra), Polybius, *Hist.*, 24.3 (4) (on Crete), 6.9.6–9, 15.21.1–2 (Cios).

62. 1 Macc. 1–14, 4 Macc. 1:11, 6:28–30, 10:1–17:22, cf. 2 Macc. 5:28, 7:32–3, 37, 3 Macc. 2:28–33, cf. J. Downing, 'Jesus and Martyrdom', *Journal of Theological Studies* 14 (1963), 281–5. Eusebius' Christian martyrological sources, of course, are not to be forgotten; cf. H. Musurillo (ed.), *The Acts of the Christian Martyrs* (Oxford 1972).

63. E.g., Ezra, 4:1–6:3, 13, Neh. 4:1–6:15, Acts 5:7–41, 11:19–12:25, 14:1–22, 16:19–40, 19:9–41, 21:27–28:31. Cf. G. Miles and G. W. Trompf, 'Luke and Antiphon', *Harvard Theological Review* 69 (1976), 259–67.

64. Trompf, *Recurrence*, 233–4, and on Augustine, 209, 211, 236–7.

65. Eusebius' judgment to document those matters which were 'profitable' (cf. ὠφελεία, 2.3) should be added to the list of principles conditioning the historiography and selection methods of his successors. Cf. G. Downey, 'The Perspective of the Early Church Historians', *Greek, Roman and Byzantine Studies* 6 (1965), 57–70.

66. Details as to the precise contextual manifestations of these weaknesses within the Church are lacking. Church historians tend to evade the issue; e.g. H. Lietzmann, *A History of the Christian Church* (trans. B. L. Woolf) (London 1961), vol. 3, 57–9.

67. μῖσος ἐπαύξοντες οἷά τε τυραννίδας τὰς φιλαρχίας ἐκθύμως διεκδικοῦντες.

68. A play on words? ἐπισκοπή can also denote the visitation of divine wrath, or punishment (cf. e.g., *Comm. in Isa.*, 84 (24:17–20) [p.158, *ll.* 22–3], Athanasius, *Expos. in Pss.*, 63:10). It is interesting to ask whether the forbidding associations of this term were of consequence sociologically (in discounting or enhancing the image of the Church).

69. Lactantius, *De Ira Dei*, 20–1; Orosius, *Hist. adv. pag.*, 7.37, 39, cf. 4.17.

70.   And in the first edition, of Licinius; cf. 9.11.9.

71.   Eusebius disagrees with an alternative view in 5.28.2–3.

72.   2.1.10–12, 13.1–15; 3.26.1–4, 32.8; 4.7.1–14, 10.1–5 (Gnosticism), 2.27.1–29.4; 6.17 cf. *DE* 7.1 (316b) (Ebionites and related), *HE*, 5.4.4–4.2, 16.1–19.4 (Montanism); 5.13.1–9 (Marcionites); 4.22.7, 24.1, etc. (various).

73.   Esp. *HE*, 2.14.2; 8.1.6–3.1; 10.4.57, cf. 3.26.4, 27.1; 4.7.1–2, 10; 14.1; 6.43.4; 7.31; *VC*, 3.12.

74.   *The Conflict between Paganism and Christianity in the Fourth Century* (Oxford 1963), 90. Cf. Eusebius, *DE*, 4.9–10 (159c–164b) on the Devil (or Chief Daimon) and the Fall of Angels at the beginning of Time.

75.   On the problems of dating this epidemic and the Dionysian Festal Epistles see Lawlor and Oulton, *op. cit.*, vol. 2, 250–3.

76.   Cf. Polybius, *Hist.*, 32.4.2.

77.   See G. E. Wright, *God Who Acts (Studies in Biblical Theology 8)* (London 1952). For background on πρόνοια, see esp. Diodorus Siculus, *Bibliot.*, 1.1.3; 3.58.1; 4.47.1, 48.7, etc., Philo, *De Provid.*, 4 Macc. 9:24, 17:22, Clement of Alexandria, *Epist.*, 8, etc.; and in the imperial language of Eusebius' day, cf. *HE*, 10.5.18. Cf. also *DE*, 4.10 (164b).

Paul the Deacon and Secundus of Trento

Ken Gardiner

It has long been recognised that for parts of his *History of the Lombards*, Paul the Deacon must have relied upon a lost chronicle by Secundus of Trento. When discussing the Frankish invasions of Italy in the late sixth century, Paul comments upon the Lombard victory of 588 and remarks that he is astonished that Secundus, 'who wrote something about the doings of the Lombards', should pass over such a victory in silence.[1] Here surely the implication is that Paul had searched through the work of Secundus for a notice of this event (which he himself had taken from Gregory of Tours: *HF* 9.25) without being able to find it; evidently the chronicle of Secundus was a work to which Paul had access and not simply a title of which he may have heard. There are two other references to Secundus, but only one of these mentions his chronicle. This is the notice of his death in Book 4: 'In the following March, Secundus, that servant of Christ whom we have often had occasion to mention, died in Trento. He had composed a brief outline of the deeds of the Lombards down to his own day. In the same year King Agilulf renewed the truce he had concluded with the Emperor. At the same time also the Frankish king Theudebert was killed, and a bitter conflict took place amongst that people' (*HL* 4.40). The war between Theuderich of Burgundy and Theudebert of Austrasia which led to the death of the latter is known from the so-called *Chronicle of Fredegar* (4.38) to have taken place in 612. Thus if Paul's chronological indications are to be taken at their face value (and Paul is notoriously vague about chronology), then Secundus must have died in March 612. Paul describes the work as a 'brief outline' (*usque ad sua tempora succinctam de Langobardorum gestis conposuit historiam*), but without other evidence this ambiguous phrase gives little idea of the type of work which Secundus actually wrote. However, like other writers of his day, Paul frequently transcribed whole sections from his sources, as for example his use of Gregory of Tours in Book 3. We may therefore be alerted by any noticeable difference of style and content in a large section of his *History* and suspect the ghost of a lost chronicle.

This observation applies particularly to the first forty chapters of Book 4. Until this point, extended narrative has predominated. Sometimes this is taken over with very little change from a known source, as with the first eight chapters of Book 3, which are derived from Gregory of Tours. At other times, the narrative passages are apparently based on saga-type material which may well represent oral tradition: examples of this are the story of Alboin and Thorisind (*HL* 1.23, 24) or the story of Alboin's death and the nemesis of his murderers (*HL* 2.28–30). With the opening of Book 4, however, the style changes abruptly: the reader is confronted with a number of chapters outlining the events of the day in terse annalistic entries, looking in fact very much as if they had been excerpted from a chronicle similar to that written by Marius of Aventicum (Avenches) in the late sixth century. The principal exceptions are chapters 37 and 38, which represent a reversion to the earlier 'saga-style'. Chapter 37, the longest in the entire work, centres around the youth of Grimoald, later Duke of Benevento and later still King of the Lombards. It seems to form part of a fairly lengthy 'saga' of Grimoald, which surfaces again in Book 5. The rest of the chapter deals with the traditions of Paul's own family. Chapter 38 deals with the deaths of two of Grimoald's brothers and gives an account which is interestingly at variance with that found in the *Chronicle of Fredegar*. One may suspect that much or most of this material came from oral tradition.

As they stand, chapters 37 and 38 are very different from the chapters of annalistic material, about which two further general points may be made. First, this annalistic material covers only a brief section of Lombard history, virtually beginning with the accession of King Agilulf at the end of Book 3 (in 590), and ending with Book 4.40, just before Agilulf's death, less than twenty-five years later. This mass of detail covering such a narrow chronological span is unparalleled in other parts of the *History* (unless perhaps by the account of Liutprand in Book 6 — which, however, lacks the annalistic character of Book 4).[2] The character of these chapters of Book 4, and the amount of information they contain, is underlined by the fact that the reigns immediately succeeding Agilulf's are the worst documented of any in the *History*: in less than ten chapters Paul surveys the period 615/16–661, which covers five reigns. Moreover, for one of these kings (Arioald) Paul himself admits that he had virtually no information (*HL* 4.43). This abrupt change suggests that with Book 4.40, Paul came to the end of an important body of source material. Significantly, this is the same chapter which deals with the death of Secundus of Trento who 'composed a brief outline of the deeds of the Lombards down to his own day'. This in itself might indicate that, if we are to see behind the annalistic chapters of Book 4 some sort of chronicle (similar perhaps to that written by Marius of Aventicum in the sixth century), it is no coincidence that this chronicle ends with the death of Secundus.

Chronology and weather

So far we have dealt merely with the form and style of the annalistic chapters of Book 4. It remains to be determined whether there are features of content which are peculiar to this part of Paul's work. A remarkable fact is that it is in this part of the *History* that we get almost the only exact dates. In the last chapter of Book 3, King Authari, the immediate predecessor of Agilulf, is said to have died on 5 September of a year which is quite certainly 590.[3] This is the only exact date of death which is available for any of the Lombard kings chronicled by Paul. Paul also knows the date of Authari's marriage to Theudelinda (15 May, 589 or 590, *HL* 3.30). A further exact date is found in 4.27 — this time in specific connection with Secundus, for we are told that Secundus himself received from the font the child Adaloald, Agilulf's son, 'when Easter Day fell upon the seventh of April' which could only be in 603. Clearly here is an item of information which must have come from the work of Secundus and which shows that as a chronicler Secundus did include the exact date of events which fell within his own personal experience. Only twice after this are events dated by month and day in Paul's *History*; both examples come from 4.28, where we are told, 'At this time hostilities were still going on between the Lombards and the imperial forces . . . Hence King Agilulf left Milan in July, and went to lay siege to the city of Cremona. He took the city on 21 August and razed it to the ground. In the same way he stormed Mantua . . . on 13 September'. After this there is no further example of dating by month and day in the rest of Paul's *History*.[4]

This type of chronological indication is a fairly strong sign that we are dealing, even if it is not at first hand, with the evidence of a contemporary. The same is true of the various notices concerning weather, which begin as early as 2.10, where the winter following the Lombard invasion of Italy (in 568) is said to have been one of exceptional severity, being followed by a bumper harvest in the summer. In 3.23, Paul describes torrential rains and floods in the autumn of a year which is evidently 589, including a flood in the city of Verona on 17 October. Paul could have taken the notice of this flood from Gregory the Great's *Dialogues* — but then he would not have found in the *Dialogues* any reference to the fire which, as he notes towards the end of his chapter, destroyed most of Verona just two months after the flood.[5] Nor indeed would he have found any reference there to the actual date of the flood itself.

References to weather, to celestial phenomena and something certainly thought to be related to them, to outbreaks of plague, become especially frequent in Book 4. We have mention of a drought which is said to have lasted from January to September in 591, and this is connected with a reference to locusts in the territory of Trento (*HL* 4.2). The drought also affected France and is mentioned by Gregory of Tours in the last chapter of his history (*HF* 10.30). But naturally enough Gregory says nothing of Trento, and it would seem certain that the locusts, if not the drought, would have been taken from the lost chronicle of Secundus. Two chapters later, apparently referring to the year 594, Paul mentions an outbreak of plague in north-eastern Italy and another very severe winter, with a rain of blood in the Brenner Pass — again an area near Trento. Celestial phenomena mentioned in this part of the *History* include a comet in January 595 (*HL* 4.10), and another in April and May 607 (*HL* 4.32). In both cases Paul is vague about the years, but the exact dates of the spectacular comets he mentions can be checked against the much more precise notices in the Chinese dynastic history covering this period — the *Sui-shu*, written in the mid-seventh century.

Comets might be invented by a historian writing later, but in this case they would hardly correspond with the actual dates on which these bodies are known to have been visible. Similarly, notices of drought and exceptional cold are not necessarily the work of a contemporary; but on the whole they are more likely to have attracted the notice of someone writing at the time these events actually occurred. Once again we should notice that Secundus was such a writer, and two of the weather notices, as already seen, relate to his home territory. The observations recall those included by Gregory of Tours in his account of sixth-century France, in that part of Gregory's writing where he is dealing with the events of his own lifetime.[6]

It is clear that, as well as detecting Paul's probable debts to an earlier writer, this line of argument allows a clearer idea of the actual character of the lost work of Secundus. The fact that it included precise dates and notices of weather confirms the earlier suggestion that Secundus composed a book in which entries were arranged year by year. It was an arrangement which Paul broke up, incorporating material from other sources, such as the letters of Pope Gregory the Great in 4.9 and 4.19. Part of the dislocation must also spring from Paul's fundamental disregard for chronology. The unfortunate result is that when there is no parallel entry in another source, be it Frankish or Chinese, then the actual date of an event is often impossible to disinter from Paul's narrative alone.

Frankish material

Another feature of Paul's *History* which mostly disappears slowly from 4.40 onwards is the reference to Frankish affairs. Since Paul lived during the Frankish conquest of Italy and since he also visited the Court of Charlemagne in France, he might well be expected to have felt an interest in this aspect of history even when it was not strictly germane to his theme. However, the way in which Frankish affairs disappear completely from his pages at the end of Book 4 and for the whole of Book 5 (a few scraps of information surface in Book 6) seems quite significant.

For the period before 591, Paul drew heavily upon the *History* of Gregory of Tours, of which he appears to have seen a text which contained all ten books, unlike the author of the so-called *Chronicle of Fredegar*, who seems to have known only the first six books.[7] Gregory's work ends in 591, but Paul's record of events amongst the Merovingian Franks continues until 612. Now, this period was covered in two Frankish chronicles: the eighth-century Neustrian *Liber Historiae Francorum* (also known as the *Gesta Francorum*) and the fourth book of the *Chronicle of Fredegar*. Of these two, the first has a much looser chronological structure, at least in its earlier chapters, and in this respect it is closer to Paul's *History*. However, a comparison of versions of the same events in the three texts makes it clear that Paul was not using either of the Frankish chronicles. Thus in 4.4 — immediately before the account of the bitterly cold winter — Paul tells us that 'Childebert waged war against his cousin, Chilperic's son; in this conflict as many as thirty thousand men lost their lives'. This is the famous battle of Droizy, which took place in 594 and is tersely noted in the *Chronicle of Fredegar*: 'In this year Wintrio, Duke of Champagne, invaded in force the kingdom of Chlothair; but the king and his warriors went to meet him and they put him to flight. Both sides suffered great losses'.[8] This account differs from Paul's in that it indicates the result of the battle, although it does not give the number of the slain. Similarly, the *Liber Historiae Francorum* gives an elaborate and highly coloured account of the battle (which includes an anticipation of Malcolm Canmore's use of Dunsinane Wood), but it ends by stating that 'an innumerable multitude' of the Austrasians were slain.[9] Clearly Paul's figure of thirty thousand must have come from another source.

Other references to Frankish affairs in Book 4 show similar discrepancies. Both the *Liber Historiae Francorum* and 'Fredegar' mention the death of Childebert, King of Austrasia and Burgundy (apparently in 596),[10] but it is only in Paul's writing that we find the information that his wife died at the same time, and that the deaths were said to be due to poison (*HL* 4.11). Similarly, Paul goes on to report an invasion of Austrasia by the Avars, which apparently happened soon after Childebert's death, while his mother Brunhild was regent for her young grandsons, Theudebert and Theuderich — and Brunhild, Paul alleges, was obliged to buy peace from the invaders. But this entire episode is completely unknown to the Frankish chroniclers. There are also other examples of such events which are recorded in this part of Paul's work but which are passed over in silence by the Frankish chroniclers, for instance a bitter war between the Franks and Saxons, *c.* 605 (*HL* 4.28).

What then was the independent source for the history of the Franks which Paul consulted? Significantly, it appears to run out with Book 4.40 in Paul's *History*. Book 4.40 contains the last mention of Frankish affairs for almost a century (in other words, well into Book 6) with a reference to the battle which brought about the death of Theudebert of Austrasia in 612. The terse annalistic character of these Frankish entries, and the point that they disappear from Paul's pages just where the rest of the annalistic material taken from Secundus gives out, suggests strongly that these Frankish entries are themselves taken from Secundus' lost work. Secundus' interest in Frankish affairs is hinted at in 4.1, where we have an account of the visit of Bishop Agnellus of Trento to France in order to ransom Lombard captives, which is followed by praise of the generosity of Queen Brunhild and a report of another visit to France, by the Duke of Trento himself. The location of Trento virtually ensured that its ruler would be more concerned with events amongst the Franks than were Lombard leaders in other parts of Italy. Thus it does not seem too far-fetched to suggest that, like the accounts of weather and comets, the references to Frankish affairs in Book 4 are also derived from Secundus.

Avars, Bavarians and others

How much, then, of Paul's Book 4 should we see as derived from the pages of Secundus? We know that Secundus was an important cleric, apparently a supporter of the Three Chapters Schism, and one who had close relations with the Lombard Court, as seen from the fact that he received Prince Adaloald from the font in 603. This situation would have given him an excellent vantage point to observe the diplomacy of King Agilulf and Queen Theudelinda; and probably the favourable press which these rulers receive in Paul's *History* derives partly from Secundus.[11] Two of the other recurrent themes in this part of the book – relationships with the Avars, and the repeated truces with the Byzantine exarch – are probably taken from Secundus. Both occur only in the form of 'annalistic' items in the relevant part of Paul's work, that is, the first forty chapters of Book 4. Moreover, if Secundus was a friend of Queen Theudelinda, as seems likely, this may have given him an interest in Bavarian affairs, for Theudelinda was a Bavarian princess. For references to Bavarian affairs, like the other features discussed, are confined to this same part of Paul's *History*. At the same time, however, a position close to the Lombard Court would also have had its liabilities: there were doubtless matters which the chronicler from Trento would have thought it advisable not to record. Here another comparison between Paul's *History* and the so-called *Chronicle of Fredegar* is suggestive. In one of the last passages apparently taken from Secundus (in 4.40 again) Paul writes: 'Gundoald, Queen Theudelinda's brother, who was Duke of Asti, was slain by an arrow . . .; it is not known who instigated the deed', while the contemporaneous Burgundian writer of *Fredegar* 4.34 wrote of the same event: 'Since Gundoald was too popular with the Lombards, Ago [i.e. Agilulf] and Theudelinda, already suspicious, caused him to be shot with an arrow while he was relieving nature. Thus he died'.[12] There is no way of knowing whether the Burgundian chronicler was here simply reporting unfounded rumour, or whether Paul, following Secundus, was suppressing an unpleasant fact.

Much has been said about Paul's debt to Secundus in this part of his *History* (Book 4 and the latter part of Book 3); nevertheless there remain interpolated passages of material plainly derived from other sources. Some of this comes from extant works, such as the letters of Gregory the Great, quoted in 4.9 and 19. The account of the sack of Monte Cassino by Zotto's Lombards (*HL* 4.17) is also taken from Gregory, this time from *Dialogues* 3.17. Then again the description of Lombard costume in 4.22 is unlikely to be from Secundus. It is clearly written at a distance from the world of the late sixth century, and probably derives from Paul's own observations of the frescoes at Monza. The tell-tale comparison with the 'Angli-Saxones' would never have occurred to Secundus, and probably reflects Paul's own interests and his reading of Bede. Moreover, if we are correct in believing that the lost work of Secundus was essentially a chronicle with terse annalistic entries, then it seems doubtful that any of the passages of extended narrative which occasionally surface in this part of

Paul's *History* came from Secundus. An independent origin has already been suggested for 4.37 which consists either of material from the 'Grimoald saga' or the oral traditions of Paul's own family; much the same is likely to be true of the romantic tale of Authari's marriage to Theudelinda in 3.30, even though such an outstanding scholar as Bognetti was inclined to ascribe this too to Secundus.[13] The obvious literary tone of this passage, replete with imaginary speeches, is very different from the terse 'annalistic' style which we have regarded as the hallmark of Secundus. Either Secundus' work contained other chapters in a very different style, or, as I suspect, Paul is here dressing up an oral tradition, as he is almost certainly doing in the story of Guntramn's dream which follows in 3.34.

Where did Secundus stop?

So far I have attempted to point out the special character of the writing in Book 4 (and some earlier chapters) of Paul's *History*, and to suggest that types of content which are found in this part of his work and nowhere else are probably derived from the lost chronicle of Secundus. However, 4.40 itself clearly poses a problem, since this chapter, which is the last in the 'annalistic' style, gives the date of Secundus' death as March of the year in which King Theudebert was killed, that is, March 612. Obviously Secundus could not have composed a chronicle entry recording the date of his own death! Nor could Secundus, even if he had continued writing until his last breath, have known about the death of King Theudebert of Austrasia. According to the *Chronicle of Fredegar* 4.38, it was not until May 612 that Theuderich collected his armies to march against Theudebert; there then followed a protracted campaign involving two major battles before Theudebert was finally eliminated. Did Paul therefore have some other source for these notices? If so, this strikes at the foundation of our ideas about the character of Secundus' writing as argued above. In fact, the solution is not so difficult. We do not know when and where the chronicle of Secundus stopped. Gregory of Tours ended his *History of the Franks* in 591, three years before his own death. But it seems quite possible that whenever Secundus stopped writing, a disciple of his may have continued the chronicle as far as the death of its original author, which may have appeared a natural terminus, along with the events of that year. Alternatively, the information about the events of 612 may have been derived from a colophon to Secundus' work.

More of a problem is presented by Paul's account of the patriarchs of Aquileia, adherents of the Three Chapters Schism, and therefore perhaps of special interest to Secundus. Once again we are dealing with material which is confined to the second, third and fourth books of Paul's work. He first refers to the patriarchs of Grado when mentioning the flight of the patriarch Paul (Paulinus) to Grado from Aquileia in 568, the year of the Lombard invasion of Italy. He then refers to the succession of patriarchs at intervals in the third and fourth books, until the death of Patriarch Severus (in 607) in 4.33. On the death of Severus there was a disputed succession. Paul records a series of two patriarchs — Candidianus and Epiphanius — being elected in Grado, while a certain John the Abbot was appointed patriarch in old Aquileia with the consent of King Agilulf and the Duke of Friuli. 'After this,' says Paul, 'there were always two rival patriarchs'. Now, figures for the length of tenure of the patriarchate by Severus and his successors in Grado can be found in the writing of John the Deacon, a Venetian chronicler of the early eleventh century. John inserts a certain Marcianus between Severus and Candidianus, and gives Severus a patriarchate of twenty-eight years. This would put his death in 614 and place the accession of Epiphanius, the last of the series, long after the death of Secundus and long after the latest information which we have ascribed to the lost chronicle. If the chronology of the somewhat later *Chronicle of the Patriarchs of Grado* is preferred, this gives Severus twenty-one years.[14] His death would then have occurred in 607, and this seems correct for other reasons. However, Marcianus still appears — apparently his tomb was shown in Grado — with a patriarchate of three years, and Candidianus with one of five, thus putting the accession of Epiphanius at 615 — again too late for our purposes. We are therefore left, it would seem, with three possible explanations: either Paul used a source for his account of the patriarchs which was *not* Secundus' chronicle, but which nevertheless ran out within a few years of the end of that text; or he used a copy of the chronicle which had been extended to cover the reigns of the Gradentine patriarchs down to Epiphanius — but apparently no other information after 612; or (and this is the explanation which I would see as more likely) the eleventh-century figures for the lengths of the patriarchates involved have to be rejected. It seems that John the Deacon was wrong about the patriarchate of Severus; it is therefore possible that the figures for his three successors in Grado are also in error, and that all three have to be accommodated between 607 and 612, which would bring them within the bounds of the Secundus chronicle as it appears to have been known to Paul.

Conclusion

We may well regret the loss of the original text of the chronicle of Secundus. In spite of its terse annalistic quality, the record of a contemporary is always invaluable to historians, particularly in a period as ill-documented as the late sixth and early seventh centuries. Yet, fortunately, we can show that the chronicle is not entirely lost to us. It still subsists in the very considerable and still detectable borrowings made from it by Paul the Deacon. We may regret the chronological blurring which has taken place when the work of an annalist is subsumed into that of a historian, but perhaps this is part of the penalty which is paid when a larger task is attempted. As it stands, Paul's *History* ends abruptly with the reign of Liutprand, at about the time of Paul's own birth. Presumably this interruption is due to Paul's death. Had he survived to write an account of the Lombards of his own day, then he too might have ended up noting down events as he had witnessed them, just as Secundus seems to have done. As it stands, however, his work surveys a past of several centuries, and over this vast period he has evidently attempted to harmonise discrepant accounts and sources as various as the *History* of Gregory of Tours, the letters and *Dialogues* of Pope Gregory, the papal lives of the *Liber Pontificalis* collection, and Lombard oral tradition. We may feel a lack of sophistication in Paul's crude juxtapositions of one source with another; we may complain about his chronological blunders and the tangles which they create — but recognisably Paul is attempting the task of the historian. There is no evidence to show that Secundus ever did this.

154   *Gardiner*

Notes

1.   *HL* 3.29: 'aliqua de Langobardorum gestis scripsit'.

2.   Superficially Book 3 might seem to cover only the short six-year reign of Authari; however, Paul's chronological vagaries bring in events of much later date, while much of the Book consists of chapters taken over from Gregory of Tours with little or no direct connection with Lombard affairs.

3.   Cf. the notice of the death of King Aptachar (= Authari) in the fifteenth year of Childebert II (= 590) in Gregory of Tours, *HF* 10.3.

4.   One earlier example of an exact date which should be noticed is that of the flood in Verona (cf. above, p.149) dated to 17 October in a year which is evidently 589. See *HL* 3.23.

5.   See Gregory the Great, *Dialogues* 3.19, where the flood is associated with a most un-likely miracle. The flood shut people inside the church; it did not penetrate into the building through the doors and windows; when the people inside felt thirsty they were able to help themselves to a drink from the wall of water.

6.   See for example *HF* 3.37 (a severe winter); comets and pestilence in 4.41 and 6.13; drought in 10.30, etc.

7.   See J. M. Wallace-Hadrill, *The Fourth Book of the Chronicle of Fredegar* (London 1960), xiv.

8.   *ibid.*, 10–11.1.

9.   *Liber Historiae Francorum [LHF]* 36.

10.   *LHF* 37 and *'Fredegar'* 4.16; the latter text follows the mention of Childebert's death with an account of a major battle between the Neustrian forces and those of Childebert's sons Theudebert and Theuderich, concerning which Paul is silent.

11.   There are a few indications – such as the death of Ansul in 3.30, and the alleged poisoning of Theudelinda's first husband, Authari in 3.35 – which hint at a darker side to life at the Court of Agilulf and Theudelinda. Cf. the account of Gundoald's death (above, p.151).

12.   Translation of Wallace-Hadrill, *op. cit.*, 22.

13.   See G. P. Bognetti, 'La Storiografia di Paolo Diacono', in *L'Età Langobarda*, 3 (Milan 1967), 167.

14.   Edited by Waitz in the same volume as his *MGH* edition of Paul the Deacon, 394.

The West and the Roman Past; from Theoderic to Charlemagne

John Moorhead

There is a sense in which medieval and much modern cultural and intellectual history is the product of a sustained relationship with the classical past. Greek and Roman Antiquity has exerted a powerful attraction over subsequent eras of European history. But however great its mystique, later periods have chosen to define their relationships to it in different ways: twelfth-century scholars saw themselves as dwarfs perched on the shoulders of ancient giants, and fifteenth-century *littérateurs* perceived themselves as the revivers of desirable classical standards of excellence. I offer this paper as part of an enquiry into medieval perceptions of the past; and I wish to address the question of how writers and the subjects of their discourses in the approximate period 500 to 800 assessed their relationship with the Roman past.

It need hardly be said that any coverage will be selective. I am not familiar with hagiographical literature, and so leave untouched the figure of the Roman in saints' lives. I shall have next to nothing to say about art, for despite its interest the relationship of an artist to his models remains obscure to one whose training lies elsewhere. Further, I must own at the outset to being a medievalist, not a classicist, and a historian, not a philologist; and when I move beyond the period which could be described as late Antiquity it will be to suggest that we then enter a period in which people began to see themselves as enjoying a new relationship with Antiquity.

The fall of the Roman Empire in the West excited little interest in what had formerly been its continental provinces, the inhabitants of which continued to see themselves as living within the Roman *oikoumene*.[1] This is made clear by our sources for Ostrogothic Italy. According to the *Excerpta Valesiana* Theoderic had been sent to Italy by the Emperor Zeno (474–91), having come to an agreement that he would rule in Zeno's place [*loco eius*] until the Emperor came,[2] and evidence from a number of sources suggests that the Roman inhabitants of Italy looked at Theoderic in ways usually reserved for emperors.[3] In 499 a synod of the Roman church acclaimed Theoderic in exactly the same way that imperial images were later acclaimed.[4] Cassiodorus, in his *Chronicle*, described Theoderic's visit to Rome in 500 in terms suggestive of an imperial *adventus*: Theoderic came to Rome, held discussions with his Senate, and with wondrous kindness gave *annonae* to the Roman people (s.a. 500, *MGH AA* 11). Needless to say, Cassiodorus was an apologist of Ostrogothic power. In his letters written on behalf of Ostrogothic monarchs, he strove to suggest a return to earlier imperial and even republican times by means of *imitatio* and *renovatio*,[5] and claimed that in his lost *History*, 'Originem Gothicam historiam fecit esse Romanam',[6] which may

155

make one inclined to doubt his implicit assimilation of Theoderic into an imperial model. But the description of Theoderic's coming to Rome given by the *Excerpta Valesiana* is similarly indicative of a contemporary perception that Theoderic fulfilled the role of an emperor:

> Pope Symmachus and all the senate and people of Rome came out of the city with great joy. Then, coming to the city and entering it, [Theoderic] went to the senate, and spoke to the people at the Palma. He promised that with the help of God he would preserve inviolate what Roman leaders [*principes*] had ordained formerly.[7]

Theoderic carried out a building programme which Cassiodorus again placed in relation with earlier times:

> Under this happy government [*felici imperio*] many cities were renewed [*renovantur*], fortresses were built, splendid palaces arose, and old marvels were overcome by his great works.[8]

Similarly Ennodius proclaimed that, thanks to the building in the reign of Theoderic, Rome, the mother of cities whose limbs had been withered by age, became youthful again (*pan. Theod.* 11). Some decades later, when Italy had been conquered by the armies of Justinian, it was only natural for Cassiodorus to assume in one of his Biblical commentaries that Rome still stood.[9] In the two books of his *Institutiones* Cassiodorus was not only content to direct the attention of his monastic readers to classics produced in a bygone age. He was also able to recommend the works of Eugippius 'quem nos quoque vidimus', (*Inst.* 1.23.1) and in the context of a discussion of Dionysius Exiguus, a man of *nostris temporibus*, he noted that in his day the Catholic church produced noteworthy men who shone with the beauty of sound doctrine.[10] The works of Boethius were also cited.[11]

It seems clear that Italians in the sixth century were able to assert continuity with Antiquity. It could be argued that Italy was a special case: given the large, traditionally-minded Senate, the tolerant policies of at least Theoderic among the Ostrogothic kings, and, later, the circumstance of the Byzantine conquest, the perception of continuity is easily understood. But a similar perception may be found in Gaul, where the period of early Frankish rule witnessed attempts to locate their rule within a reputable classical Roman framework. It was alleged that the origin of the Franks was Trojan,[12] and that Childeric, the father of Clovis, had been ordered to go to Gaul by the Emperor Maurice (that is, Marcian).[13] The contents of Childeric's tomb have been interpreted as showing that he saw himself as the successor of the Roman rulers of Gaul.[14] In a famous passage, Gregory of Tours relates that the Emperor Anastasius (491–518) made Clovis consul, whereupon he wore purple, distributed largesse among the people of Tours, and became known as consul and *Augustus*.[15] Clovis' grandson Childeric also seems to have deliberately imitated the conduct of an emperor. He built amphitheatres in Soissons and Paris so that he could offer shows to the people, took it upon himself to propound an original formulation of Christological doctrine and, presumably in imitation of Claudius, invented three new letters for the Latin alphabet, which he ordered to be used in place of unspecified old ones.[16] Thus in Gaul as in Italy there seems to have been a prolongation of Roman forms of life and a feeling among both Romans and barbarians of continuity with the immediate Roman past.[17]

I suspect that a decisive shift in consciousness may first have appeared in Visigothic Spain, and that it is related to a number of curious features in the works of Isidore of Seville (*c.* 570 –636). In his *Etymologi* Isidore enumerates the ecumenical councils (*principales synodi*) of the church. He lists four, starting with Nicaea and finishing with Chalcedon.[18] Yet a fifth council, Constantinople II, had been held at the behest of Justinian in 553, and its decrees had been accepted, although under protest, by Pope Vigilius and subsequent popes. Elsewhere in his works Isidore frequently refers to the policies adopted by Justinian's council, of which he invariably expresses disapproval [19] — a response which presumably accounts for his failure to recognise it as an ecumenical council. In the same way, Isidore's list *De auctoribus legum* is truncated, for it extends only to Theodosius II and ignores Justinian's claim to be a promulgator of laws (*Etym.* 5.1). It would seem reasonable to assume that some hostility towards Justinian is operating here. I would suggest that it was bound up with a general animosity towards the Byzantines arising from their attempted conquest of Spain which began in 554, animosity which was so bitter that it paradoxically ruined the posthumous reputation of Hermenigild, the first Catholic convert among Visigothic royalty (on the grounds of his collaboration with the Byzantines).[20] Before the mass conversion of the Visigoths to Catholicism they called Catholics *Romani*,[21] but after the conversion in the reign of Reccared and the abolition of restrictions on intermarriage between Goths and Romans by his predecessor Leovigild the only contemporary application of the term was to the hated Byzantine invaders.[22] Pejorative contemporary connotations coloured the term, and it may well be that they were bound up with sentiments strongly favourable to the Goths and a feeling of pleasure that they had earlier taken Spain from the *Romani*. Consider Isidore's *De laude Spaniae*:

> And so rightly did golden Rome, the head of peoples, yearn for you long ago, and first that glorious Romulean strength was allowed to pledge itself to you. But, again, the most flourishing people of the Goths eagerly seized and loved you, and enjoys you still amid royal ornaments and abundant wealth in the secure felicity of empire.
>
> (*MGH AA* 11, 167).

Similarly, in the *Recapitulatio* at the end of his *Historia Gothorum* Isidore observes that Rome, who had been victorious over all peoples, had been brought to the yoke of captivity by Gothic triumphs, so that the mistress of all races (*gentium*) was now their subject handmaiden (*Recap.* 67). Isidore looked with favour on a transition from Roman to Gothic periods in Spanish history. We have come a long way from Theoderic.

The documentation for the period after Isidore is patchy, but the evidence suggests that seventh-century Spanish culture was self-confident, prepared both to look Antiquity in the eye and also to see itself as moving beyond it. Bishop Braulio of Saragossa described Isidore as one whom Antiquity claimed as its own, and as one whom his own age saw as possessing the knowledge of Antiquity (*PL* 82,65). Isidore, Braulio believed, was one raised up by God *novissimis temporibus*: 'for the purpose of restoring the monuments of the ancients, and giving us something to lean against, as it were' (*PL* 82,67). Ildefonsus of Toledo did not think it absurd to claim that Pope Gregory surpassed Anthony in holiness, Cyprian in eloquence, and Augustine in wisdom (*PL* 96,198). The period after the end of the sixth century saw the hitherto opposed Gothic and provincial-Roman artistic forms come together:[23] while the golden crowns of seventh-century Visigothic monarchs symbolised 'an idea of kingship deeply embedded in the popular imagination, without reference to the ancient Roman past'.[24] Coronation ceremonial was expanded to incorporate a new element of unction by clergy.[25]

In short, by the seventh century Visigothic Spain was prepared to assert equality with the Roman past, if not positive advance beyond it. We have no way of knowing how this high degree of self-regard in the face of Antiquity would have developed in Spain, for in the early eighth century the Visigothic kingdom was abruptly terminated by Muslim conquest. But such development can be traced in Francia. The Franks were slow developers. While the Byzantines were attacking Spain, Gregory of Tours was busy incorporating Byzantine material in his *History*, apparently ignoring the substantial irrelevance because of its inherent fascination.[26] It also seems that Gregory failed to make a connection between *Romani* and Byzantines. Only once does he term the Byzantines Romans, and on this he is quoting from an inscription on a medallion sent to Francia by the Emperor Tiberius (*HF* 6.2). Elsewhere it almost seems that Gregory avoids applying a proper noun to the inhabitants of the Empire, except in conjunction with their activities in Spain — where they are called *Graeci* (*HF* 5.38, 6.40).

Just as holiness, for Gregory, was vested in the material remains of the long-dead,[27] so the concept of Rome belonged to the past, but it was a past which had never come to a clear end. A century before Gregory, Sidonius Apollinaris had playfully compared the members of his literary circle to classical worthies in terms suggestive of equality (*carm.* 2, 4.446, 5.97). Gregory, who was by no means impressed with the literary culture of his time and who felt himself open to the accusation of being *rusticus*,[28] could never have done this. Nor could he have accepted the estimate of immediately preceding culture which had been made by Cassiodorus,[29] and as for the later historian who wrote under the name Fredegarius, 'mundus iam senescit'. Fredegarius believed that no-one of his time was similar to earlier *oratores*, or could even pretend to be similar. For himself, *rusticitas* and *stermitas* [sic] were all he could lay claim to.[30] One has the feeling of someone working in a tradition which he feels to have been hopelessly debased and beyond his power to restore, yet which is still operative. Only in the eighth century did the inhabitants of Francia confidently move into a post-Roman world.

The self-esteem of the eighth-century Franks in the face of Antiquity is well caught in the prologue to a revised edition of the Salic Law. The prologue begins:

> The famous race of the Franks, established through God its founder, strong in arms, steadfast in peaceful alliance, deep in counsel, in body noble, entire in its integrity, in appearance outstanding, bold swift and fierce, [when] converted to the Catholic faith, free from heresy; while still held by pagan[31] practice, by the inspiration of God, searching for the key of knowledge according to the nature of its customs, it sought justice and maintained piety.[32]

Perhaps there is little to wonder at here, although it would be interesting to know what Gregory of Tours would have made of the glorification of a pagan people and the claim that it enjoyed divine inspiration. The prologue proceeds to give a brief account of the history of the Salic Law, asserts a close relationship between Christ and the Franks, and goes on to draw a comparison between Franks and Romans which is favourable to the former:

> Long life to him who loves the Franks, Christ who guards their kingdom. May the light of his grace fill their leaders, protect their army, and give strong faith; may

Jesus Christ the Lord of lords grant unto them of his goodness the joys of peace and prosperous times. For this is a people which is powerful while strong in body. They shook off the most hard yoke of the Romans by fighting, and after receiving baptism the Franks adorned with gold and precious stones the bodies of the holy martyrs which the Romans had consumed by fire, butchered by the sword, or thrown before beasts.[33]

The Franks, rejoicing in their prowess and faith, are superior to the Romans.

Also indicative of growing self-esteem among the Franks are some eighth-century *Laudes regiae* chants in the form of a litany which are discussed by Kantorowicz.[34] The litany begins with a threefold cry 'Christus vincit, Christus regnat, Christus imperat', and continues with a series of intercessions. Christ is asked to look with favour on, and groups of saints are invoked to help, the Pope, Charlemagne, 'the most noble royal progeny' and 'all the judges and the entire army of the Franks'. Noteworthy is the group of saints which is invoked to help the judges and the army — Hilary, Martin, Maurice, Dionysius, Crispin, Crispinianus, and Gereon. Each of these figures has strong Gallic, if not Frankish, connotations. Then, after further acclamations of the might of Christ, there follows a series of descriptions of Christ's military qualities applied to the Franks (for example, *victoria nostra, arma nostra invictissima, murus noster inexpugnabilis*), in each case followed by the acclamation *Christus vincit*. The *laudes* conclude with the ascription of empire, glory and power, strength, fortitude and victory, and honour, praise and jubilation to Christ — together with some utterances which appear, to a non-specialist, to be liturgical commonplaces. As with the prologue to the Salic Law, this text too confronts us with an apparent fusion between the military characteristics of the Franks and the favour of God. The *laudes* contain no mention of the Romans, but it is easy to conjecture that in any comparison with the Franks they would come off second best. For, as the continuator of Fredegarius makes clear, his hero Charles Martel was to be seen as God's chosen.[35] We have moved far beyond the sub-Roman world of Gregory of Tours, and by the late eighth century we have moved into a world which perceived itself as being explicitly post-Roman. Hence, for example, the subtle alteration made by the Biblical commentator Peter of Pisa to a passage of Jerome.[36] The same point was made in the ninth century by the historian Notker, locating himself (in a characteristically confused way) in a tradition of historical periodisation based on a prophecy of Daniel, and he went beyond Peter to suggest that the Romans had been replaced by Charlemagne:

He who ordains the fate of kingdoms and the march of the centuries, the all-powerful Disposer of events, having destroyed one extraordinary image, that of the Romans, which had, it was true, feet of iron, or even of clay, then raised up, among the Franks, the golden head of a second image, equally remarkable, in the person of the illustrious Charlemagne.[37]

It was a simple matter to suggest that the transition from Roman to Frankish power in Gaul was not the peaceful process that we can infer from sixth-century evidence. Rather, it was a remarkably abrupt changeover. According to a ninth-century notation on a manuscript, Clovis exterminated all the Romans who then lived in Gaul, so that scarcely one could be found.[38]

With the ninth century we reach the end of a road. As we have seen, the cessation of Roman power in the West was followed by a reluctance (or an inability) on the part of both

Romans and barbarians to admit the reality of the situation. In Francia one almost has the impression of a society living off cultural capital accumulated in earlier times, and despising itself for so doing. But first the Visigoths, and then more confidently the Franks, were the subjects of exaltation at the expense of the Romans. Historical consciousness developed, and Europe moved into an explicitly post-Roman world.

The Carolingians' perception of the relationship between their own intellectual life and that of classical Antiquity can be located within this trend whereby the West gradually distanced itself from Rome. Under Charlemagne (768–814) and Louis the Pious (814–40) in particular, the lands of the Franks enjoyed an expansion of cultural activities. This was made possible by the happy circumstances of relative political stability,[39] of enlightened patronage,[40] and possibly by the availability of economic resources which could be directed towards the non-essential.[41] The Carolingians frequently drew connections between themselves and the Chosen People of Israel, and themselves and their own Germanic past, while the concept of *Europa* also played a role in their thought.[42] When, however, they sought to locate their present with respect to an area of the past, in the great majority of cases – as the most casual perusal of Carolingian writing would indicate – they looked to classical Antiquity, and in particular to Rome.

This can be seen, for example, in their political rhetoric. As early as 781 Charles was described as consul (*MGH. Poet.* 1.95, *l.*18); before the imperial coronation Alcuin wrote to Charles of his *christianum imperium*:[45] bishop Modoin of Autun referred to him as Caesar (*MGH. Poet.* 1.571, *l.*86; 572, *l.*102) as did Benedictus (*MGH. Poet.* 2.673); while Ermoldus Nigellus applied the same title to Louis the Pious (*de rebus gestis Ludovici: PL* 115, 571). Einhard's biography of Charlemagne, based on Suetonius' lives of the Caesars and apparently making a conscious break with early medieval biographical tradition,[44] writes of Charlemagne using the vocabulary Suetonius used to describe his subjects.[45] Echoing Vergil's famous description of the activities proper to the Roman, in 800 Alcuin advised Charles:

Erige subiectos et iam depone superbos.[46]

Elsewhere, in a letter to Charlemagne, he recommended the sentiment of 'a certain one of the old poets', on this occasion quoting Vergil correctly (*MGH. Ep.* 4, 294). Charlemagne built at Aachen what was described as a *Roma secunda*, complete with forum and holy senate (*MGH. Poet.* 1.368, *ll.*94, 99 cf. *Aen.* 1.426), and members of his Court delighted to bestow on each other classical nicknames.[47] Paul the Deacon was compared to Homer, Vergil, Philo, Tertullus, Horace and Tibullus.[48] Not only was Charlemagne's prudence deemed broader than the Nile, more abundant than the icy Danube, greater than the Euphrates, and not less than the Ganges (*MGH. Poet.* 1.484, *ll.*25ff.), but he surpassed the famous observations of the illustrious Cato, he overcame the great Cicero in sweetness of discourse, and the eloquent Homer yielded to his sayings (*MGH. Poet.* 1.368, *ll.*72–4).

Such expressions show an obvious concern by Carolingian authors to assert connections between themselves and classical culture, but for more precise indications of what they felt these connections to be we must turn elsewhere. The most helpful evidence I have discovered is the first letter of the correspondence between Lupus, subsequently abbot of Ferrières, and

Einhard, the biographer of Charlemagne (*PL* 119, 431–6). It is a fascinating document. A young scholar, Lupus, takes it on himself to solicit the friendship of an admired elder, together with the loan of some of his manuscripts. He reveals a good deal of the intellectual preoccupations of Carolingian scholars, and he also shows how he perceives the relationship between his own day and classical Antiquity.

He begins by explaining that he has long hesitated to write to Einhard, but now seeks his friendship. His point is buttressed by a quotation from Horace and by an argument drawn from Christian ethics. From his earliest childhood, states Lupus, he has had an innate *amor litterarum*, although he has suffered from a lack of teachers. He then proceeds to make observations on the place of scholars in the community, which he adorns with a tag from Cicero. He finds works written in his age [*nostra aetate*] not to his taste, for they stray from the *gravitas* of Cicero and others — something which the outstanding writers of the Christian religion were able to rival. But Einhard's account of the deeds of Charles has now come into his hands, and he has fallen in love with its good taste, lack of conjunctions, and short sentences. Earlier he knew Einhard by reputation, but now he feels he must meet him. As it happens, he has crossed to the eastern side of the Rhine for study. He would also like copies of some books: Cicero on rhetoric, his dialogue *de Oratore*, a commentary on Cicero, and the *Attic Nights* of Gellius. There are many other books he would like to see as well, and perhaps he will be able to borrow these when he has returned the first lot.

Lupus' taste is obviously classical. Tags from Roman authors drop with apparent effortlessness from his pen, and in his enthusiasm for obtaining classical manuscripts (as in the strongly Ciceronian cast of his classical interests) he strongly foreshadows the later Italian humanists. Fifteenth-century humanism is also foreshadowed in another important respect. Lupus laments that modern works have fallen short of the style of Cicero, but now Einhard has written outstandingly [*clarissime*] and apparently satisfies Ciceronian criteria. It is not entirely clear in what spirit this encomium is to be taken, for in the preface to his biography (which Lupus had presumably read) Einhard confessed to falling short of Cicero's talent, a bad grasp of Latin, and foolishly disregarding Cicero's advice to would-be authors.[49] But the main point is clear. A style which had been lost is being practised again, and Lupus would have seen in Einhard one of those described by Notker: 'moderni Galli sive Franci antiquis Romanis et Atheniensibus aequarentur' (*Taten* 2.1).

Variously expressed, this theme runs through much of Carolingian intellectual activity. One of the forms it frequently took was to be found in attempts made to regain contact with the earlier Christian centuries (which, as we have seen, Lupus linked with Cicero) by means of the production of textually sound editions of standard works. So, for example, various attempts were made to correct and improve the text of the Bible,[50] and it was said that Charles himself died the day after he had corrected the text of the Gospels with reference to Greek and Syriac versions.[51] Projects to obtain sound texts of the *Rule of Benedict*, the mass, the homiliary and canon law were also undertaken.[52] A story later told of Charles by the Deacon John in his Life of Pope Gregory neatly brings out the wish to return *ad fontes*. When some Romans and Franks were arguing as to whose collection of church chants was the older, the king asked whether the spring or the brook would be likely to have purer water.[53]

Intellectual concerns of this kind, and the florid use of classical rhetoric, express a genuine sense of seeking and, in some areas at least, of obtaining a new relationship with classical Antiquity. The estimate which the Carolingians made of this relationship coloured their estimate of their own achievement. The most concise statement of how their achievement was regarded occurs in an inscription on the seal ring which Charles adopted after his imperial coronation. It consists of four words. In the centre is the word ROMA, around which is the expression RENOVATIO ROMANI IMPERII.[54] Any interpretation of these words must be cautious. Perhaps the term is used merely in a political sense, from which it would be unwise to generalise. Furthermore, the concept of *renovatio* is by no means unknown in Roman times,[55] and one may choose to contemplate the Carolingians adopting an old idea of renewal. Nevertheless, we find the same idea, with a form of the same key word, in one of Alcuin's letters. Writing to Charles in April or May 799, Alcuin observes that the rules of proper pronunciation are rarely followed, but that thanks to Charles' concern a style worthy of learned discourse has begun to be revived (*renovari incipit: MGH. Ep.* 4, 285). According to the poet Modoin:

> Rursus in antiquos mutataque saecula mores
> Aurea Roma iterum renovata renascitur orbi;[56]

and again

> Aurea securis nascuntur regna Latinis;
> > (*MGH. Poet.* 390, *l.*92);

while Charles' buildings at Aachen were interpreted as bringing a second Rome into being.[57] According to the account of Charles' imperial coronation which is given in the Royal Frankish Annals, Charles was adored by the Pope 'more antiquorum principum' (*Annales, anno* 801). This is the only account to make the point; presumably therefore it reflects a conjunction between Charles and classical emperors which the Court particularly wished to make. Another piece of evidence which may point in this direction is Charles' mysterious removal of a statue in Ravenna which is thought to be that of the Ostrogoth Theoderic. It could be argued, as it is by Löwe, that this indicates that Charles thought of Theoderic in connection with himself.[58] Our source for this incident, however, stresses Charles' admiration of the beauty of the statue, and it may be well to see the incident as no more than another case of the plundering of Italy by Franks seeking splendid classical materials.[59]

Thus the Carolingians saw themselves as effecting a cultural and indeed political rapprochement with classical Antiquity.[60] This entailed another judgment. Given their high estimate of classical civilisation, and the renewal of it which they saw themselves bringing about, there followed of necessity the existence of an intervening period which fell short of these classical standards. The judgment which Carolingian scholars passed on the attainments of their immediate predecessors was negative. So Walahfrid Strabo in his prologue to Einhard's biography: when Charles took over, the breadth of the kingdom entrusted to him by God was full of darkness and almost blind, but he restored light to that which had been barbarous.[61] A capitulary issued in 782 already makes this point: it is Charles' concern to restore letters, 'almost obliterated by the indolence of our ancestors'.[62] The text of the Bible has been corrupted by the lack of skill of copyists.[63] In one of his letters, Alcuin makes one of his teachers in Northumbria refer to the faintheartedness of many of his contemporaries (*nunc pusillanimitas multorum*) who are not interested in knowing the nature of things, and compare them with the wisest of men who discovered knowledge of this (*MGH. Ep.* 4.239).

According to Notker at the beginning of Charles' reign 'the pursuit of letters was almost forgotten throughout the length and breadth of [his] kingdom and the worship of the true God was at a very low ebb'.[64] But it was believed that the situation had improved, and in 799 Alcuin was able to refer to the *rusticitas* of earlier writers.[65] — the very quality which Fredegarius admitted to possessing.[66] Alcuin, apparently, was prepared to accept the earlier author at his own valuation, and although he frequently refers to his own *rusticitas* (for example, *MGH. Ep.* 4.32) there is a feeling of conventional modesty. The difference which he perceived between Fredegarius and himself was *rusticitas* rampant in the former, but overcome in the latter.

In their different ways Walahfrid, Charles, Alcuin, Notker and Lupus all postulated a disjunction with the past. The perception of this is by no means uniform among Carolingian authors, and could take odd forms. In the mid-ninth century the Biblical commentator Angelomus distinguished between two sorts of earlier commentators: the *antiqui*, ranging from Origen to Isidore, and the *moderni*, who included Bede, Alcuin and Hrabanus.[67] Confronted with differences between classical Latin and Christian Latin, the eccentric Smaragdus seems to have regarded the developments as improvements.[68] But as we have seen the disjunction with the past generally took one form. In the time of Charles a break was made with corrupt tradition. The break was the obverse of the renewal of classical culture. The Carolingians felt themselves able to look back at classical Antiquity across a barbarous intervening middle age.

It has been my aim in this paper to examine the development of how people in western Europe perceived their relationship with Rome. I have suggested that during a period of about three centuries people came to cease thinking of themselves as inhabiting a sub-Roman world in favour of a view of a post-Roman world. The conclusion may seem banal, if not foreordained, in the sense that this development in perception was merely an inevitable function of the passage of time, the writers being merely a few centuries late in accommodating themselves to reality. But, for whatever reason, people were finally able to postulate a definite break with the Roman past, which left them free to conceive of a revival of its desirable culture. This, of course, involved the writing off of the period which came between themselves and that past. The Carolingians were able to formulate the categories of renaissance and a preceding age of barbarousness.

These categories were both novel and influential. Modern scholarship has been by no means backward in the discovery of a host of 'renaissances' in post-Roman Europe — in what has sometimes resembled an exercise in ornithology, with prizes for spotting the most implausible specimens. In the pre-Carolingian period, scholars have identified a renaissance of Hellenism under the Ostrogoths,[69] an Isidorian renaissance,[70] and a number of renaissances beginning in the late seventh century.[71] I would argue that these movements, however real their existence, were different in kind from the self-defined renaissance of the Carolingians, and from the self-defined Ottonian, twelfth-century and Italian renaissances which followed. The outcome of the process described in the first part of this paper was the development of the historical construct described in the second part. This construct which has been exceptionally influential in subsequent European thought stands as a noteworthy response to a task that each generation is called to carry out: that of defining itself with reference to its past.

Notes

1. On the impact of the deposition of the last western emperor in 476 consult M. Wes, *Das Ende des Kaisertums im Westen des römischen Reichs* (The Hague 1967); A. Momigliano, 'La caduta senza rumore di un impero nel 476 d.C.' *Rivista Storica Italiana* 85 (1973), 5–21.

2. *Anonymi Valesiani pars posterior* 11.49 *MGH. AA.* 9, 316. For Theoderic's constitutional position see A. H. M. Jones, 'The Constitutional Position of Odoacer and Theoderic', *Journal of Roman Studies* 52 (1962), 126–30.

3. Note that what we think of as barbarian successor states may have appeared in quite a different light to contemporaries: cf. K. Hauck, 'Von einer spätantiken Randkultur zum Karolingischen Europa', *Frühmittelalterlichen Studien* 1 (1967), 54–7, and in particular the citation of Mommsen 55f., and H. Löwe, 'Von Theoderich dem Grossen zu Karl dem Grossen', *Deutsches Archiv für Erforschung des Mittelalters* 9 (1952), 353–401.

4. E. Kantorowicz, *Laudes Regiae. A Study in Liturgical Acclamations and Medieval Ruler Worship* (Berkeley 1946), 16f., n.7.

5. See the examples from his correspondence given by F. Heer, 'Die "Renaissance" – Ideologie im frühen Mittelalter', *Mitteilungen Institut für Österreichische Geschichteforschung* 57 (1949), 40 nn. 124f.

6. *Variae* 9.25 (*MGH. AA.* 12, 292, *ll.*2–3). Cassiodorus, it has been suggested, was closely followed in this aim by Jordanes: A. Momigliano, 'Cassiodorus and Italian Culture of his time', *Proceedings of the British Academy* 41 (1955), 207–45. (rp. in *Studies in Historiography* (London 1966)). Jordanes also stressed the similarity of the Goths to the Greeks (*Getica* 40).

7. 12.65f. I suspect that speculation on the possible significance of the term *principes* would not be rewarding.

8. *Chron. ad ann.* 500. Theoderic's activities as a builder are discussed by G. Della Valle, 'Teodorico e Roma', *Rendiconti della Academia di Archeologia Lettere e Belle Arti* (Naples) n.s. 34 (1959), 119–76.

9. *Complexiones in epistulis apostolorum: epistula secunda ad Thessalonicenses* 2 (*PL* 70. 1351f.).

10. *ibid.*, 1.23.2. A few decades later Pope Gregory I made a similar point concerning the working of miracles: introductory exchange between Peter and Gregory in Gregory, *Dialogorum libri IV* ed. V. Moricca (Rome 1924).

11. *Institutiones* 2.3.18, 2.4.7, 2.6.3. Elsewhere Boethius is cited without acknowledgment: 2.3.8, 2.3.11, appendix C. Differences in citations of Boethius' works in various families of manuscripts may reflect fluctuations in Boethius' posthumous reputation in the later part of the sixth century. Note too Cassiodurus' enthusiasm for a presumably traditional Christian education at an earlier time of his life: H.-I. Marrou, 'Autour de la bibliothèque du Pape Agapit', *Mélanges d'archéologie et d'histoire* 48 (1931), 122–69.

12. See the discussion of G. J. F. Kurth, *Histoire poétique des Mérovingiens* (Paris 1983), 505–16 and J. M. Wallace-Hadrill, *The Long-Haired Kings* (London 1962), 70–89. I have not been able to consult B. Luiselli, 'Il mito dell'origine troiana dei Galli, dei Franchi e degli Scandanavi', *Romanobarbarica* 3 (1978), 89–121. This belief was to have a long future: see, for example, the twelfth-century *Ecclesiastical History of*

Orderic Vitalis (ed. and trans. M. Chibnall) (Oxford 1969), Book 4, p.274; Book 5, p.54.

13. *Chronicarum quae dicuntur Fredegarii Scholastici libri IV* (*MGH. Scriptores rerum Merovingicarum*, 2.96).

14. P. Lasko, *The Kingdom of the Franks: North-west Europe before Charlemagne* (London 1971), 25f.

15. Gregory of Tours, *HF* 2.38. On the significance of *ingressus* and *profectio* see Hauck, *op. cit.*, 30–7. For Gregory, Clovis was 'novos [sic] Constantinus': *HF* 2.31.

16. Gregory, *HF* 5.17, 5.44. The continuing use of an amphitheatre at Arles is attested, perhaps with irony, by Procopius, *Wars* 7.33.5. For Claudius' alphabetical reform: Suetonius, *Claud.* 41; Tacitus, *Ann.* 11.13f.

17. According to Ammianus Marcellinus (28.5.11) the Burgundians knew themselves to be related to the Romans.

18. *Etymologi* 6.16.6–10, ed. W. M. Lindsay (Oxford 1911). These councils are presumably to be identified with the *generalia concilia* of 6.16.2.

19. *De vir. ill.* 4 (5), 19 (25), 31 (4), 32 (42) (ed. *PL* 83); *chron.* 397 a (ed. *MGH. AA.* 11).

20. E. A. Thompson, *The Goths in Spain* (Oxford 1969), 76–8; J. Hillgarth, 'Coins and Chronicles: Propaganda in Sixth-century Spain and the Byzantine Background' *Historia* 15 (1966), 483–508.

21. Gregory of Tours, *Liber in gloria martyrum* 24.

22. On Isidore's use of the word *Romani*: H. J. Diesner, *Isidore von Sevilla und seine Zeite* (Stuttgart 1973), 66ff.

23. K. Stroheker, *Germanentum and Spätantike* (Zurich 1965), 114.

24. P. Brown, *The World of late Antiquity* (London 1971), 182; illustrations in P. de Patol, *Arte hispanico de la epoca visigoda* (Barcelona 1968), nos.114–7.

25. See for example R. Collins, 'Julian of Toledo and the Royal Succession in Seventh Century Spain', in P. H. Sawyer and I. N. Wood (eds), *Early Medieval Kingship* (Leeds 1977), 30–49.

26. See Averil Cameron, 'The Byzantine Sources of Gregory of Tours', *Journal of Theological Studies* n.s.26 (1975), 421–6. (rp. in *Continuity and Change in Sixth Century Byzantium* (London 1981).)

27. P. Brown, *Relics and Social Status in the Age of Gregory of Tours* (Reading 1977) (= The Stenton Lecture 1976, rp. in *Society and the Holy in Late Antiquity* (London 1982), 222–50.); J. Moorhead, 'Thoughts on some Early Medieval Miracles', in E. and M. Jeffreys and A. Moffatt (eds), *Byzantine Papers* (Canberra 1981), 1–11.

28. See in particular the celebrated preface to the *HF*, and *HF* 10.28 (ed. Krusch, 536, *l.* 14); also H. Beumann 'Gregor von Tours und der Sermo Rusticus', in *Wissenschaft vom Mittelalter* (Cologne 1972), 41–70 (orig. pub. in *Festgabe für Max Braubach* (Munster 1964), 69–98).

29. Above, p.156.

30. *The Fourth Book of the Chronicle of Fredegarius with its Continuators* (ed. and trans. J. M. Wallace-Hadrill) (London 1960), prologue p.2.

31. *Barbaro*. I have ignored for the purposes of this paper the question of the development in meaning of the word *barbarus*.

32. K. A. Eckhardt (ed.), *Lex Salica 100 Titel-Text* (Weimar 1953), 82–4.

33. *Ibid.*, 88–90. There are interesting similarities between the prologue of the *Lex Salica* and a description of the Franks by the twelfth-century author Guibert of Nugent (*Gesta Dei per Francos* 2.1: *PL* 156,697f.). Much work remains to be done on Guibert.

34. *Laudes regiae* 13–64; on the date 53f. The text is also printed in *Dictionnaire d'archéologie chrétienne et de liturgie* 8, 1900–3.

35. Ed. Wallace-Hadrill, chaps. 6, 13, 15, 19, 20.

36. By the changing of *delenda sunt* to *deleta sunt*. Jerome, *Comm. in Dan.* (*CCL* 75A 847); Peter of Pisa: *PL* 76.1354. I owe these references to W. Ullmann, *The Carolingian Renaissance and the Idea of Kingship* (London 1969), 140 n.2.

37. Notker, *Taten Kaiser Karls des Grossen* (ed. H. F. Haefele) (Berlin 1962), 1.1. I reproduce the translation of L. Thorpe, *Two Lives of Charlemagne* (Harmondsworth 1969), 93. For a simple introduction to historical thinking based on Daniel, see B. Smalley, *Historians in the Middle Ages* (London 1974), 35ff.

38. Quoted with reference by E. Ewig, 'Volkstum und Volksbewusstsein im Frankenreich des 7. Jahrhunderts', *Caratteri del secolo VII in occidente* (Spoleto 1958), 587–648 at 648. Note the catastrophic impact attributed to the Goths and Vandals by Notker, 2.1 (ed. Haefele, 51).

39. Although this could easily be overestimated. Insecurity has been stressed by D. Bullough, *The Age of Charlemagne* (London 1973), 58f.; an attempted rebellion occurred when Charles's reign was at its zenith (*Annales regni Francorum* (ed. F. Kurze, Hannover 1895) *anno* 792 revised version); and even the early years of the reign of Louis were fraught with danger: P. R. McKeon, '817: une année déstastreuse et presque fatale pour les Carolingiens', *Le moyen âge* 84 (1978), 5–12. See now K. Brunner, *Oppositionelle Gruppen im Karolingerreich* (Vienna 1979).

40. For which Charlemagne was well-rewarded: see for example the extraordinary piling up of adjectives by the author of the epic 'Karolus Magnus et Leo Papa' (*MGH. Poet.* 1, 367, ll.61–6). Discussion of this work in D. Bullough, '*Europae Pater*: Charlemagne and his Achievement in the Light of Recent Scholarship', *English Historical Review* 85 (1970), 59–105 at 66f.

41. H. Fichtenau, *The Carolingian Empire* (Oxford 1967), 79–82.

42. S. Epperlein, 'Zur Bedeutensgeschichte von "Europa", "Hesperia" und "occidentalis" in der Antike und im frühen Mittelalter', *Philologus* 115 (1971), 81–92 at 86f.

43. *MGH. Ep.* 4, 241 *l.*24, 292 *l.*26. Given the imprecision with which the term *imperium* was used, however, this example must be treated with caution (cf. above n.8).

44. Bullough, *op. cit.* (n.40 above).

45. See among many discussions F. L. Ganshof, 'Einhard Biographer of Charlemagne', in his *The Carolingians and Frankish Monarchy* (London 1971), 1–16, at 3f.

46. *MGH. Poet.* 1, 259 *l.*67; cf. *Aen* 6.852f. On the possible significance of Alcuin's use of the term *subiecti* after the imperial coronation in 800, see R. Folz, *The Coronation of Charlemagne* (London 1971), 157.

47. For example, *ibid.*, 387 *ll.* 85, 87. The whole poem is an excellent example of Carolingian classicising, as is the letter in which Alcuin playfully develops the notion of Angilbert as Homer: *MGH. Ep.* 4.141f.

48. *MGH. Poet. l.*48.11.5. Who can Tertullus be? Paul denied the justice of the comparison: *ibid.*, 49.12.4f.

49. Einhard, *Vita Karoli Magni* (eds G. H. Pertz and G. Waitz) (Hanover 1911), p.2.

50. G. W. H. Lampe (ed.) *The Cambridge History of the Bible*[2] (Cambridge 1969), 133–9.

51. *Karl der Grosse Lebenswerk und Nachleben*, 2 (ed. B. Bischoff) (Düsseldorf 1965), esp. B. Fischer, 'Bibeltext und Bibelreform unter Karl dem Grossen', 156–216; C. Vogel, 'La réforme liturgique sous Charlemagne', 217–32; B. Bischoff, 'Panorama der Handschriftenüberlieferung aus der Zeit Karls des Grossen', 232–54.

52. Thegan, *Vita Hludowici Imperatoris* (ed. G. H. Pertz *MGH. Script.* 2), 592.

53. John the Deacon, *Vita Gregorii* 2.9 (*PL* 75).

54. Folz, *op. cit.*, (n.46 above) illust. 12.

55. Heer, *op. cit.*, (n.5 above), 23f.; G. Ladner, 'Eineuerung', *Reallexion für Antike und Christentum* 6 (1966), 245f., 262–4.

56. *MGH. Poet.* 385 *ll.*26f. (cf. *novae Romae l.*24). There are clear allusions here to Calpurnius *Ecl.* 1.42 and Ovid *Ars amatoria* 3.113, so that again we are faced with the apparently paradoxical situation of authors borrowing old language to express a concept of renewal. I am content here merely to point to a common problem in interpreting classical and scriptural allusions in medieval authors: it is often impossible to tell whether they are unconsciously reproducing familiar expressions, showing off, or flashing to literate readers signals of meaning which are now hard to decode. An elaborate study by Walter Ullmann (*Carolingian Renaissance . . .*) is devoted to the application of the concept of rebirth in this period, although some of the author's erudition seems misplaced. As in other of Ullmann's works, I suspect that too much of the argument hinges upon the imputation of necessary understanding by the medieval authors of fine shades of meaning which they may well not have perceived.

57. According to Notker (1.28) his cathedral was more excellent than the old works of the Romans. See in general R. Krautheimer, 'The Carolingian Revival of Early Christian Architecture', *Art Bulletin* 24 (1942), 1–38.

58. *Agnelli liber pontificalis ecclesiae Ravennatis* 94 (ed. *MGH. Scriptores rerum Langobardicarum et Italicarum saec. VI–IX*, 338 *ll.* 19–21). See the discussion of Löwe, *op. cit.* (n.3 above), and W. Kaemmerer, 'Die Aachener Pfalz Karls des Grossen', *Karl der Grosse* 2, 322–48.

59. The taking of marble columns from Rome and Ravenna to Aachen is mentioned by Einhard (*Vita* 26), and the removal of mosaic and marble from Ravenna in a letter of Pope Hadrian (*MGH. Ep.* 1, 614).

60. See also the discussion of W. von den Steinen, 'Der Neubeginn', *Karl der Grosse* 2, 9–27.

61. Preface to Einhard, *Vita* xxviii. Walahfrid probably wrote in the 840s; in the part of his prologue immediately following he complained of a decline in learning in his own day.

62. *Encyclica de emendatione librorum et officiorum ecclesiasticorum* (*MGH. Leges* 1, 44f.).

63. *Karoli epistola generalis* (*MGH. Capitula regum Francorum* 1 no.30 80 *ll.*25–30).

64. *Taten* 1 (trans. Thorpe, 93).

65. *MGH. Ep.* 4, 285. Note that, according to Braulio, Isidore had been raised up by God to prevent the people of Spain from growing old *in rusticitate* (*PL* 81, 16D–17A).

66. Above n.30.

67. M. L. W. Laistner, 'Some Early Medieval Commentaries on the Old Testament', *Harvard Theological Review* 46 (1953), 27–46, at 29f.

68.   J. Leclercq, 'Smaragde et la grammaire chrétienne', *Revue du moyen âge Latin* 4 (1948), 15–22.

69.   P. Courcelle, *Late Latin Writers and their Greek Sources* (Cambridge, Mass. 1969), 271ff.

70.   J. Fontaine, *Isidore de Seville et la culture dans l'Espagne visigothique* (Paris 1959), 863ff.

71.   P. Riché, *Education et culture dans l'occident barbare 6ᵉ–8ᵉ siècles* (Paris 1962), 410ff.

Epilogue: Old and New in Late Antique Historiography

Roger Scott

The title of the conference at which these papers were originally delivered ('Old and New in Late Antique Historiography') suggests that it is useful to reflect briefly on what these papers have proposed about change and continuity in the writing of history between the fourth and seventh centuries. For this purpose the papers can be classified loosely into three groups: those that discuss the 'old', that is, history written in the classical tradition (namely Ammianus Marcellinus, Procopius and Agathias); the 'new' which amounts to the emergence of the Byzantine world chronicle and also the rather different Western chronicle; and a third properly miscellaneous and amorphous group of papers which look at other forms of literature (the exegetical, the panegyrical and the antiquarian) which reveal new ways of moulding history and of showing an awareness of the past.

First the old. What emerges from these papers is the strength of the old, though perhaps in a lopsided and unexpected way. For it is only on the Greek side that the classical historiographical tradition survives. Not that this implies a high quality of Greek historical writing but rather, as Katherine Adshead (above, pp.82–7) points out for Agathias, there is a quality in the imitation of classical models which is not limited to language but which extends even to structure and ideas. Adshead shows that however much we may grumble at Agathias' limited understanding of his subject-matter, he did have a wider knowledge and understanding of classical historiography than he has lately been given credit for. Agathias then (and the same point can be made for his predecessor Procopius) provides evidence for the strength of the Greek tradition in the sixth century, a strength which only fails after Theophylact Simocatta at the beginning of the seventh century. But it is the emphasis in these papers, notably those of Matthews (pp.30–41), Emmett (pp.42–53) and Austin (pp.54–65), on the Greekness of Ammianus Marcellinus in the fourth century that is important here. That he wrote in Latin and has long been considered as *Tacitus continuatus* must not hide the fact that he was a Greek speaker with a Greek background for whom Antioch remained the focal point. This transfer of Ammianus back to the Greek tradition, though it strengthens the case for the continuity of that tradition, makes it difficult to talk at all about a Latin classical tradition in history after Tacitus. We can dredge up the names of histories and historians to be sure, such as Symmachus' friend Nicomachus Flavianus (cos. 394) from the end of the fourth century and his imitator Q. Aurelius Memmius Symmachus (cos.485) who wrote early in the sixth century.[1] But we know virtually nothing of these works nor will any amount of dredging bring a surviving classical tradition of Latin historiography to the surface.

The classical tradition in Latin historiography had never been strong. There are only three great names: Sallust, Livy and Tacitus. None of these survives in full and only a slight thread preserves even what we do have. The remnants of Tacitus' *Annals* are preserved in single manuscripts; Livy of whom the bulk is lost, perhaps owes even his partial survival to the antiquarian interests of Symmachus' scholarly coevals,[2] while Sallust's *Histories* have disappeared virtually completely and what survive are unique biographical monographs. Edwin Judge (above, pp.13–29) has drawn attention to the failure of the contemporary historians to understand the radical changes in society in the fourth century as opposed to the success of the philosophers, and he asks whether the traditional forms of writing history had proved a hindrance rather than a help. His point concerns the inability of historians to realise the limitations of the conventions of their art. I wonder if we can go further and ask whether their readers too had for several centuries also found conventional history an unsatisfactory medium, or at least a less satisfactory medium than biography.

Even if traditional history-writing was inadequate, there was certainly no lack of interest either in the past or in recording and explaining the present. There is no need to dwell here on the strength of the biographical tradition and the use of Suetonius as a model in the late Empire and in mediaeval times.[3] That it is Sallust's *Jugurtha* and *Catiline* which survive rather than his more conventional *Historiae* is probably part of the same phenomenon. In addition to biography, some of late Antiquity's new trends in writing history are well known. In particular there is the epitome and then the chronicle as well as polemical history, especially Christian propagandist history, such as Salvian and Orosius' *History against the Pagans*, and more moderate ecclesiastical history.[4] But these papers widen the field by drawing attention to the variety of other ways in which the past was studied. There is the strength and influence of the antiquarian tradition (Maslakov, pp.100–6), the use of biblical exegesis to present a 'sound' basis for knowing the past and so interpreting the present (Rousseau, pp.107–15), as well as the interest shown by philosophers (Judge, pp.13–29) and panegyrists (Nixon, pp.88–99) in recording and understanding contemporary events and their skill in so doing. We should also mention hagiography, another late antique development in the writing of history.[5] But this varied interest in the past during late Antiquity still assumed a continuity of Roman traditions and an identification with the Roman world. John Moorhead (pp.155–68) shows how this identification gradually disappeared, how it in turn produced, by Carolingian times, a radically different way of viewing the past. And at the same time we get the creation of a new *genre*, the national histories of the barbarian nations.

In the East, however, the Byzantines continued to think of themselves as *Romaioi* till 1453 and beyond. The imitation (*mimesis*) of classical literature there likewise remained as an ideal.[6] I have already drawn attention to the survival of a classical tradition in historiography until the early seventh century. But here too change was taking place behind that Byzantine facade of statuesque immutability. Procopius, for all his classicising vocabulary and technique, can still produce a sixth-century Christian interpretation of events where holy men and bishops play an increasingly important role in which God's plan for the world is decisive.[7] Yet neither the classicising history nor even the ecclesiastical histories, of which there had been a lively output, emerge from the darkness of the seventh century nor are they revived until much later. What did survive was the Christian world chronicle. Its origins are discussed in this volume by Brian Croke (pp.116–31) while Elizabeth Jeffreys' paper on its earliest surviving example, Malalas, is published elsewhere.[8] The Christian world chronicle was indisputably at odds with the Hellenic tradition of historiography but it did allow, indeed insisted, that Byzantines continue to see themselves as *Romaioi* while simultaneously presenting a Christian interpretation of history with some force. I have argued elsewhere that there is a biographical and propagandist approach in the chronicles and that these features are important for an understanding of later Byzantine historiography.[9] Undoubtedly we still find classical trappings in later Byzantine historians (the carefully worded preface, the formal speeches, the learned digressions) and often highly intelligent adaptations of classical models. But in this classical revival, which begins in the tenth century, as with the later western Renaissance's discovery of Livy and Tacitus, the imitation of classical models may disguise but does not prevent a fundamental difference in approach between model and imitator. The chronicle, it may be added, continued to live on independently, unaffected by such classical revivals, so that this product of late antique historiography continued to give its idiosyncratic account of the ancient world almost unchanged up to at least the eighteenth century.[10]

Notes

1.   The sole testimony to Flavianus' work (*ILS* 2948) does not permit us to decide what period his *Annals* covered: some think the Roman republic (e.g. J. Matthews, *Western Aristocracies and Imperial Court A.D. 364–425* (Oxford 1975), 231); others more recent times (e.g. F. Paschoud, *Cinq études sur Zosime* (Paris 1975), 150ff.; cf. T. D. Barnes, *Classical Philology* 71 (1976), 267–8). Symmachus' *Roman History* is preserved in a solitary enigmatic fragment of Jordanes' *Getica* (B. Luiselli, 'Note sulla perduta *Historia Romana* di Q. Aurelio Memmio Simmaco', *Studi Urbinati* 49 (1975), 529–35).

2.   Cf. H. Bloch, 'The Pagan Revival in the West at the End of the Fourth Century,' in A. Momigliano (ed.), *The Conflict between Paganism and Christianity in the Fourth Century* (Oxford 1963), 215–6.

3.   G. B. Townend, 'Suetonius and his Influence' in T. A. Dorey (ed.) *Latin Biography* (London 1967), 79–111. In the same volume note also the contributions of A. R. Birley, T. A. Dorey, D. H. Farmer and R. Brooke.

4.   The most convenient discussion of these developments is A. Momigliano, 'Pagan and Christian Historiography in the Fourth Century A.D.' in Momigliano, *op. cit.*, 79–99.

5.   For the relationship between biography and hagiography see A. Crabbe, 'Life after Martyrdom: A Literary Perspective' (unpublished).

6.   H. Hunger, 'On the Imitation (*mimesis*) of Antiquity in Byzantine Literature', *Dumbarton Oaks Papers* 23/4 (1969/70), 15–38 and 'The Classical Tradition in Byzantine Literature: the Importance of Rhetoric' in M. Mullett and R. Scott (eds), *Byzantium and the Classical Tradition* (Birmingham 1981), 35–47; G. Moravcsik, 'Klassizismus in byzantinischen Geschichtsschreibung' in *Polychronion Festschrift F. Dölger z. 75 Geburtstag* (Heidelberg 1966), 366–77.

7.   For a full discussion we must wait for Averil Cameron's forthcoming book on Procopius. In the meantime see Averil Cameron, *The Sceptic and the Shroud* (Inaugural Lecture, King's College, University of London 1980), 5–6 and 'Images of Authority: Elites and Icons in Late Sixth-Century Byzantium', *Past and Present* 84 (1979), 30–2 (= Mullett and Scott, *op. cit.*, 230–1) — both papers now reprinted in Averil Cameron, *Continuity and Change in Sixth-Century Byzantium* (London 1981).

8.   E. M. Jeffreys, 'Malalas and Mythical History', *Byzantine Studies in Australia News-letter* 8 (1981), 5–11.

9.   R. Scott, 'The Classical Tradition in Byzantine Historiography' in Mullett and Scott, *op. cit.*, 61–74.

10.   C. Mango, *Byzantium. The Empire of New Rome* (London 1980), 193–201 and 'Discontinuity with the Classical Past in Byzantium' in Mullett and Scott, *op. cit.*, 53–5.

General Index

Alexandria
6, 20, 21, 26, 27, 32, 40, 116,
118, 119, 120, 121, 122, 123,
129, 133, 140

Anecdotes – see also Digressions
55

Annals – see also Chronicles
2, 3, 37, 104, 119, 120, 123,
124, 128, 147–153, 169

Antioch
6, 8, 20, 21, 22, 23, 24, 31, 32,
34, 36, 58, 64, 72, 116, 120
122, 126, 169

Antiquarians
37, 47, 48, 100–106, 120, 169,
170

Apologists
3, 14, 29, 102, 103, 116, 118,
120–127, 136, 140

Asceticism
22, 107, 114

Audience
2, 3, 7, 8, 42, 45, 91, 93, 94,
98, 125, 135

Autobiography
5, 34, 42, 49, 54–65

Barbarians
1, 2, 3, 8, 9, 12, 16, 70, 82,
155–168, 170
Huns: 55, 57, 59, 86
Vandals: 58, 63
Visigoths: 2, 3

Bible – see also Exegesis
8, 17, 18, 20, 21, 28, 29,
107–115, 118, 122, 123, 124
125, 126, 129, 130, 134, 135,
138, 140, 161, 162, 167
Genesis 1: 121
Deuteronomy: 138
Chronicles: 138
Ezra 4:24: 124
Job: 138
Psalms: 121, 138
Jeremiah 12:1: 138
Daniel: 121, 122, 125
Maccabees: 136, 138, 144, 145
Matthew: 17, 18, 87, 107–115
Mark: 17
Luke: 124, 134, 135, 138, 143
John: 138
Acts: 110, 115, 134, 135, 143

Biography – see also Saints' lives
2, 37, 52, 92, 93, 94, 107, 160,
161, 170, 171

Britain
9, 53, 80, 90, 151

Byzantine historiographical tradition
– see also Christian World
Chronicle
7, 8, 11, 12, 22, 38, 45, 117,
128, 131, 165, 169–172

Byzantium – see Constantinople,
Byzantine historiographical
tradition

Causes in history – see also Fate,
Fortune, Providence
5, 6, 85, 107–115, 139, 170

Gallienus, Julian, Justinian,
Licinius, Marcus Aurelius,
Maximinus Daia, Theodosius I,
Theodosius II
6, 8, 20, 32, 35, 36, 38, 39, 46,
68, 75, 76, 77, 80, 89, 92, 93,
94, 97, 98, 124, 134, 155, 156

Epitomes
2, 37, 42, 49, 55, 100, 120, 170

'Eternal City' – see also Rome
3, 33, 48, 53, 93, 156, 157,
158, 162

Exegesis
107–115, 127, 136, 139, 169, 170

Exempla
34, 86

Eyewitness accounts – see also
Contemporary history
1, 31, 34, 36, 37, 47, 54–65,
141

Fasti
117, 119, 120, 129

'Fate'
5, 6, 35, 85, 139

Formulas introducing digressions
34, 44, 45, 51

Fortune
5, 6, 64, 84, 85, 135, 144

Gallienus
142

Gaul
3, 9, 10, 32, 34, 36, 37, 42, 45,
47, 48, 55, 66–81, 90, 94, 95,
96, 98, 105, 126, 156, 159

Geography
32, 42, 46, 47, 52, 60, 66–81,
99, 123, 141

Greek language and cultural tradition
31, 32, 33, 37, 38, 45, 117,
118, 119, 124, 127, 128, 135,
138, 140, 169–172

Hagiography – see Saints' lives

Hebrew history – see also Bible, Jews
117, 118, 122, 123, 124, 133,
138, 140, 143

Hellenism
20, 22, 116, 120, 135, 140

Heretics
21, 25, 112, 139

Historical method
14, 47, 49, 59, 62, 82–86
Method of composition: 43,
44, 82–87

Historiography – see Annals, Antiquarians, Autobiography,
Biography, Byzantine historiographical tradition, Christian
history, Chronicles, Classical
tradition, Documents, Eyewitness accounts, Geography,
Historical method, Military
history, Mimesis, Models,
Propaganda, Romance, Sources,
Utility of history

History of historiography
1, 101, 102, 105, 128, 169–172

Ireland
116, 127, 128

Jerusalem
6, 19, 112, 135

Jews – see also Hebrew history
16, 17, 107–115, 118, 133,
135, 136, 138

Julian
27, 28, 31, 34, 38, 39, 45, 48,
49, 52, 55, 61, 88, 138, 141
Persian campaign of: 22, 32,
34, 35, 45, 48, 55, 56, 57, 60,
61, 64, 72

Justinian
5, 6, 56, 62, 83, 84, 157

Kaisergeschichte
40, 50

Index of Ancient Authors Cited